Scriptures
of the West

Scriptures of the West

Edited by

James Fieser
University of Tennessee at Martin

John Powers
Australian National University

Boston   Burr Ridge, IL   Dubuque, IA   Madison, WI
New York   San Francisco   St. Louis
Bangkok   Bogotá   Caracas   Lisbon   London   Madrid   Mexico City
Milan   New Delhi   Seoul   Singapore   Sydney   Taipei   Toronto

McGraw-Hill

A Division of The **McGraw·Hill** *Companies*

SCRIPTURES OF THE WEST

This book is printed on acid-free paper.

1 2 3 4 5 7 8 9 0 DOC/DOC 9 0 9 8 7

ISBN 0-07-021022-5

Editorial director: Phillip A. Butcher
Sponsoring editor: Sarah Moyers
Marketing manager: Dan Loch
Project manager: Pat Frederickson
Production supervisor: Karen Thigpen
Designer: Larry J. Cope
Compositor: Shepherd Incorporated
Typeface: 10/12 Palatino
Printer: R. R. Donnelley & Sons Company

Library of Congress Cataloging-in-Publication Data

Scriptures of the West / edited by James Fieser, John Powers.
    p. cm.
  Includes bibliographical references and index.
  ISBN 0-07-021022-5 (alk. paper)
  1. Sacred books. I. Fieser, James. II. Powers, John, 1957–
BL70.S36 1998   97–29507
291.8'2--dc21   CIP

http://www.mhhe.com

Contents

Judaism   27

Christianity 87

Islam   147

Baha'i Faith   *199*

Endnotes   233

Acknowledgments   239

About the Authors

JAMES FIESER is an assistant Professor of Philosophy at the University of Tennessee at Martin. He received his BA. from Berea College (1980), and his MA and PhD from Purdue University's Department of Philosophy (1983, 1986). He has published articles on the topics of the philosophy of religion, rights theory, environmental ethics, moral skepticism, David Hume, and Thomas Aquinas. He has edited and annotated David Hume's *The Natural History of Religion* for Prentice Hall Publications and has created several World Wide Web sites in philosophy, including the Internet Encyclopedia of Philosophy.

JOHN POWERS is a senior lecturer in the Faculty of Asian Studies, Australian National University. He received his PhD from the University of Virginia in Buddhist Studies. His research interests include Indo-Tibetan Mahayana Buddhism, Indian philosophy, and contemporary human rights issues. He is the author of 7 books and 35 articles, including *Introduction to Tibetan Buddhism* (Ithaca: Snow Lion, 1995) and *Hermeneutics and Tradition in the Saṃdhinirmocana-sutra* (Leiden: E J Brill, 1993). He teaches courses on Asian Religions, Methodology, and Contemporary India.

Preface

Several avenues are open for understanding the world's religions. One could dialog with believers of the various religions, visit their sacred sites and temples, or attend classes for converts. A more practical approach would be to read surveys of the various religions, some written by believers defending their faith, others by critics, and even more by academic historians, anthropologists, psychologists, and philosophers. Yet another avenue is to examine the collected sacred texts revered by these religions. Each of these avenues offers only a single perspective on one of the most complex phenomena of world civilization, and none alone can claim primacy.

The present text introduces the world's religions through selections from their scriptures. There are special benefits to this avenue of exploration. In most cases the sacred texts are the oldest written documents in the tradition, and one gains a sense of immediate connection by studying the same documents that followers have been reading for millennia. The texts are also foundational to a religion's most important doctrines, rituals, and social and ethical positions. Thus, they explain the authoritative basis of traditions that might otherwise seem incomprehensible, or even groundless. Finally, the texts have become the most sacred symbols of these traditions, implying that one is on holy ground each time a sentence is read.

We have prepared our selection of scriptures in different formats. The volume titled *Scriptures of the East* contains the sacred writings of Hinduism, Jainism, Buddhism, Sikhism, Confucianism, Taoism, and Shinto. *Scriptures of the West* contains those of Zoroastrianism, Judaism, Christianity, Islam, and the Baha'i Faith. The volume titled *Scriptures of the World's Religions* contains all the material in the East and West volumes.

Since very few scriptures were originally written in the English language, these are selections of *translated* scriptures. Efforts have been made to find the most recent and readable translations available. Many scripture anthologies rely heavily on older public-domain translations, presumably as a means of cutting production costs. The trade-off is that the public domain selections are often outdated both in terms of scholarship and readability. We do not believe the trade-off is worth it and, when possible, have always preferred more recent translations. A few scriptures are still available only in older translation, such as the Shinto *Nihongi,* and therefore are the default choice. We modernized some of these translations in view of recent scholarship. We have also been sensitive in our selection among competing translations. For example, in the *Judaism* chapter we opted for the Jewish Publication Society's translation of the *Tanakh* rather than translations of the Old Testament that are more associated with Christianity. Similarly, in the *Christianity* chapter we used the Scholar's Version of the New Testament gospels, a new translation that was prepared free of ecclesiastical and religious control. Unique to this anthology are several scriptures in Asian languages newly translated by John Powers.

An exhaustive collection of world scriptures would be over a thousand volumes in length. Selectivity, therefore, is necessary. The first difficult choice was to confine the texts to those of religions that are practiced today. This excludes dead traditions that are mainly of academic interest, such as ancient Greek, Mesopotamian, and Egyptian religions. Second, emphasis is placed on religions that are historical in the sense that they have a body of written literature. Indigenous religious practices known only through secondary descriptions by anthropologists are excluded, such as those of African and Native American peoples. Third, preference is given to texts that discuss the lives and teachings of religious founders and present central doctrines. These are not only of greater intrinsic interest, but assure that the essential differences between religions emerge. Fourth, the scriptures selected are those accessible to lay practitioners, and not those intended mainly for theologians. Finally, emphasis is placed on religions that have a wide sphere of influence, specifically Hinduism, Buddhism, Judaism, Christianity, and Islam. Less influential religions, specifically Jainism, Shinto, Sikhism, Zoroastrianism, and the Baha'i Faith, are covered more briefly.

In spite of the above boundaries of inclusion, the notion of *scripture* used here is sufficiently broad to include three strata of religious texts. The first stratum involves texts that the religions themselves deem most sacred. The term *protocanonical* is typically used in reference to this level, which includes the Buddhist *Pali Canon,* the Muslim *Qur'an,* and the Jewish *Tanakh.* The second stratum involves more peripheral sacred texts, often termed *deuterocanonical,* that are usually derived from oral law and oral tradition. This includes collections of oral law, such as the Jewish *Talmud* and the Muslim *Hadith,* as well as texts on the lives of religious founders, such as the Sikh *Janam-sakhi.* The third stratum involves sectarian texts that at some time in the history of that religion were considered scripture by members of that sect. This final category allows for a broader range of texts than are found in most scripture anthologies, and includes sacred writings from the religion's mystical tradition. Examples are the Jewish *Zohar* and Christian writings of Pseudo-Dionysius.

A high priority was placed on including material that is of interest to women. Religious texts and practices throughout the ages have been biased in favor of men and often against women. Religious scriptures are almost entirely written by men, religious institutions are dominated by men, and religion is frequently used to keep women socially subordinate. Unfortunately, this male bias is perpetuated in the text selections in virtually all world religion anthologies. Considering recently evolving attitudes about gender issues in the field of religious studies, it is important to avoid perpetuating this bias. We have therefore also sought out scriptures in all of the represented religions that support the interests of women, present women in positions of leadership, or are written by women. Some of these are Judaism's *Song of Deborah* in the *Tanakh,* the Christian *Gnostic Gospel of Mary,* the mystical sayings of Rabi'a in Islam, Buddhism's *Liberation Songs of the Nuns,* and the Jain debates on enlightenment of women.

We recognize that each religion's canon of scripture presents unique problems of selection, and that no fixed criteria of selection can be rigidly applied. The canons of Hinduism and Buddhism, for example, contain hundreds of volumes of writings, whereas those of the Western religions contain only a few volumes. Accordingly, selections from Buddhism and Hinduism are often shorter, covering a wide range of scriptures. A special problem is presented by the fact that the majority of readers of the anthology will be of Western backgrounds, and thus will generally have greater familiarity with the Judeo-Christian tradition than with other religions. Thus, to make the selections on Judaism and Christianity most profitable to those already familiar with the Judeo-Christian tradition, several important yet historically dated scriptures are included, such as those from the *Pseudepigrapha,* the Dead Sea Scrolls, and Gnosticism. The introductory comments to the selections also reflect the varying scholarly traditions of the religions. Form criticism dominates Jewish and Christian biblical scholarship, yet is virtually unknown in many Asian religions. Qur'an scholarship is dominated by devout believers is Islam. Zoroastrianism has seen comparatively little scholarly interest in its scriptures recently.

The readings within each religion are categorized according to the inherent structure of the scriptural canons themselves, following a sequence of historical narrative or their dates of composition. This is preferred over topical arrangement, influenced by anthropological studies of religion, which eliminates narrative and historical context. We believe that our arrangement is more harmonious with the way each religion understands its own canon and that it is more consistent with how religious studies scholars understand a given religion's scriptures. In addition, it allows readers to gain a sense of the historical development of ideas and practices. This is important, since all religious traditions are dynamic systems that create new paradigms in response to changing social conditions and religious ideals, while striving to maintain a perceived connection with their origins. The dynamic relation between tradition and innovation is critical to understanding and interpreting living religious systems. It is hoped that by arranging texts in a roughly chronological sequence readers will gain a sense of the relations between the origins of religions as reported in early canonical works and subsequent developments.

We thank friends and colleagues who have generously offered advice on this book's contents. Alphabetically, they are Ronald C. Bluming, Christopher Buck, Stevan L. Davies, Richard Detweiler, Richard Elliot Friedman, Norman Lillegard, William Magee, Rochelle Millen, Robert J. Miller, Moojan Momen, Joseph H. Peterson, Habib Riazati, Kenneth Rose, Betty Rosian, Aziz Sachedina, Chaim E. Schertz, Robert Stockman, Mark Towfiq, and Mark Tyson.

Scriptures of the West

Zoroastrianism

With little more than 100,000 followers, Zoroastrianism today is a shadow of its former self when it was a dominant religion of the Near East. Zoroastrianism developed in Iran and southern Russia around 1200 B.C.E., and at its height was the state religion of Persia's empires from the third century C.E. until the expansion of Islam in the seventh century. Although the face of Zoroastrianism changed over its long history, several doctrines have remained consistent: (1) Ahura Mazda is worshipped as the one supreme God; (2) Zarathushtra[1] is said to be Ahura Mazda's prophet who delivers his unique revelation; (3) the universe is a battleground between opposing good and evil forces, and this cosmological dualism accounts for the presence of good and evil everywhere. Angra Mainyu, the primary evil spirit that embodies evil, is to be opposed; (4) Ahura Mazda created several divine beings, or Beneficent Immortals, who are to be venerated; (5) humans will be judged in the afterlife for their good or evil deeds.

HISTORY OF ZOROASTRIANISM

Background and Life of Zarathushtra

Between 2000 and 1500 B.C.E., there occurred a mass migration of Aryan people, perhaps from eastern Europe, to the region of what is now Iran. Over the next few centuries they successfully assimilated with the native people, as indicated by the name "Iran," which means home or land of the Aryans. The Aryan newcomers brought with them the an ancient polytheistic religion that involved the worship of daevas, or divine beings. After some centuries, a group of these Aryans migrated further to northern India, forming the basis of the early Hindu religion. Aryan culture had three principal social classes (priests, warriors, and cattle breeders), and different deities were associated with each. The gods of the priestly class included Mitra, Anahita, Varuna (the latter perhaps identified as Ahura Mazda). The priestly class also had religious rituals involving sacrificing oxen, imbibing the intoxicating juice of the haoma plant (*soma* in Sanskrit), and fire rituals, perhaps derived from Agni, the fire God of early India's religion.

Zarathushtra emerged as a religious reformer, reacting against both the polytheism and rituals of the Aryan religion. Little historical information is available about the life of Zarathushtra, and scholars have variously placed him between 1,500 and 500 B.C.E. The most plausible tradition places him around 1200 B.C.E.[2] in the Azerbaijan province of Northwest Iran; some linguistic and archaeological evidence, however, suggest that he was from an oasis tribal setting in Eastern Iran, near what is now the Afghanistan border.

According to later Zoroastrian tradition, Zarathushtra began his mission at age 30, after having a series of visions in which he was escorted to Ahura Mazda's presence, where he received his divine message. The first ten years of his mission were especially unsuccessful, and his only convert was his cousin. His teaching antagonized a group of priests who conspired against him and threw him into prison. At age 42, still in prison, his fortune changed with the conversion of King Vishtaspa (Hystaspes in Greek), an as yet unidentified monarch. Vishtaspa had an ill horse, and Zarathushtra healed it, leg by leg. During the process, the king was required to make certain concessions. The king was impressed, and the whole court accepted Zarathushtra's teachings.

Although Zarathushtra's life events remain hazy, there is greater knowledge about the content of his teachings and his role as a religious reformer. His foremost reform is advocating the supremacy of Ahura Mazda. The name *Ahura Mazda* means "Wise Lord," and Zarathushtra described him as holy, eternal, just, all knowing, and creator of all. Ahura Mazda is also said to be the source of all goodness, including success, glory, honor, physical health, and immortality. Zarathushtra condemned the *daevas* of the Indo-Iranian pantheon as subordinate devils, and their priests as devil followers. He also attacked many of the traditional Indo-Iranian religious rituals, especially the wasteful slaughter of great numbers of oxen, bulls, and cows in ritual sacrifices. Aspects of the haoma ritual were condemned, but Zarathushtra continued this tradition with some modifications.[3] The traditional fire rituals were also modified so as to reflect worship of Ahura Mazda, who is symbolized by undying fire.

Zarathushtra emphasized the religious conflict between good and evil. This ethical emphasis is best described as dualistic insofar as all key players—human and divine—choose either good or evil. Ahura Mazda demands ethical and ritual purity and judges the souls of people after death. The principal evil force, called the Lie (*druj*), wages war against Ahura Mazda. To assist in the war against evil, Ahura Mazda created Beneficent Immortals (*Amesha Spentas*). Later Zoroastrian tradition sees them as guardians over areas of Creation. They are: Asha Vahishta (Best Order, or Best Truth), associated with fire; Vohu Manah (Good Thought), associated with the ox; Khshathra Vairya (Desirable Dominion), associated with metals; Spenta Armaiti (Beneficent Devotion), associated with the earth; Haurvatat (Wholeness), associated with water; and Ameretat (Immortality), associated with plants. The theological status of the Beneficent Immortals is not entirely clear, and it is not certain whether they are distinct entities or merely different aspects of Ahura Mazda. Some scholars believe that their names and functions are derived from traditional Indo-Iranian deities, particularly the deities of the lower classes.

According to Zarathushtra, the cosmic ethical drama began when two twin spirits[4] chose between good and evil. The spirit Spenta Mainyu (Beneficent Spirit) allied himself with good, and Angra Mainyu (Destructive Spirit) chose evil. As Zoroastrianism developed over the centuries, Angra Mainyu became the embodiment of all evil, and even the corival of Ahura Mazda. Although his role is more limited in Zarathushtra's teachings, Zoroastrian tradition consistently describes Angra Mainyu as working for evil in the service of the Lie and is the source of misfortune, disaster, war, sickness, and death. To aid him in the assault on good, Angra Mainyu created several devils (*daevas*) which correspond with the Beneficent Immortals. The demon opposing Vohu Mano is Ako Mano (Bad Mind), against Asha Vahishta is Spozgar (Disorder), against Khshathra Vairya is Bushyasp (Sloth), against Spenta Armaiti is Asto Vidhatu (Death, literally, Bone Dissolver), against Haurvatat is Az (Greed), and against Ameretat is Tishn (Thirst). Angra Mainyu also counter-created demons/fiends which correspond to the other spiritual beings (*Yazads*).

The Rise and Decline of Zoroastrianism

Zarathushtra's new religion continued to spread after his death. During the Achaemenian Persian dynasty (550–330 B.C.E.), the first documented period of Zoroastrian influence, the religion was associated with the Magi. Although the identity and role of the Magi is unclear, they were experts in cultic ritual and claimed to be descendants of Zarathushtra's first converts. They may have originally been an early hereditary class of priests who allied themselves with Zarathushtra's teachings. When Mesopotamia was conquered by Alexander the Great, the impact of Greek culture caused a decline of Zoroastrianism. It was revived during the Parthian period (247 B.C.E.–237 C.E.), although there is little reliable information to indicate its character at this time.

Zoroastrianism peaked in influence during the Sasanian period (227–651 C.E.) when it became the state religion of Persia. Zoroastrian expansion throughout the empire was mostly the result of conversion, though at times adherents to rival forms of worship were punished. Sasanid theologians developed Zoroastrianism's great cosmological myths, dividing cosmic history into four 3,000-year periods. During the final period, Zarathushtra and his three descendent prophets appeared at 1,000-year intervals to wage war on Angra Mainyu. The world currently awaits the last prophet, Saoshyant, who will bring about final judgment and usher in a new world. The dead will then be resurrected, Ahura Mazda will judge all people according to their conduct as recorded in the book of deeds, and Angra Mainyu will be destroyed. Hell will also be dismantled, and the wicked (with few exceptions), having been purified, will be released.

Zoroastrianism gradually declined after 633 when the Muslims entered Persia and most of the population was forced to convert to Islam. Zoroastrianism was still tolerated for about three hundred more years, but persecution in the 10th century prompted many to leave Iran for India. Known as the Parsis, the immigrating Zoroastrians settled near Bombay and today total around 70,000. They are generally financially well off,[5] and many help to support the remaining Zoroastrians in Iran, who today number around 30,000. An additional 20,000 Zoroastrians live in other parts of the world.

Parallels between Zoroastrian beliefs and those of Judaism, Christianity, and Islam are striking, for example the messianic figure of Saoshyant, the Armageddon-like final battle, bodily resurrection, final judgment, and heaven and hell. Many historians of religion believe that Zoroastrianism is the source of these beliefs. However, the complex web of Zoroastrian doctrines themselves developed over time, and precisely when certain doctrines first appeared is still unclear. Until this is more firmly established, it is best to simply note the parallels.

ZOROASTRIAN SCRIPTURES

The foundational and oldest Zoroastrian scripture is the *Avesta*, a compilation of liturgical texts composed over a 1,000-year period. The original *Avesta* probably comprised 22 books and included historical, medical, and legal information along with liturgical texts. Only a small part of the original *Avesta* has survived. Zoroastrian legend recounts that two official copies were destroyed by Alexander during his campaign in the Persian capital. Priests gathered the remaining orally transmitted fragments, which were regularly recited in liturgies. The *Avesta* was kept alive through recitation until about 400 C.E., when an official edition was ordered by the Sasanid rulers. It is written in an archaic language called Avestan, which is related to Sanskrit and uses a modified Pahlavi alphabet.[6] The *Avesta* is the only surviving example of a text in this language.

In its current form, the *Avesta* is about 1,000 pages and written in different dialects from different periods of time. The most important division is the *Yasna*, a collection of prayers and liturgical formulas in 72 chapters. A 50-page section in the middle of the *Yasna*, called the *Gathas* (chapters 28–34, 43–54), contains hymns in an older dialect, and is believed to have been written by Zarathushtra himself. The other key divisions of the *Avesta* are:

Visparat (all the leaders): liturgical extension of the Yasna (22 chapters);

Vendidad (law against demons): instructions for ritual purification and moral practice to ward off evil powers, also containing myths and medical texts (22 chapters);

Khorde Avesta (*Smaller Avesta*): book of daily prayer used by the laity. Among other texts, it includes:

- *Yashts* (songs of praise): long hymns to various divine beings, some paralleling those found in the Hindu Vedas, plus epic narratives about kings and heroes;
- *Niyayeshs*: litanies to the Sun, Mithra, the Moon, the Waters, and to Fire;
- *Gahs*: dedications for each period of the day;
- *Afrinagans*: blessings;

The *Avesta* also includes several shorter fragments of lost books.

In addition to the *Avesta*, Zoroastrians have numerous scriptures from the Sasanian period which are written in a middle-Persian dialect called Pahlavi. Thus, the writings are typically called *Pahlavi texts*. Many are exegetical commentaries (called *Zand*) that translate, summarize, and explain the *Avesta*. The Pahlavi texts are more numerous than those of the *Avesta*. The primary ones are:

> *Bundahishn (Original Creation)*: 36 chapters on cosmogony, mythology, and cosmic history.
>
> *Denkard (Acts of the Religion)*: a collection of doctrines, customs, traditions, history, and literature, originally written in nine books, of which the first two are now lost.
>
> *Datastan-i Denik*: religious opinions of the high priest Manushkihar in response to 92 questions.
>
> *Zadsparam*: a collection by the high priest Zadsparam, younger brother of Manushkihar, which discusses cosmology and the life of Zarathushtra.

In addition to the Pahlavi texts, several later Zoroastrian texts are written in a more modern Persian language. The most important of these is the *Sad Dar (One Hundred Doors)*, the first Zoroastrian text known to the West, which was translated into Latin by Thomas Hyde in 1700.

SELECTIONS FROM THE AVESTA

ZOROASTRIAN CREED

Most of the surviving texts of the Avesta *were used ceremonially. The following creed from* Yasna *Chapter 12 is among the oldest and most central Zoroastrian statements of faith, perhaps initially required of converts. In both thought and deed, the believer vows to reject all evil as associated with daevas and the Lie [druj], and instead adhere to the good of Ahura Mazda, and the Beneficent Immortals [Amesha Spentas].*[7]

1. I curse the Daevas. I declare myself a Mazda-worshipper, a supporter of Zarathushtra, hostile to the Daevas, fond of Ahura's teaching, a praiser of the Amesha Spentas, a worshipper of the Amesha Spentas. I ascribe all good to Ahura Mazda, 'and all the best,' the Asha-owning one, splendid, xwarena-owning, whose is the cow, whose is Asha, whose is the light, 'may whose blissful areas be filled with light'.
2. I choose the good Spenta Armaiti for myself; let her be mine. I renounce the theft and robbery of the cow, and the damaging and plundering of the Mazdayasnian settlements.
3. I want freedom of movement and freedom of dwelling for those with homesteads, to those who dwell upon this earth with their cattle. With reverence for Asha, and (offerings) offered up, I vow this: I shall nevermore damage or plunder the Mazdayasnian settlements, even if I have to risk life and limb.

4. I reject the authority of the Daevas, the wicked, no-good, lawless, evil-knowing, the most druj-like of beings, the foulest of beings, the most damaging of beings. I reject the Daevas and their comrades, I reject the demons (yatu) and their comrades; I reject any who harm beings. I reject them with my thoughts, words, and deeds. I reject them publicly. Even as I reject the head (authorities), so too do I reject the hostile followers of the druj.

5. As Ahura Mazda taught Zarathushtra at all discussions, at all meetings, at which Mazda and Zarathushtra conversed;

6. As Ahura Mazda taught Zarathushtra at all discussions, at all meetings, at which Mazda and Zarathushtra conversed—even as Zarathushtra rejected the authority of the Daevas, so I also reject, as Mazda-worshipper and supporter of Zarathushtra, the authority of the Daevas, even as he, the Asha-owning Zarathushtra, has rejected them.

7. As the belief of the waters, the belief of the plants, the belief of the well-made (Original) Cow; as the belief of Ahura Mazda who created the cow and the Asha-owning Man; as the belief of Zarathushtra, the belief of Kavi Vishtaspa, the belief of both Frashaostra and Jamaspa; as the belief of each of the Saoshyants (saviors)—fulfilling destiny and Asha-owning—so I am a Mazda-worshipper of this belief and teaching.

8. I profess myself a Mazda-worshipper, a Zoroastrian, having vowed it and professed it. I pledge myself to the well-thought thought, I pledge myself to the well-spoken word, I pledge myself to the well-done action.

9. I pledge myself to the Mazdayasnian religion, which causes the attack to be put off and weapons put down; which upholds khvaetvadatha (kin-marriage), which possesses Asha; which of all religions that exist or shall be, is the greatest, the best, and the most beautiful: Ahuric, Zoroastrian. I ascribe all good to Ahura Mazda. This is the creed of the Mazdayasnian religion.

[*Yasna* ch. 12]

GATHA ON DUALISM

The dualistic battle between good and evil forces is the most characteristic feature of Zoroastrianism during all phases of its history. The following is from a section of the Yasna known as the Gathas—texts believed to have been written by Zarathushtra. In this Gatha, Zarathushtra describes the foundational moral conflict between Ahura Mazda and the Lie (druj). The conflict is carried on further by Ahura Mazda's twin sons, identified in other passages as the good Spenta Mainyu (Beneficent Spirit) and the evil Angra Mainyu (Destructive Spirit). This passage presents significant interpretive problems. On one interpretation, Spenta Mainyu is regarded as separate from Ahura Mazda; thus, both of these battling spirits—including Angra Mainyu—were created by Ahura Mazda. A second interpretation, by William Malandra,[8] is that the twin sons are merely ethical concepts, not spiritual beings. Thus, Zarathushtra is retelling a traditional myth that was familiar to his audience, and then reinterpreting it in the light of his own revelations. "Spenta Mainyu" then, is as a synonym for Ahura Mazda. On either interpretation, the cosmic dualism established between Spenta Mainyu and Angra Mainyu is paralleled by an ethical dualism between Druj *(the lie, evil) and* Asha *(truth, righteousness).*[9]

Now the two primal Spirits, who revealed themselves in vision as Twins, are the Better and the Bad in thought and word and action. Between these two the wise once chose aright, the foolish not so. When these two Spirits came together in the beginning, they established Life and Not-Life, and that at the last the Worst Existence [i.e., hell] shall be to the followers of the Lie [*druj*], but the Best Thought [i.e., heaven] to him that follows Truth [*asha*]. Of these two Spirits he that followed the Lie chose doing the worst things. The most beneficent Spirit chose Truth [*asha*], he that clothes him with heavy diamonds as a garment. So likewise they that are devoted to please Ahura Mazda by dutiful actions. Between these two, the *daevas* also chose not aright for delusion came upon them as they took counsel together, so that they chose the Worst Thought. Then they rushed together to Violence, that they might sicken the world of man.

To humankind came Dominion, Good Thought, and Truth [*asha*]. Piety gave continued life of their bodies, and indestructibility, so that by your retributions through the molten metal he may gain the prize over those others. So when there comes the punishment of these evil ones, then, Oh Mazda, at your command shall Good Thought establish the Dominion in the Consummation, for those who deliver the Lie, oh Ahura, into the hands of Truth [*asha*]. So may we be those that renovate the universe! Oh Mazda, and you other Ahuras, gather together the Assembly and you too the Truth [*asha*], that thoughts may meet where Wisdom is at home. Then truly on the [followers of] the Lie shall come the destruction of delight; but they that get them good name shall be partakers in the promised reward in the fair home of Good Thought, of Mazda, and of Truth [*asha*].

[*Yasna* ch. 30:3–10]

VENDIDAD ON DISPOSAL OF HAIR AND NAILS

The moral battle between good and evil not only touches the spiritual realm of thoughts and deeds, but the material realm as well. Things associated with contamination and death, for example, are deemed evil. Although no longer widely practiced today, Zoroastrian rituals concerning the removal of hair and nails vividly illustrate how physical things can be tainted by evil. The following purification rituals are from the Vendidad.[10]

Zarathushtra asked Ahura Mazda: "Oh Ahura Mazda, most beneficent Spirit, maker of the material world, holy one! Which is the most deadly deed whereby a man increases most the baleful strength of the demons, as he would do by offering them a sacrifice?"

Ahura Mazda answered: "It is when a man here below combing his hair or shaving it off, or paring off his nails drops them in a hole or in a crack. Then for want of the lawful rites being observed, demons are produced in the earth. For want of the lawful rites being observed, those Khrafstras [i.e., vermin] are produced in the earth which men call lice, and which eat up the grain in the grain-field and the clothes in the wardrobe. Therefore, oh Zarathushtra, whenever here below you shall comb your hair or shave it off, or pare off your nails, you shall take them away ten paces from the faithful, twenty paces from the fire, thirty paces from the water, fifty paces from the consecrated bundles of *baresma* [i.e., grasses used in sacrifice]. Then you shall dig a hole, ten fingers deep if the earth be hard, twelve fingers deep if it be soft. You shall take the hair down there and you shall say aloud these fiend-smiting words: 'Out of him by his piety Mazda made the plants grow up.' Thereupon you shall draw three furrows with a knife of metal around the hole, or six furrows or nine, and you shall chant the *Ahuna-Vairya* three times, or six, or nine."

[Ahura Mazda continued:] "For the nails, you shall dig a hole, out of the house, as deep as the top joint of the little finger. You shall take the nails down there and you shall say aloud these fiend-smiting words: 'The words that are heard from the pious in holiness and good thought.' Then you shall draw three furrows with a knife of metal around the hole, or six furrows or nine, and you shall chant the *Ahuna-Vairya* three times, or six, or nine. And then [say], 'Look here, oh friend-of-Truth bird! Here are the nails for you, look at the nails here! May they be for you so many spears, knives, bows, falcon-winged arrows, and sling-stones against the Mazainya devils. If those nails have not been dedicated to the bird, they shall be in the hands of the Mazainya devils. All the Lie [*druj*] followers are the Lie incarnate; those who scorn a teaching scorn all teachings; those who disobey are entirely disobedient; those who are not Truth-owning are entirely Asha-disowning, and have forfeited their bodies [i.e., mortal sinners].

[*Vendidad* 17:1–11]

VENDIDAD ON REMOVAL OF THE DEAD

The problem of physical things being contaminated by evil is most pronounced with dead human bodies. When one dies, a Corpse Demon (druj nasu) comes into the body and contaminates it and items that touch the body. Burial is not possible, since this contaminates the sacred earth, and cremation contaminates the fire. As described in the following selection from the Vendidad, *the preferred method of corpse disposal is for dead bodies to be devoured by corpse-eating dogs and birds that frighten off the Corpse Demon. To facilitate this, Zoroastrians construct Towers of Silence (dakhmas), cylindrical walled structures that expose corpses to vultures. This practice has been frequently noted in literature and is one of the most distinctive aspects of Zoroastrian ritual.[11]*

[Zarathushtra asked:] Oh Maker of the material world, holy one, to what place shall we bring, where shall we lay the bodies of the dead, oh Ahura Mazda?

Ahura Mazda answered: On the highest summits, where corpse-eating beasts and birds can most readily find it, oh holy Zarathushtra. There shall the worshippers of Mazda fasten the corpse by the feet and by the hair, with brass, stones, or horn, lest the corpse-eating dogs and the corpse-eating birds shall go and carry the bones to the water and to the trees.

[Zarathushtra asked:] If they shall not fasten the corpse so that the corpse-eating dogs and the corpse-eating birds may go and carry the bones to the water and to the trees, what is the penalty that they shall pay?

Ahura Mazda answered: They shall be whipped: two hundred stripes. . . . [12]

[Zarathushtra asked:] To what place shall we bring, where shall we lay the bones of the dead thereafter, oh Ahura Mazda?

Ahura Mazda answered: The worshippers of Mazda shall erect a receptacle out of the reach of the dog, of the fox, and of the wolf, and wherein rain water cannot pool.[13] Such a receptacle shall they erect, if they can afford it, with stones, chalk, and clay; if they cannot afford it, they shall lay down the dead man on the ground, with the earth as his bed, and the sunlight as his clothing.

Zarathushtra asked Ahura Mazda: When a man dies, at what moment does the Corpse Demon [i.e., *druj nasu*] rush upon him?

Ahura Mazda answered: Directly after death, as soon as consciousness has left the body, oh Spitama Zarathushtra, the Corpse Demon comes and rushes upon him, from the regions of the north, like the most ghastly vermin, with knees and tail sticking out, all stained with stains. . . .

[Zarathushtra asked:] If a man has been killed by a dog, or by a wolf, or by witchcraft, or by the artifices of hatred [i.e., poison], or by falling down a precipice, or by treachery, or by murderer, or by strangulation, how long after death does the Corpse Demon come and rush upon the dead?

Ahura Mazda answered: At the next watch [*gah*] after death [i.e., in a few hours], the Corpse Demon comes and rushes upon the dead. . . .[14]

[Zarathushtra asked:] If there be a number of men resting in the same place, on adjoining bedding, on adjoining pillows, be there two men near one another, or five, or fifty, or a hundred, close by one another; and of those people one happens to die; how many of them does the Corpse Demon envelope with infection, pollution, and uncleanliness?

Ahura Mazda answered: If the dead one be a priest, the Corpse Demon rushes forth, oh Spitama Zarathushtra, she falls on the eleventh and defiles the ten. If the dead one be a warrior . . . she falls on the tenth and defiles the nine. If the dead one be a husbandman . . . she falls on the ninth and defiles the eight. If it be a shepherd's dog . . . she falls on the eight and defiles the seven. . . .

[Zarathushtra asked:] What part of his bedding and pillow does the Corpse Demon defile with infection, uncleanliness and pollution?

Ahura Mazda answered: The Lie [*druj*] defiles with infection, uncleanliness, and pollution the upper sheet and the inner garment.

[Zarathushtra asked:] Can that garment be made clean that has been touched by the carcass of a dog or the corpse of a man?

Ahura Mazda answered: It can, oh holy Zarathushtra. . . . If, indeed, the garment has been defiled with semen, blood, feces, or vomit, the worshippers of Mazda shall cut it to pieces, and bury it [i.e., the defiled part] under the ground. But if it has not been defiled with semen, blood, feces, or vomit, then the worshippers of Mazda shall wash it with *gomez* [cow urine].

[Zarathushtra asked:] Can he be clean again who has eaten of the carcass of a dog or of the carcass of a man? . . .

Ahura Mazda answered: He cannot, oh holy Zarathushtra. His burrow shall be dug out, his life shall be torn out, his bright eyes shall be put out; the Corpse Demon falls upon him, takes hold of him even to the end of the nails, and he is unclean, thenceforth, for ever and ever.

[Zarathushtra asked:] Can he be clean again, oh holy Ahura Mazda, who has brought a corpse with filth to either water or fire, and made either unclean?

Ahura Mazda answered: He cannot, oh holy Zarathushtra. Those wicked ones it is, those men turned to Nasus [i.e., demons] that most increase spiders and locusts, those wicked ones it is, those men turned to Nasus, that most increase the grass-destroying drought. Those wicked ones it is, those men turned to Nasus, that increase most the power of the winter, produced by the demons [*daevas*], the cattle-killing, thick-snowing, overflowing, the piercing, fierce, mischievous winter. Upon them comes and rushes the Corpse Demon, she takes hold of them even to the end of the nails, and they are unclean, thenceforth, for ever and ever.

[Zarathushtra asked:] Can the wood be made clean, oh holy Ahura Mazda, to which dead matter has been brought from a dead dog, or from a dead man?

Ahura Mazda answered: It can, oh holy Zarathushtra. . . . If the Nasu has not yet been smitten by the corpse-eating dogs, or by the corpse-eating birds, they shall lay down, apart on the ground, the wood on the length of a *Vitasti* [i.e., five fingers] all around the dead matter, if the wood be dry; on the length of a *Frarathni* [i.e., fourteen fingers] all around, if it be wet; then they shall sprinkle it once over with water, and it shall be clean.

[*Vendidad* 6:44–51; 7:1–8, 9–29]

THE *NAM SETAYASHNE* DAILY PRAYER

The Khorde Avesta (Smaller Avesta) is a book of the Avesta that contains daily prayer used by the laity. One such text is the Nam Setayashne. An interesting theological point of this devotional is the equation of Spenta Mainyu with Ahura Mazda.[15]

1. I praise the name of that Spenta Mainyu, the increaser, worthy to be praised, who always was, always is, and always will be; whose one name is Ahura Mazda, the God who is the greatest among all, wise, Creator, supporter, protector, endurer, the lord of Asha [truth/righteousness], forgiver, and dispenser of excellent and pure justice.

2. Thanks be to the exalted Lord of the world, who, of his own power and wisdom, created six Bounteous Immortals of high rank, numerous spiritual beings [*yazads*], the shining paradise Garothman, the surrounding heavens, the hot sun, the shining moon, the numerous stars, the wind, the atmosphere, the fire, the water, the earth, the trees, the cattle, the metals, and humankind.

3. Adoration and prayers to the righteous Lord who has given us speech and the power to think, thereby making us superior to other creatures of this world. He has done this so that we might rule over people and make people walk together to fight against the Daevas.

4. I bow in the presence of the omniscient and caretaking Lord, who has sent, through Zarathushtra Spitaman of the adorable farohar [i.e., guardian angel], the wisdom of the religion, for the purpose rendering people friendly towards Him. This wisdom we gain through natural intelligence and knowledge of science, and is the best guidance for all persons who are, were and will be. Through this wisdom the soul is freed from the pains of hell, and reaches into the shining, fragrant, ever-happy, and the highest mansions of the pure.

5. Oh Lord Protector! In obedience to your command I am firm in the pure religion and I promise to think and speak and do every righteousness. Forgive me of my many sins. May I keep my conduct pure and, in accordance with your wishes, keep my six powers of the soul uncontaminated: work, speech, thought, reasoning, memory, and intellect.

6. And, in order to obtain the riches of the next world through good thoughts, good words, and good deeds, I will worship you, that I may thus open for myself the path to the shining paradise. By this, the heavy punishment of hell will not be inflicted upon me and I may, passing over the Chinvat bridge, reach into the fragrant all-adorned and eternally happy mansions of paradise.

7. I praise the Lord of gifts, who gives to those who obey his commandments the reward of righteous wishes and who will at the end liberate transgressors from hell and adorn the world with purity.

[*Khorde Avesta, The Nam Setayashne 1–7*]

SELECTIONS FROM PAHLAVI WRITINGS

THE CHINVAT BRIDGE, HEAVEN AND HELL

Zarathushtra taught that heaven awaits good people, and hell evil people. Entrance into heaven requires crossing the Chinvat Bridge which spans the abyss of hell below (Yasna 46:10, 11; 51:13). The details of this journey of the soul were worked out in later Pahlavi texts, such as the following by ninth-century Zoroastrian high priest Manushkihar from his Datastani Denik.[16] *On the fourth day after death, our souls leave our bodies and we cross the Chinvat Bridge. If we sided with good during our lives, then the bridge is as wide as seven spears and we easily pass to heaven, which is filled with beauty, light, pleasant scents, and happiness. If we sided with evil during our lives, however, the bridge turns sideways becomes as narrow as a razor's edge, and we plummet into hell which is filled with stench, filth, and pain.*

20. The nineteenth question that you ask is this: To what place do the righteous and wicked go?

    The reply is this. It is said that the souls of the dead are three nights on earth. The first night satisfaction comes to them from their good words and discomfort and punishment from their evil words. The second night come pleasure from their good words and discomfort and punishment from their evil words. The third night come exaltation from their good deeds and punishment from their evil deeds. That third night, in the dawn, they go to the place of account on Alburz [i.e., the mountain surrounding the world]. The account being rendered, they proceed to the [Chinvat] bridge. He who is righteous passes over the bridge on the ascent, and if belonging to Hamistagan [i.e., Purgatory][17] he goes there where their place is. If along with an excess of good works his habits are correct, he goes even to heaven; and if, along with an excess of good works and correct habits, he has chanted the sacred hymns, he goes even to the supreme heaven. He who is of the wicked falls from the lower end of the bridge, or from the middle of the bridge. He falls head-foremost to hell, and is precipitated to that grade which is suitable for his wickedness.

21. The twentieth question that you ask is this: How are the Chinvat bridge, the Daitih peak, and the path of the righteous and wicked; how are they when one is righteous, and how when one is wicked?

    The reply is this, as the high-priests have said: the Daitih peak is in Eranwej, in the middle of the world. The beamed-shaped spirit, the Chinvat bridge, reaches to the vicinity of that peak and is thrown across from the Alburz enclosure back to the Daitih peak. That bridge is like a beam of many sides, of whose edges there are some which are broad, and there are some which are thin and sharp. Its broad sides are so large that its width is twenty-seven reeds, and its sharp sides are so contracted that in thinness it is just like the edge of a razor. When the souls of the righteous and wicked arrive it turns to that side which is suitable to their needs, through the great glory of the creator and the command of him who takes the just account.

    Moreover, the bridge becomes a broad bridge for the righteous, as much as the height of nine spears, and the length of those which they carry is each separately three reeds. It becomes a narrow bridge for the wicked, resembling the edge of a razor. Those who are righteous pass over the bridge. Their paths are filled with pleasantness, as when they eagerly and unweariedly walk in the golden-colored spring, and with the gallant body and sweet-scented blossom in the pleasant skin of that maiden spirit. Such is the price of goodness.

Those who are wicked, as they place their feet onto the bridge, because of distress and its sharpness, fall from the middle of the bridge, and roll over headmost. The unpleasantness of this path to hell is like the worldly one in the midst of the stinking and dying things. There numbers of the sharp-pointed darts are planted out inverted and point upwards, and they come unwillingly running. These do not allow him to stay behind or delay. This pleasantness and unpleasantness to the souls is much greater than their worldly likeness, since that which is fit for the spirit is greater than that fit for the world.

26. The twenty-fifth question that you ask is this: how are the nature of heaven and the comfort and pleasure which are in heaven?

The reply is this, that it is lofty, exalted, and supreme, most brilliant, most fragrant, and most pure, most supplied with beautiful existences, most desirable, and most good, and the place and home of the sacred beings. In it are all comfort, pleasure, joy, happiness, and welfare, more and better even than the greatest and most supreme welfare and pleasure in the world. There is no want, pain, distress, or discomfort at all in it. Its pleasantness and the welfare of the angels are from that constantly-beneficial place, the full and undiminishable space, the goodness and boundless world. The freedom of the heavenly from danger of evil in heaven is like their freedom from disturbance, and the coming of the good angels is like the heavenly ones' own good works provided. This prosperity and welfare of the spiritual existence is more than that of the world, as much as that which is unlimited and everlasting is more than that which is limited and demoniacal.

27. The twenty-sixth question that you ask is this: How are the nature of hell, and the pain, discomfort, punishment, and stench of hell?

The reply is this, that it is sunken, deep, and descending, most dark, most stinking, and most terrible, most supplied with wretched existences, and most bad, there is the place and cave of the demons and fiends. In it is no comfort, pleasantness, or joy whatever. In it are all stench, filth, pain, punishment, distress, profound evil, and discomfort. There is no resemblance of it whatever to worldly stench, filthiness, pain, and evil. Since there is no resemblance of the mixed evil of the world to that which is its sole-indicating good, there is also a deviation of it from the origin and home of evil.

So much more grievous is the evil in hell than even the most grievous evil on earth, as the greatness of the spiritual existence is more than that of the world. More grievous is the terror of the punishment on the soul than that of the vileness of the demons on the body. The punishment on the soul is from those whose home it has become, from the demons and darkness—a likeness of that evil to hell—the head of whom is Angra Mainyu the deadly.

The words of the high-priests are these, that where there is a fear of every other thing it is more than the thing itself. But hell is a thing worse than the fear of it.

[*Datastani Denik*, ch. 20, 21, 26, 27]

CREATION AND THE MILLENNIA

In later Pahlavi Zoroastrian writings, Angra Mainyu has a more elevated role in cosmic history. The following selection from the Bundahishn, *a Pahlavi text on cosmogony and cosmic history, describes the initial confrontation between Ahura Mazda and Angra Mainyu and their ensuing 12,000-year battle. During the first 3,000 Ahura Mazda created the Beneficent Immortals and the world. Angra Mainyu responded by creating helper demons. They then agreed to limit the struggle to an additional 9,000 years.[18]*

As revealed by the religion of the Mazda Worshipers [i.e., Zoroastrians], so it is declared that Ahura Mazda is supreme in omniscience and goodness, and unrivalled in splendor. The region of light is the place of Ahura Mazda, which they call "endless light," and the omniscience and goodness of the unrivalled Ahura Mazda is what they call "revelation."

Revelation is the explanation of both spirits together. One is he who is independent of unlimited time, because Ahura Mazda and the region, religion, and time of Ahura Mazda were and are and ever will be. Meanwhile, Angra Mainyu in darkness, with backward understanding and desire for destruction, was in the abyss, and it is he who will not be. The place of that destruction, and also of that darkness, is what they call the "endlessly dark." Between them was empty space, that is, what they call "air," in which is now their meeting.

Both are limited and unlimited spirits, for the supreme is that which they call endless light, and the abyss that which is endlessly dark, so that between them is a void, and one is not connected with the other. Again, both spirits are limited as to their own selves. Secondly, on account of the omniscience of Ahura Mazda, both things are in the creation of Ahura Mazda, the finite and the infinite. For, this they know is that which is in the covenant of both spirits. Again, the complete sovereignty of the creatures of Ahura Mazda is in the future existence, and that also is unlimited forever and everlasting. The creatures of Angra Mainyu will perish at the time when the Final Body occurs, and that also is eternity.

Ahura Mazda, through omniscience, knows that Angra Mainyu exists, and whatever he schemes he infuses with malice and greediness till the end. Because he accomplishes the end by many means, he also produced spiritually the creatures which were necessary for those means, and they remained three thousand years in a spiritual state, so that they were unthinking and unmoving, with intangible bodies.

The evil spirit, on account of backward knowledge, was not aware of the existence of Ahura Mazda. Afterwards, he arose from the abyss, and came into the light which he saw. Desirous of destroying, and because of his malicious nature, he rushed in to destroy that light of Ahura Mazda unassailed by fiends. He saw its bravery and glory were greater than his own, so he fled back to the gloomy darkness, and formed many demons and fiends. The creatures of the destroyer arose for violence.

Ahura Mazda examined the creation of the Destructive Spirit, which were terrible, corrupt, and bad, and considered them not commendable. Afterwards, the evil spirit saw the creatures of Ahura Mazda. There appeared many creatures, and they seemed to him commendable. He commended the creatures and creation of Ahura Mazda. Then Ahura Mazda, with a knowledge of which way the end of the matter would be, went to meet the evil spirit, and proposed peace to him, and spoke thus: "Evil spirit! Bring assistance to my creatures and offer praise, so that, in reward for it, you and your creatures may become immortal and undecaying, without hunger and thirst."

The evil spirit shouted, "I will not depart, I will not provide assistance for your creatures, I will not offer praise among your creatures, and I am not of the same opinion with you as to good things. I will destroy your creatures forever and everlasting. Moreover, I will force all your creatures into disaffection to you and affection for myself." The explanation for this is that the evil spirit reflected that Ahura Mazda was helpless as regarded him. Therefore, Ahura Mazda offered peace, and Angra Mainyu did not agree, but continued on even into conflict with him.

Ahura Mazda spoke: "You are not omniscient and almighty, oh evil spirit, so that it is not possible for you to destroy me, and it is not possible for you to force my creatures so that they will not return to my possession. Through omniscience, Ahura Mazda knew if he did not grant a period of contest, then it would be possible for Angra Mainyu to seduce his creatures. As even now there are many of the intermixture of humankind who practise wrong more than right. Ahura Mazda spoke to the evil spirit: "Appoint a period so that the intermingling of the conflict may be for nine thousand years." For he knew that by appointing this period the evil spirit would be undone. Then the evil spirit, unobservant and through ignorance, was content with that agreement, just like two men quarrelling together, who propose a time thus: Let us appoint such-and-such a day for a fight.

Through omniscience, Ahura Mazda also knew that, within these nine thousand years, for three thousand years everything proceeds by the will of Ahura Mazda. In the next three thousand years, there is an intermingling of the wills of Ahura Mazda and Angra Mainyu. In the last three thousand years the evil spirit is made powerless, and they keep the adversary away from the creatures.

Afterwards, Ahura Mazda recited the *Ahunvar* [the Zoroastrians' most sacred prayer].[19] He also exhibited to the evil spirit his own triumph in the end, and the impotence of the evil spirit, the annihilation of the demons, and the resurrection and undisturbed future existence of the creatures forever and everlasting. The evil spirit, who perceived his own impotence and the annihilation of the demons became confounded, and fell back to the gloomy darkness. . . . He became confounded and impotent as to the harm he caused the creatures of Ahura Mazda, and he remained three thousand years in confusion.

Ahura Mazda created his creatures in the confusion of Angra Mainyu. First he produced Vohu Manah (Good Thought), by whom the movement of the creatures of Ahura Mazda was advanced. The evil spirit first created Mitokht (Falsehood), and then Akoman (Evil Thought). The first of Ahura Mazda's creatures of the world was the sky, and his good thought, by good procedure, produced the light of the world, along with which was the good religion of the Mazda Worshipers. This was because the resurrection which happens to the creatures was known to him. Afterwards arose Ardavahist, then Shatvairo, then Spendarmad, then Horvadad, and then Amerodad [the Beneficent Immortals]. From the dark world of Angra Mainyu were Akoman and Andar, then Sovar, then Nakahed, and then Tairev and Zairik. Of Ahura Mazda's creatures of the world, the first was the sky, the second water, the third earth, the fourth plants, the fifth animals, and the sixth mankind.

[*Bundahishn* ch. 1]

LIFE OF ZARATHUSHTRA

During the second 3,000-year period of cosmic history, Angra Mainyu stays in darkness only to wage a full-scale assault on creation during the third 3,000-year period. The fourth and final 3,000-year period begins with the birth of Zarathushtra, who rallies humans to the cause of Ahura Mazda. The following describes the miraculous conception of Zarathushtra, attempts to kill him at an early age, his encounter with Vohu Manah and his call to prophethood at age 30. The selections are from the Pahlavi Denkard, *a Pahlavi compendium of Zoroastrian doctrine, and the* Zatspram, *a collection of doctrines from ninth century* C.E. *Zoroastrian high priest Zatspram.*[20]

One marvel before the birth of Zarathushtra is this which is declared, that the creator passed on that divine grace of Zarathushtra through the material existences of the creatures to Zarathushtra. When the command arose from Ahura Mazda, the coming of that glory from the spiritual existence to the worldly, and to the material substance of Zarathushtra, was manifested as a great wonder to the multitude. Just as revelation mentions it thus:[21] "Thereupon, when Ahura Mazda had produced the material of Zarathushtra, the glory then, in the presence of Ahura Mazda, fled on towards the material Zarathushtra, on to the germ. From that germ it fled on, and to the light which is endless. From the light which is endless it fled on to that of the sun. From that of the sun it fled on to the moon. From that moon it fled on to those stars. From those stars it fled on to the wife which was in the house of Zoish. From that it fled on to the wife of Frahimrvana-Zoish, when she brought forth that girl who became the mother of Zarathushtra.

[*Denkard,* Book 7, ch 2.2 ff]

When the child had been born, Porushaspo [his father] called one of the five brothers of the race of Priests [*Karaps*], and spoke thus: "Fully observe the marks and specks of my son Zarathushtra."

The priest went and sat down before Zarathushtra, and the head of Zarathushtra was thereupon severely twisted by him, in order that he should be killed. But he, being fearless, watched the priests whose terror was distressing. As it was in those ten nights for hospitality, Ahura Mazda sent Spandarmad, Ardvisur, and Arda-frawash [i.e., the Holy Guardian Angel] down to the earth, by way of female care. Thereupon no marks (of evil) were observed on the child, and, further, the hand of that priest was withered, and that priest demanded the life of Zarathushtra from Porushaspo for the harm from him, which sprang upon himself from his own action.

At the same time Porushaspo took Zarathushtra, and gave him to the priest, that he might do with him according to his own will. He seized him and threw him out, at the feet of the oxen who were going on a path to the water. The leader of that herd of oxen stood still beside him, and 150 oxen, which walked behind it, were kept away from him thereby. Porushaspo took him, and carried him back to the house. . . .

The third day, firewood was gathered together by the priest, and Zarathushtra was deposited on it by him, the fire was stirred up by him, yet with the same result, the child was not burnt by it. . . .

[*Zatspram,* ch. 16]

On the completion of thirty years beyond his birth, the archangel Vohu Manah came on in commemoration of Ahura Mazda, when Zarathushtra was bringing his Haoma-water from the river Aevatak. . . . The words of Vohu Manah were: "Oh Zarathushtra, about what is your foremost distress? About what is your foremost endeavor? For what is the tendency of your desire?" Zarathushtra's reply was thus: "About Asha [truth/righteousness] I consider my foremost distress. About Asha [truth/righteousness] my foremost endeavor, and for Asha the tendency of my desire." The words of Vohu Manah were: "Oh Zarathushtra, that which is Asha is existing, so that whatever is that which is Asha is thus what is one's own." Zarathushtra spoke thus: "That which is Asha exists, and concerning that I am completely clear and aware. But where and how is the radiance which is that whose arrival is through Vohu Manah." Vohu Manah spoke to him thus: "O Zarathushtra, deposit this one garment which you carry, so that we may confer with him by whom you are produced and by whom I am produced, who is the most propitious of spirits, who is the most beneficent

of existences, and who is he that I, who am Vohu Manah, am testifying."
Thereupon, Zarathushtra thought thus: "Good is he who is the creator,
who is better than this reminder." Then they proceeded in company, Vohu
Manah and Zarathushtra, Vohu Manah first and Zarathushtra after.

[*Denkard*, Book 7, ch. 3:51, 56–63]

COMING OF SAOSHYANT THE SAVIOUR

*After Zarathushtra, three additional saviors are to come at 1,000-year intervals. They
will be born from virgins who bathe in a lake guarded by 99,999 angels who preserve
Zarathushtra's seed. The saviors are Hushedar, Aushedar-Mah, and Saoshyant.
Saoshyant's coming marks the end of the 12,000-year cosmic struggle between Ahura
Mazda and Angra Mainyu. The following, from the Pahlavi* Denkard, *describes the
birth of Saoshyant and his defeat of Angra Mainyu in the final battle.[22]*

10. Thirty winters prior to the close of the tenth century [in the final mil-
    lennium], the maiden Eredat-fedhri walks up to the waters. She is the
    mother of that testifying Saoshyant who is the guide to conveying
    away the opposition of the destroyer. . . . [Just as revelation states,]
    "That maiden whose title is All-overpowerer is thus all-overpowering.
    This is because through giving birth she brings forth him who over-
    powers all, both the affliction owing to demons, and also that owing
    to mankind." Then she sits in that water, when she is fifteen years old,
    and it introduces into the girl him whose name is the Triumphant Ben-
    efiter [i.e., Saoshyant], and his title is the Bodymaker. Such a benefiter
    as benefits the whole embodied existence, and such a body-maker,
    alike possessing body and possessing life, as petitions about the dis-
    turbance of the embodied existences and mankind. Not before that has
    she associated with men; nor yet afterwards, when she becomes preg-
    nant, has she done so before the time when she gives birth. When that
    man becomes thirty years old, the sun stands still in the zenith of the
    sky for the duration of thirty days and nights, and it arrives again at
    that place where it was appointed by allotment.
11. In his fifty-seventh year there occur the annihilation of the fiendish-
    ness of the two-legged race and others, and the subjugation of disease
    and decrepitude, of death and persecution, and of the original evil of
    tyranny, apostasy, and depravity. There arise a perpetual verdant
    growth of vegetation and the primitive gift of joyfulness. For seven-
    teen years everyone abstains from meat, then there are thirty years
    where people subsist on water alone, and then ten years where subsis-
    tence is on spiritual food alone.
       All the splendor, glory, and power which have arisen in all those
    possessing splendor, glory, and power, are in him on whom they ar-
    rive together and for those who are his, when many inferior human be-
    ings are aroused splendid and powerful. Through their power and

glory all the troops of the fiend are smitten. All mankind remain of one accord in the religion of Ahura Mazda, owing to the will of the creator, the command of that apostle, and the resources of his companions.

At the end of the fifty-seven years the fiend and Angra Mainyu are annihilated, the renovation for the future existence occurs, and the whole of the good creation is provided with purity and perfect splendor. Just as revelation states thus: "When that millennium has fully elapsed, which is the third of the religion of the Mazda-worshippers, that Mazda-worshipper whose name is so Triumphant then marches forward from the water Kasava with a thousand companions and also maidens of restrained disposition and blindly striving-behavior. He smites the wicked people who are tyrannical, and annihilates them."

Then those Mazda-worshippers smite, and none are smiting them. Then those Mazda-worshippers produce a longing for a renovation among the existences, one ever-living, ever-beneficial, and ever desiring a Lord. "Then I, who am Ahura Mazda, produce the renovation according to the longing among the existences, one ever-living, ever-beneficial, and ever desiring a Lord."

[*Denkard*, Book 7, ch. 10.15ff, 11.4ff]

RESURRECTION OF THE DEAD, FINAL JUDGMENT

After the defeat of Angra Mainyu in the final battle, the dead will resurrect on the spot where they died, and Ahura Mazda will judge everyone. The evil of the world will be purged with molten metal, Angra Mainyu will be destroyed, and a new universe will come into being. These events are described in the following passage from the Pahlavi Bundahishn.[23]

On the nature of the resurrection and future existence it says in revelation, that, whereas Mashya and Mashyang [Adam and Eve], who grew up from the earth, first fed upon water, then plants, then milk, and then meat, men also, when their time of death has come, first desist from eating meat, then milk, then from bread, till when they shall die they always feed upon water. So, likewise, in the millennium of Hushedar-mah, the strength of appetite will thus diminish, when men will remain three days and nights in superabundance through one taste of consecrated food. Then they will desist from meat food, and eat vegetables and milk. Afterwards, they abstain from milk food and abstain from vegetable food, and are feeding on water. For ten years before Saoshyant comes they remain without food, and do not die.

After Saoshyant comes they prepare the raising of the dead . . . . First, the bones of Gayomard [the primordial human] are roused up, then those of Mashya and Mashyang, then those of the rest of mankind. In fifty-seven years Saoshyant will raise all the dead. Whoever is righteous and whoever is wicked, every human creature, they rouse up from the spot where its life departs. Afterwards, when all material living beings assume again their bodies and forms, they will give them their protoplasm. Of the light accompanying the sun, one half will be given to Gayomard, and one half will give enlightenment among the rest of men, so that the soul and body will recognize that this is my father,and this is my mother, and this is my brother, and this is my wife, and these are some other of my nearest relations.

Then the assembly of Isat-Vastar will meet, where all mankind will stand at this time. In that assembly everyone sees his own good deeds and his own evil deeds. A wicked man becomes as conspicuous as a white sheep among those which are black. Whatever righteous man was friend of a wicked one in the world, and the wicked man complains of him who is righteous, thus, "Why did you not make me acquainted, when in the world, with the good deeds which he practised yourself?" If he who is righteous did not inform him, then it is necessary for him to suffer shame accordingly in that assembly.

Afterwards, they separate the righteous from the wicked. The righteous is carried to heaven, and they cast the wicked back to hell. Three days and nights they inflict punishment bodily in hell, and then he beholds bodily those three days' happiness in heaven. As it says that, on the day when the righteous man is parted from the wicked, the tears of everyone, thereupon, run down to his legs. When, after they separate sons from their fathers, a brother from his brother, and a friend from his friend, they suffer, everyone for his own deeds, and weep, the righteous for the wicked, and the wicked about himself. For there may be a father who is righteous and a son wicked, and there may be one brother who is righteous and one wicked. Those for whose peculiar deeds it is appointed . . . as those deserving death, undergo a punishment no other men undergo. They call it "the punishment of the three nights."

Among his producers of the renovation of the universe, those righteous men of whom it is written that they are living, fifteen men and fifteen damsels, will come to the assistance of Saoshyant. As Go-chihar [a meteor] falls in the celestial sphere from a moonbeam onto the earth, the distress of the earth becomes as that of a sheep when a wolf falls upon it. Afterwards, the fire and halo melt the metal of Shatvairo, in the hills and mountains, and it remains on this earth like a river. Then all men will pass into that melted metal and will become pure. When one is righteous, then it seems to him just as though he walks continually in warm milk. But when wicked, then it will seems to him as though he walks continually in world of melted metal.

Afterwards, with the greatest affection, all men come together, father and son and brother and friends ask one another: "Where were you these many years, and what was the judgement upon your soul? Have you been righteous or wicked?" The first soul of the body sees; it enquires of it with those words. All men become of one voice and administer loud praise to Ahura Mazda and the archangels.

Ahura Mazda completes his work at his time, and the creatures become so that it is not necessary to make any effort about them. Among those by whom the dead are prepared, it is not necessary that any effort be made. Saoshyant, with his assistants, will perform the rite for the restoration of the dead [*Yazishn*]. They slaughter the ox Hadhayos for this rite. From the fat of that ox and the white haoma they prepare the immortal beverage [*Hush*], and give it to all men, and all men become immortal forever and everlasting. Whoever had been an adult, they restore him then with an age of forty years. They who have been little when not dead, they restore them with an age of fifteen years. They give everyone his wife, and show him his children with the wife, so they act as now in the world, but there is no begetting of children.

Afterwards, Saoshyant and his assistants, by order of the creator Ahura Mazda, give every man the reward and recompense suitable to his deeds. . . . Afterwards, Ahura Mazda seizes on the evil spirits . . . and the dragon Go-chihr will be burnt in the melted metal, and the stench and pollution which were in hell are burned in that metal, and hell becomes quite pure. Ahura Mazda sets the hiding place into which the evil spirit fled, in that metal. He brings the land of hell back for the enlargement of the world. The renovation arises in the universe by his will, and the world is immortal forever and everlasting. This earth becomes an iceless, slopeless plain.[24] Even the mountain, whose summit is the support of the Chinvat bridge, they keep down, and it will not exist.

[*Bundahishn* ch. 30]

SIX RITUAL OBLIGATIONS

Zoroastrians have a variety of rituals, such as seven holy days of obligation, rites of passage, including the navjote *initiation ceremony for young adolescents, and rituals of cleansing and purification. Six primary ritual obligations are discussed in the following from the* Sad Dar (Hundred Doors), *a text on a hundred subjects which is written in Persian.[25]*

1. The sixth subject is this, that of the many good works there are of those which, when they accomplish them, obtain great rewards; and if one does not perform them severe punishment seizes upon one at the head of the Chinvat bridge.
2. One is the celebration of the season festivals [*Gahambars*]. The second is keeping the days of the guardian spirits [fravashis, the last ten days of the religious year]. The third is attending to the souls of fathers, mothers, and other relations. The fourth is reciting the Sun Litany [*Khwarshed Nyaish*] three times every day. The fifth is reciting the Moon Litany [*Mah Nyayis*] three times every month, once when it becomes new, once when it becomes full, and once when it becomes slender. And the sixth is celebrating the Rapithwin ceremony once every year.
3. If not able to celebrate them oneself, it is requisite to order them, so that they may celebrate them every single time.

4. These six good works are things indispensable unto every one.
5. When any one of them is not performed—be it that which, if omitted at its own time, it is not possible to accomplish, or if it be that one time one omits an occasion, and another time they accomplish twice as much—one should consider that as an advantage, which occurs in retribution for it, or as atonement for the transgression.
6. Because they call the transgression of each of these six a bridge-sin; that is, every one through whom a transgression of these may have arisen they keep back, at the head of the Chinwad bridge, till punishment for it happens to him, and no good work is possible in this place, which is torment and punishment for him.
7. Therefore it is necessary to make an effort, that they may be performed each one at its own time, so that they may obtain a recompense, and not a severe punishment.

[*Sad Dar*, 6:1–7]

VIRTUES AND SOCIAL OBLIGATION

In addition to ritual obligations, Zoroastrians have strict codes of moral obligation that encourage virtues and condemn vices. Often these moral instructions are in the form of aphorisms (Andarz), *such as the following from the* Denkard.[26]

23. There are five best things in religion. These are: truthfulness, generosity, being possessed of virtue, diligence and advocacy. This truthfulness is best: one who acts (in such a manner) to the creatures of Ahura Mazda that the recipient of his action has so much more benefit when he acts like that to him. This generosity is best: One who makes a present to a person from whom he has no hope of receiving anything in reward in this world, and he has not even this (hope), namely, that the recipient of his gift should hold him abundantly in gratitude and praise. This possession of virtue is best: One who makes battle against the non-material demons, whatever they may be, and in particular does not let these five demons into his body: Greed, Envy, Lust, Wrath and Shame. This diligence is best: One who does the work which he is engaged in doing in such a manner that at every moment he has certainty in himself with regard to the following: were he to die at that hour it would not be necessary to do anything whatsoever in a way different from that in which he is doing it. That advocacy is best: One who speaks for a person who is inarticulate, who cannot speak his own misery and complaint; that person speaks out the voice of his own soul and of that of the poor and good person to the people of this world and these six Amesha Spentas.
24. They held this too: Wisdom is manifest in work, character in rule, friend in hardship.

C82. When food offerings [*myazd*], seasonal festivals [*gahambar*] and acts of charity to good people diminish, there is increase of evil government for men, pain for grain plants, bad husbandry, diminution of the fertility of the land and rains. When the virtue of consanguine marriage diminishes, darkness increases and light diminishes. When worship of the gods and the protection and advocacy of good people diminish, the evil government of rulers and unlawful action increase, and evil people gain the upper hand over good.

[*Denkard* 6:23, 24, C82]

ZURVAN WRITINGS

ZURVAN AND HIS TWIN SONS

The Zurvan sect of Zoroastrianism flourished between the fifth and tenth centuries C.E. *Zurvan, a minor deity mentioned in the* Avesta, *is the supreme God of the sect.* Yasna *30 of the* Avesta *states that "Truly there are two primal Spirits, twins renowned to be in conflict. In thought and word, in act they are two: the better and the bad." The Zurvan sect interprets this literally and sees Ahura Mazda and Angra Mainyu twin sons of Zurvan. The good and evil twins create the world and wage war on each other, and the evil twin is ultimately defeated. The following is a fragment from a lost fourth-century Pahlavi Zurvan text, as cited by Eznik of Kolb, an Armenian Christian Apologist.[27]*

1. Behold what Zarathushtra said concerning the begetting of Ahura Mazda and Angra Mainyu. When nothing at all yet existed, neither heaven nor earth nor any other creature which is in heaven or on earth, there existed the great god Zurvan, whose name is to be interpreted as "fate" or "fortune. For one thousand years he offered sacrifice in order that he might perhaps have a son who would be called Ahura Mazda, and who would make the heavens and earth and all which they contain.

2. For one thousand years he offered sacrifice. Then he pondered in his heart and said: "Shall I truly have profit of these sacrifices, and shall I have a son called Ahura Mazda? Or do I strive thus in vain?" And even while he reflected in this manner, Ahura Mazda and Angra Mainyu were conceived in the womb: Ahura Mazda through the offered sacrifice, Angra Mainyu through the doubt.

3. When he became aware of this, Zurvan said: "Lo, two sons are in the womb. Whichever of them appears swiftly before me, him I shall make king." Ahura Mazda, being aware of their father's purposes, revealed them to Angra Mainyu. . . .

4. And Angra Mainyu, having heard this, pierced the womb and came forth and presented himself to his father. And Zurvan, beholding him, knew not who he might be, and asked "Who are you?" And he said: "I am your son." Zurvan answered him: "My son is fragrant and bright,

and you, you are dark and noisome." And while they spoke thus, Ahura Mazda, being born at the due time, bright and fragrant, came and presented himself before Zurvan. And Zurvan, beholding him, knew that he was his son, Ahura Mazda. And taking the rods which he held in his hand, and with which he had offered sacrifice, he gave them to Ahura Mazda and said: "Until now it is I who have offered sacrifice for you. Henceforth it is you who will offer it for me."

5. And while Zurvan was giving the rods to Ahura Mazda and blessing him, Angra Mainyu, having drawn near to Zurvan, said to him: "Have you not made this vow, that whichever of my two sons shall first come before me, him I shall make king? And Zurvan, that he should not violate his oath, said to Angra Mainyu: "Oh false and injurious one! The kingship shall be granted you for nine thousand years; and I shall establish Ahura Mazda as ruler over you. And after nine thousand years. Ahura Mazda shall reign and do all that he will wish to do."

6. Then Ahura Mazda and Angra Mainyu set to fashioning the creatures. And all that Ahura Mazda created was good and straight, and all the Angra Mainyu made was evil and crooked.

[Pahlavi fragment reported by Eznik of Kolb]

GLOSSARY

Ahura Mazda   (Ohrmazd in Pahlavi) literally, "Wise Lord"; supreme God and originator of all good.

Amesha Spentas, or Beneficent Immortals   servant angels who assist Ahura Mazda in the battle against evil; alternatively, they are sometimes seen as aspects of Ahura Mazda.

Angra Mainyu   (Ahriman in Pahlavi) literally, "Destructive Spirit" (antonym of "beneficent spirit"); the evil rival of Ahura Mazda in later Pahlavi texts.

Asha   literally, "The Truth"; the good moral principle in opposition to the *druj* (the lie).

Avesta   literally, "Basic Text"; the oldest and most sacred collection of Zoroastrian scriptures, written in the Avestan language.

Chinvat Bridge   literally, "separator bridge"; bridge by which people enter heaven; it spans the abyss of hell below.

Daevas   literally, "Heavenly Beings" in early Aryan religion; evil devils, demons in Zoroastrianism.

Druj   literally, "The Lie"; evil spirit or spirits that wage war against Ahura Mazda, and are opposed to Truth (*Asha*).

Magi   Zoroastrian priests, or, perhaps, cult leaders who claimed to be descendents of Zarathushtra's first converts.

Pahlavi   an early form of the Persian language, in which later Zoroastrian scriptures were written.

Saoshyant   literally, "Savior"; final descendent of Zarathushtra and the spiritual leader who will usher in the final judgment.

Spenta Mainyu   literally, "Beneficent Spirit"; the good son of Ahura Mazda in the *Avesta,* or, perhaps, a synonym for Ahura Mazda.

Zurvan   literally "time", supreme God of the Zurvan sect, who is the father of Ahura Mazda and Angra Mainyu.

SUGGESTIONS FOR FURTHER READING

BOYCE, MARY A. *Zoroastrians: Their Religious Beliefs and Practices* (1979).
——. *Textual Sources for the Study of Zoroastrianism.* Chicago: University of Chicago Press, 1990.
——. *A History of Zoroastrianism,* 2 vol. Leiden: 1975–1982.
DHALLA, MANECKJI. *History of Zoroastrianism.* New York: 1977.
——. *Zoroastrian Theology from the Earliest Times to the Present Day.* New York: 1914.
DUCHESNE-GUILLEMIN, JACQUES. *Symbols and Values in Zoroastrianism.* Bombey: 1966.
——. *The Western Response to Zoroaster* (1958).
MALANDRA, WILLIAM W. *An introduction to Ancient Iranian Religion: Readings from the Avesta and Achaemenid Inscriptions.* Minneapolis: University of Minnesota Press, 1983.
MOULTON, JAMES H. *Early Zoroastrianism.* London: 1913.
RANDERIA, JER D. *The Parsi Mind: A Zoroastrian Asset to Culture.* Munshiram Manoharlal Publishers, 1993.
SHAKED, SHAUL. *Wisdom of the Sasanian Sages.* Boulder, Colorado: 1979.
ZAEHNER, R. C., *The Dawn and Twilight of Zoroastrianism.* New York: Putnam, 1961.
——. *The Teachings of the Magi: A Compendium of Zoroastrian Beliefs* (1956).

Judaism

Judaism, with its 3,000-year existence, is one of the world's oldest living religions. Like all religions, Judaism has evolved over time, but several key beliefs pervade its rich history. First and foremost is the belief that YHWH (usually pronounced Yahweh) is the only God and creator of all. Second, humans should obey God's law as found in both written and oral law. Third, God made a series of covenants with the Jews to designate their lineage as chosen. The most significant of these covenants are with Abraham, who received the promise of a nation, with Moses, who received the Law, and with David, who received the kingdom. Fourth is the belief that a coming King-Messiah will free the Jews from foreign domination. Unlike the other major monotheistic religions in the Western tradition—Christianity and Islam—Judaism is distinguished by being *this-worldly*. Although a doctrine of the afterlife can be found in its teachings, greater emphasis is placed on the nation, the land, and traditions.

HISTORY OF JUDAISM

Beginnings

Judaism is inseparably tied to the history of the Jewish people; their scriptures, feasts, and worship practices recall events of the past. The earliest historical archaeological record derived from the period of Israel's settlement in its land is from the 12th century B.C.E., during the period of the Judges. At this time the Israelites were occupied with capturing territory from the previous inhabitants of perhaps a thousand years, the Canaanites, and settling into agrarian life. The land, *Israel* to the Jews and *Canaan* to the Canaanites, is an area about the size of New Jersey, located on the southeast shore of the Mediterranean sea. Some of the Israelite stories defined their identity as a nation and entitled them to the land. In these stories, their lineage is traced back to Abraham, a Mesopotamian nomad from a few hundred years earlier. Abraham made a special pact with God whereby God would make him the father of a nation. Abraham and his clan migrated to Canaan, the land later given to him by God. Two generations later famine drove his descendants to Egypt. For a while all was fine, until the Pharaoh of Egypt resorted to forced labor for his building projects. Abraham's descendants were then enslaved for this purpose. Eventually, they were led by

Moses out of Egypt and into the desert, where they wandered for 40 years. During the journey, Moses received detailed codes of law directly from God. The story further recounts that Moses' successors led the Israelites into Canaan to capture the land promised to Abraham.

Politically, Canaan was a decentralized collection of tiny independent kingdoms. Religiously, they performed plant and animal sacrificial rites in temples and open-air places, and fertility rites of prostitution. Key deities of the Canaanites were El the creator, Asherah the consort of El, Baal the son of El and god of storm, and Anat daughter of El and goddess of war. The Israelites and Canaanites already shared a common ethnic and language family, which was Semitic. As they occupied the land and eventually controlled the region, many intermarried with the locals and adopted the Canaanite ways, including worship of their deities. Politically the Israelites were a loose confederation of 12 tribes. A political balance of power was held in Israel between the chosen tribal leaders, legal and military judges, prophets, and priests from a 13th and landless group or tribe, Levi. Geographically there was a more delicate balance of power between two southern tribes, Judah (the largest of the twelve) and Benjamin, and the remaining ten tribes located primarily in the north, who felt threatened by Judah's size and political dominance.

United and Divided Kingdoms

An unexpected influx of warring invaders from the northeast Mediterranean area forced the Israelites to unify politically. These invading Philistines had a special military advantage in iron weaponry. Bronze weapons were less effective, especially in the hands of an Israelite army of drafted civilians. The need for a monarchy arose to facilitate a more concerted effort to block the Philistine power. The first King, Saul, died in battle with the Philistines. The Kingdom and military leadership passed to his son-in-law, David, who instituted a standing professional army. Equipped with iron weapons, David's army effectively put an end to the Philistine threat. Through military and diplomatic maneuvers, the Kingdom of Israel took control of territory as far south as Egypt, and as far north as Mesopotamia. At David's death, the throne passed to his young son, Solomon. Legendary for his wisdom and multiple diplomatic marriages, Solomon launched monumental building projects, including several fortified cities, a palace, and Israel's first permanent temple. Although Solomon taxed the entire country to fund his projects, benefits were seen primarily in Judah, which further alienated the northern tribes.

Solomon died about 922 B.C.E., and the throne passed to his son, Rehoboam. When Rehoboam announced that he would continue his father's policy of taxation, the northern tribes split from the south and proclaimed their own kingdom. The southern kingdom was thereafter referred to as *Judah*, while the northern kingdom retained the name *Israel*. During this period, both the northern and southern kingdoms continued to be influenced by Canaanite religious practices and efforts were made at monotheistic reform in both kingdoms by prophets and kings.

After a 200-year existence, the northern kingdom was conquered by the Assyrian empire. For several decades, the north had tried several strategies of resistance, but in 722 B.C.E. its kingdom was annexed as an Assyrian province. Some Israelites were deported, while others fled to Judah. Colonists from Mesopotamia settled in the region and intermarried with the remaining inhabitants, forming the Samaritans, a remnant of which remains today. The southern kingdom escaped immediate annexation by becoming a vassal of the Assyrians. Two decades later, though, Judah's King Hezekiah broke with the Assyrians, prompting a military confrontation that ended in loss of territory for Judah and a return to vassal status. He, and later King Josiah, made valiant efforts at monotheistic reform, but each time the populous reverted to Canaanite practices.

Exile and Restoration

In Mesopotamia, the power structure shifted and the Babylonians overtook the Assyrians. The new Babylonian Empire invaded surrounding countries to bring them within its control, and in three separate invasions (596, 587, and 583 B.C.E.), two of which were provoked by the Judeans, Judah was crushed. Cities and homes were destroyed, thousands of skilled craftsmen and potential troublemakers were deported to Babylon, and thousands more fled to Egypt, some of whom came to the Island of Elephantine. Most significantly, Solomon's temple was destroyed.

Although events during the Babylonian captivity are sketchy, the trauma of the exile apparently forced the Israelites to reexamine and solidify their religious beliefs. In the absence of the temple, the *Torah*, or books of Moses, became more important. Their understanding of Yahweh may also have changed to view him as sovereign authority over the universe. The term *Jew* became common at this time, which means someone from Judah.

Yet again the power structure in Mesopotamia shifted. In 539 B.C.E., the Persian emperor Cyrus overthrew the Babylonians, returned forty thousand Jews to Judah, now known by its Greek pronunciation *Judea*, and authorized the rebuilding of the temple. Judea, however, remained a province of the Persian empire. The Jews who stayed in Babylon continued to prosper and populate, and their views may have been influenced by Zoroastrianism, the Persian religion at the time. Angeology and demonology become more prominent themes in postexilic writings. Greater emphasis was placed on the resurrection of the dead, cataclysms of the end times, and the age of a redeemer or Messiah. In 458 B.C.E. an additional 17 thousand people returned to the land under the leadership of the priest Ezra. He returned from Babylon with a complete *Torah* in the form we have today, which is the five books of Moses. He and governor Nehemiah instituted a theocratic state with power vested in the priests. The Jews were required to take an oath to observe the Torah, tithe, sacrifice, and attend feasts. Marriage with foreigners was condemned in order to assure cultural and religious survival. He also established a council called *The Great Synagogue* to formulate doctrine and perhaps compile the texts of the *Tanakh*. Indeed, Ezra's and Nehemiah's reforms set a new direction for the Jewish religion.

Maccabean Revolt and the Hasmonean Dynasty

The Persian Empire collapsed in 333 B.C.E. during Alexander the Great's campaign for world domination. The next year Judea also fell under his control. After Alexander's death, the empire was divided between four of his generals, whose dynasties were committed to Hellenization, the propagation of Greek culture. Judea was passed back and forth between two dynasties of the divided empire: the Selucid Dynasty of Persia, and the Ptolemaic Dynasty of Egypt. From 301 to 198 B.C.E. life was peaceful under the Ptolemies. Then it changed hands to the Selucids. By 165 B.C.E., the extreme Hellenizing policies of Selucid King Antiochus Epiphanes reduced central Jewish religious rites to capital crimes. For many young Jews their heritage became an embarrassment, as evidenced by a frequently practiced surgical reversal of circumcision. The ultimate assault against the Jewish religion was the erection of an altar to Zeus in the temple upon which pigs were sacrificed. Further plans were made to confiscate land from Jews who followed their traditions. In revolt, an old priest named Mattathias killed a commissioner who had ordered him to sacrifice to Zeus. Gathering his five sons and followers, he fled to the desert. From there his son Judas Maccabeus launched a guerrilla attack, recapturing Jerusalem, and restoring worship. Although the Selucid army responded to the revolt, the Selucids could not engage in a protracted guerrilla war, and ultimately recognized Judea as a semi-independent temple-state. The Maccabean leaders declared themselves a dynasty of Priest Kings, also called the Hasmonean Dynasty, and for the next hundred years engaged in relatively independent, although frequently despotic, rule.

The Hasmoneans greatly expanded Judea's borders and fortified key cities. It is probably during this time that synagogues emerged as centers for local religious education and worship. According to Josephus, noted Jewish historian of the first century C.E., three religious orders also emerged: the Pharisees, the Sadducees, and the Essenes. The Pharisees were priests and lay people who adopted a priestly life; they were proponents of oral tradition, purity rituals, a Messianic kingdom, and the resurrection of the dead. They were also dedicated teachers of these doctrines to the masses. The Sadducees were aristocratic and priestly rivals of the Pharisees, and denied many of their doctrines, especially those listed above. They also competed with the Pharisees for political influence in the Sanhedrin, the legislative assembly of Judea. The Essenes shared key doctrines with the Pharisees, such as food rituals, a Messianic kingdom, and the resurrection of the dead. However, they became disgusted with the tyrannical rule of the Hasmoneans and the quarreling religious leaders, and established a monastic community in the desert along the Dead Sea.

Roman Domination

Hasmonean rule of Judea ended in 63 B.C.E. when a civil war broke out between Jewish parties. Roman general Pompey was called in to arbitrate, but instead occupied Judea and declared it a Roman province. The first Roman governors were particularly brutal, enslaving or crucifying those who disobeyed. A cunning Jewish governor from Galilee, Herod the Great, was soon appointed King of the Jews in 37 B.C.E. Herod had non-Jewish ancestry and was never completely accepted by the Jews. Preoccupied with conspiracies against him, Herod built massive fortifications for protection. He also rebuilt Jerusalem and the temple on a grand scale. But taxation for these projects economically crippled the peasant population. After Herod's death in 4 B.C.E., the Romans appointed a series of governors who where insensitive to the religious practices and economic concerns of the people. Growing anti-Roman sentiment among the peasants led to a series of minor revolts in which thousands of Jews were massacred. Incited by an oracle that a Jewish messiah would rule the world, a territory-wide peasant revolt finally erupted in 66 C.E. Although initially successful, the Romans marched on the rebellious Jewish territories, destroying everything in their path. Most importantly, the elaborate new temple in Jerusalem was destroyed, bringing an end to temple sacrifices in 70 C.E. Many Jews were sold as slaves, and the Jewish territories forfeited statehood status within the Roman Empire. With the temple in ruins for three generations, in 132 C.E. Jewish peasants and leaders were easily seduced by the messianic leader Simeon Bar Kokhba, who promised to restore the temple. His unsuccessful three-year revolt brought more destruction to the country and a massive disbursement, or Diaspora, of the Jews throughout Europe. Jerusalem became officially off limits to all Jews, and the country was ironically renamed *Palestine*, after the ancient Philistines, arch-enemies of the early Israelites.

Diaspora

With the Diaspora, the center of Judaism shifted from Jerusalem to Babylonia, where a large population of Jews remained after the 586 B.C.E. exile. At its peak, one million Jews lived in Babylon in the years following the exile and restoration. The figure of the Rabbi emerged at this time as an authority in scriptural interpretation and Jewish law, culminating in the creation of the Babylonian *Talmud*, the ultimate repository of Jewish oral law and commentary. Babylonian Jews remained the dominant voice of Judaism until the Arab conquest of the region in the seventh century C.E.

In the centuries following, Jews of the Diaspora attempted to settle in communities throughout Europe, only to be forced out as host countries became intolerant of them. In the reshuffling, two distinct groups emerged, each with their own distinct language and religious rituals. The Saphardic Jews were expelled from Spain and Portugal and moved to the Ottoman Empire. The Ashkenasic Jews were expelled from other countries and moved to eastern Europe.

Beginning in the 18th century, Judaism evolved in several directions. In reaction to impersonal rabbinic legalism and widespread disillusionment in the absence of the expected Messiah, the Hasidic movement was founded by

Baal Shem Tov. Hasidism offered a more mystical and joyous approach to Judaism, particularly for the laity. Although Hasidim were at first persecuted by traditional rabbinic schools, eventually half of the traditional rabbis joined them.

It was not until the 18th century Enlightenment that European countries finally granted civil rights to their Jewish citizens. As an outgrowth of their freedom, Reformed Judaism was founded in Germany by Abraham Geiger in the 19th century. Geiger believed that Judaism should be confined more to the sphere of religion than to culture and that Jewish worship practices should be modified to parallel those of Protestant Christians. In reaction, the Orthodox denomination reaffirmed the traditional elements of Judaism. In an attempt to mediate between the reformed and orthodox views, the Conservative denomination emerged as an attempt to "conserve" historical traditions that the Reformed denomination had eliminated. Finally, in the 20th century the Reconstructionist denomination was founded by Mordecai Kaplan as a development from the Conservative denomination. Reconstructionists offer a more pragmatic approach in the modern world, placing more emphasis on the cultural development of Judaism rather than on its religious elements.

JEWISH SCRIPTURES

Scriptures within the history of Judaism may be classed into four key divisions, corresponding to three periods of literary activity: (1) the *Tanakh*, (2) post-exilic sectarian writings, (3) Rabbinic writings, and (4) mystical writings. Each of these groups will be briefly examined.

The Tanakh

The most sacred collection of writings for Judaism is the *Tanakh*. The word "Tanakh" is an acronym coined in the middle ages from the initials of its three divisions: the Torah (Law), the Neviim (Prophets), and the Ketuvim (Writings). The 24 books of the *Tanakh* are traditionally categorized as follows:

Torah: Genesis, Exodus, Leviticus, Numbers, Deuteronomy

Neviim:

Former Prophets: Joshua, Judges, Samuel, Kings

Latter Prophets: Isaiah, Jeremiah, Ezekiel, The Twelve (Hosea, Joel, Amos, Obadiah, Jonah, Micah, Nahum, Habakkuk, Zephaniah, Haggai, Zechariah, Malachi)

Ketuvim: Psalms, Job, Proverbs, Ruth, Song of Songs, Ecclesiastes, Lamentations, Esther, Daniel, Ezra-Nehemiah, Chronicles

The books of the *Tanakh* were written and compiled over a period of 1,000 years, from approximately 1100–100 B.C.E. Each book has a detailed history of authorship, editing, and reediting. The writings appear in a variety of literary genres, including song lyrics, historical chronicles, wisdom literature, laws, prophecies, and apocalypses. The oldest stories and poems, such as the *Song of Deborah*, included below, may have been orally transmitted before taking written form. Much of the *Tanakh* bears the mark of post-exilic Judaism, either in composition or in editing. The books and main divisions of the *Tanakh* were in place when in 90 C.E. a Sanhedrin council in the Palestinian city of Jabneh gave the list its official stamp.

Of all writings within Judaism, the five books of the Torah have always been considered the most sacred. Thus, an understanding of its development is important. The term *Torah* means law, in the sense of instruction or teaching, which traces its authority to Moses. More specifically, *Torah* has come to mean the collection of writings consisting of Genesis, Exodus, Leviticus, Numbers, and Deuteronomy. Any account of the origin and authorship of the *Torah* must take place against the backdrop of a theory in biblical scholarship known as the Documentary Hypothesis, most famously articulated by Julius Wellhausen (1844–1918). According to this, the *Torah* is a fabric sewn from four distinct textual sources identified as J, E, P, and D. The J source acquired its name from its continued use of the word *Yahweh* (often mispronounced *Jehovah*) for God in early parts of the narrative (prior to the revelation of the divine name of God to Moses). The E source is so named for its pervasive use of the term *Elohim* for God. The D source refers to the bulk of the text of Deuteronomy with its unique style. Finally, the P source derives its name from the priestly content of its text.

Since Wellhausen, biblical scholars have identified more precisely the authors and dates of the four sources. One interpretation is that the J source was written by an author of the southern kingdom and reflects the political interests of Judah. Sometimes this involves besmirching the north. The E source, by contrast, was written by an author of the northern kingdom, possibly a Levitic priest, who endorsed the north's political structure but attacked its religious establishment.[1] Both J and E appear to have been written between 922 and 722 B.C.E. Shortly after the fall of the north to the Assyrians in 722 and during Hezekiah's reign in the south, J and E were spliced or *redacted* together into a single document as a conciliation to the northern Israelites who had migrated to Judah. In reaction to the influx of northern priests, the P source was created as an alternative to the JE story. One hundred years later, during the reign of Josiah, the framework of the D source was written around an old law code as a catalyst for religious reform. The D source is the first part of a larger historical sequence encompassing Joshua, Judges, Samuel, and Kings, compiled and edited by a single historian. The complete sequence of texts, called the Deuteronomistic History, details God's covenant with David for an unbroken royal lineage and rejection of local altars in favor of a single sacrificial site at the temple in Jerusalem.[2] Finally, all four sources (JE, P, and D) were redacted together into the five books of Moses, the *Torah*, by a priest (possibly Ezra) during or shortly after the Babylonian exile.

Post-Exilic Sectarian Writings

From 300 B.C.E. until about 200 C.E. the notion of an official Jewish canon of scriptures was fluid, even after the council of Jabneh in 90 C.E. Hundreds of religious texts appeared which were considered authoritative by many at this time. Although the authority of these texts was rejected by later Jewish scholars, even today they continue to have historical importance. These writings are classified into three collections: Apocrypha, Pseudepigrapha, and Dead Sea Scrolls.

The term *Apocrypha* is Greek for *concealed* and refers to 13 texts which at one time were associated with the Jewish canon but were officially rejected at the council of Jabneh. The original source of the Apocrypha is a Greek translation of the Jewish scriptures called the Septuagint (meaning "70"), so called because 72 Jewish scholars were brought to Egypt to create a Greek translation of Jewish scriptures between 285 and 246 B.C.E. Legend has it that each translated the first five books within 72 days, compared the various translations, and found them to be exactly the same. Completed around 100 B.C.E., the Septuagint contains the 13 Apocryphal books interspersed among the other books of the *Tanakh,* with no clear distinction in importance. The 13 books include Esdras 1 and 2, Tobit, Judith, the rest of the book of Ester, the Wisdom of Solomon, Ecclesiasticus (Sirach), Baruch, a Letter of Jeremiah, additions to the Book of Daniel (the Song of the Three Children, Susanna, and Bell and the Dragon), the Prayer of Manasseh, and Maccabees 1 and 2.

The term *Pseudepigrapha* means "writings with false subscriptions" and refers to a collection of 52 Jewish religious writings from 200 B.C.E. to 200 C.E., attributed to ideal figures in Jewish history such as Abraham and Moses. In literary styles paralleling those of the *Tanakh,* its four theological themes are the origins of sin and evil, God's transcendence, a coming Messiah, and the resurrection of the dead. The Pseudepigrapha is important in showing the diversity of Jewish theology at this time and the development of doctrines such as the Messiah, which are only hinted at in the *Tanakh.*

The Dead Sea Scrolls are a collection of writings and fragments discovered between 1947 and 1960 C.E. in the Qumran Valley area on the northwest shores of the Dead Sea. The religious community of Qumran was established around 200 B.C.E. as a desert haven against the oppressive political and religious realities of the time, and was destroyed in 70 C.E. by the Romans during the Jewish revolt. The Messianic community was preparing to be joined by angels for a final war against evil on earth. Although the Qumran community is often identified with the Essenes as described by Josephus, its association with that or any other sect is uncertain. Scriptures of the Qumran community were discovered in 1947, and made fully public in 1991. The writings include the earliest copies of many texts of the *Tanakh* as well as an array of previously unknown religious texts. When first discovered, the new documents were thought to represent the unique views of the post-exilic monastic community. More recently, however, some historians believe they originated in Jerusalem, the center of Jewish religious activity, and thus, like the Pseudepigrapha, reflect the quantity of Jewish scripture at the time.

Rabbinic Writings

During the first five centuries C.E., Judaism witnessed a dramatic flourishing of literary activity among Rabbis. One such was the composition of verse-by-verse commentaries on the *Tanakh*, known collectively and stylistically as *midrash*. Another and more important type of activity was the development of oral law, culminating in the texts of the *Mishnah* and the *Talmud*. Traditionally, the oral law of Judaism is believed to have been given to Moses by God at Mount Sinai, and orally transmitted for 1,500 years. In view of its divine origin, the oral law is on the same scriptural plane as the *Tanakh*. Historically, the foundation of the oral law tradition is thought to have been laid with Ezra's *Great Synagogue*, continuing through the Pharisees, and then extensively developed by the *Tannaim*, scholarly Rabbis who lived during the first two centuries C.E. Although the *Tannaim* resisted committing the oral traditions to writing, in 200 C.E. the Palestinian Rabbi Judah Ha-Nasi did just that. This work is the *Mishnah*, a collection of sayings attributed to specific *Tannaim* and Rabbinic schools from the first two centuries C.E. The sayings are stylistically rhythmic, which facilitated their early memorization. Much of its content derives from the legal codes in the Torah, although it rarely quotes the *Tanakh* directly. The text contains six key divisions: agricultural rules, laws governing the Sabbath and holidays, laws on marriage and divorce, the system of civil and criminal law, rules of temple sacrifices, and rules of purities and impurities.

Early Rabbis developed a tradition of commenting on the contents of the Mishnah. One collection, called the *Tosefta*, was written by the *Tannaim* themselves. After the Tannaim, two other groups of Rabbis continued commenting on the Mishnah: the *Amoraim* (200–500 C.E.), and the *Saboraim* (500–700 C.E.). Their comments became the basis of the *Talmud*, the grandest expression of this Rabbinic tradition. A first version of the *Talmud* appeared in 450 C.E. in Jerusalem, and a second and longer version in 500 C.E. in Babylon. Material was added to each version in the following century. Both the Jerusalem and Babylonian Talmuds have two parts: first, the text of the *Mishnah*, and second, the *Gemara*, which is a several-thousand-page collection of comments on the *Mishnah* written by the *Amoraim* and *Saboraim*. Both Talmuds are structured according to the main divisions of the *Mishnah*, although the Babylonian *Talmud* covers more divisions than its Jerusalem counterpart and, thus, is more definitive.

Mystical Writings

One of the earliest Jewish mystics was Philo of Alexandrea (20 B.C.E.–50 C.E.) who wrote a Hellenized, mystical commentary on the Pentateuch. Anticipating Plotinus, he believed there was a primary, concealed level of God, and two secondary levels: the logos, and the sensible universe. Union with God involves the awareness that we are part of the logos. *Tannaim* of the first two centuries C.E., such as Rabbi Aqiba and Rabbi Ishmael, emphasized mysticism by describing visions of the divine palaces (*keikhalot*) and the divine chariot (*merkavah*). This introduced a cosmic hierarchy into Jewish mysticism. A second-century text called the *Shi'ur Qomah* (Measurement of the Divine Height) describes the limbs of the God as metaphors for his nature, and thereby offers a mystical investigation into the nature of God. In the fourth century, the *Sefer Yesirah* (Book of Creation) introduced the concept of the ten *sefirah*, which are ten emanations of God. Since the 12th century, the most dominant school of Jewish mysticism has been Kabbala, which draws from all of the above expressions of mysticism. The classical statement of early Kabbala is found in two 13th-century texts: *Sefer ha-Bahir* (Book of Brightness), and *Sefer ha-Zohar* (Book of Splendor). The multivolume *Zohar* was so influential that within a few centuries it attained the status of sacred text among Kabbalists. This epic text was written between 1280 and 1286 by Moses de Leon, a Spanish Jew from Guadalajara. The hero of the book, Rabbi Shim'on, a second-century C.E. *Tannaim*, presents to his followers a verse-by-verse mystical *midrash* on several books of the *Tanakh*. To gain a receptive audience and lend authenticity to its content, Moses de Leon claimed that his work was a recently discovered ancient text written by Rabbi Shim'on himself. For almost 600 years, Kabbalists took Moses de Leon at his word. The next major development in Kabbala involved a 16th-century mystical revival in the Palestinian city of Safed which maintained that mystical union should be achieved by every person, not just specialists. From this revival grew certain messianic movements in the 17th century, and Hasidic mysticism in the 18th century.

SELECTIONS FROM THE TANAKH[3]

CREATION

The first 11 books of the Tanakh *present a continuous historical narrative from the creation of the world until the Babylonian exile. Genesis opens with two creation stories, one from the P or Priestly source, and one from the J or Yahwist source. Central to both is the idea that humans are the pinnacle of God's creative activity. The P source creation story, presented below, emphasizes the cosmic structure of creation, as opposed to the earlier and perhaps agrarian-oriented account of the J source. Also, the writer sees creation involving three mandates. First, humans are to fill the earth and master it. Second, humans are to eat plants for food. Finally, the seventh day of the week is declared holy.*

When God began to create heaven and earth—the earth being unformed and void, with darkness over the surface of the deep and a wind from God sweeping over the water—God said, "Let there be light"; and there was light. God saw that the light was good, and God separated the light from the darkness. God called the light Day, and the darkness He called Night. And there was evening and there was morning, a first day.

God said, "Let there be an expanse in the midst of the water, that it may separate water from water." God made the expanse, and it separated the water which was below the expanse from the water which was above the expanse. And it was so. God called the expanse Sky. And there was evening and there was morning, a second day.

God said, "Let the water below the sky be gathered into one area, that the dry land may appear." And it was so. God called the dry land Earth, and the gathering of waters He called Seas. And God saw that this was good. And God said, "Let the earth sprout vegetation: seed-bearing plants, fruit trees of every kind on earth that bear fruit with the seed in it." And it was so. The earth brought forth vegetation: seed-bearing plants of every kind, and trees of every kind bearing fruit with the seed in it. And God saw that this was good. And there was evening and there was morning, a third day.

God said, "Let there be lights in the expanse of the sky to separate day from night; they shall serve as signs for the set times—the days and the years; and they shall serve as lights in the expanse of the sky to shine upon the earth." And it was so. God made the two great lights, the greater light to dominate the day and the lesser light to dominate the night, and the stars. And God set them in the expanse of the sky to shine upon the earth, to dominate the day and the night, and to separate light from darkness. And God saw that this was good. And there was evening and there was morning, a fourth day. God said, "Let the waters bring forth swarms of living creatures, and birds that fly above the earth across the expanse of the sky. God created the great sea monsters, and all the living creatures of every kind that creep, which the waters brought forth in swarms, and all the winged birds of every kind. And God saw that this was good. God blessed them, saying, "Be fertile and increase, fill the waters in the seas, and let the birds increase on the earth." And there was evening and there was morning, a fifth day.

God said, "Let the earth bring forth every kind of living creature: cattle, creeping things, and wild beasts of every kind." And it was so. God made wild beasts of every kind and cattle of every kind, and all kinds of creeping things of the earth. And God saw that this was good. And God said, "Let us make man in our image, after our likeness. They shall rule the fish of the sea, the birds of the sky, the cattle, the whole earth, and all the creeping things that creep on earth." And God created man in His image, in the image of God He created him; male and female He created them. God blessed them and God said to them, "Be fertile and increase, fill the earth and master it; and rule the fish of the sea, the birds of the sky, and all the living things that creep on earth."

God said, "See, I give you every seed-bearing plant that is upon all the earth, and every tree that has seed-bearing fruit; they shall be yours for food. And to all the animals on land, to all the birds of the sky, and to everything that creeps on earth, in which there is the breath of life, [I give] all the green plants for food." And it was so. And God saw all that He had made, and found it very good. And there was evening and there was morning, the sixth day.

The heaven and the earth were finished, and all their array. On the seventh day God finished the work that he had been doing, and He ceased on the seventh day from all the work that He had done. And God blessed the seventh day and declared it holy, because on it God ceased from all the work of creation that He had done. Such is the story of heaven and earth when they were created.

[Genesis 1:1–2:3]

COVENANT WITH NOAH

The first great covenant in the Tanakh *is between God and Noah. The P text story relates how God finds all the earth's inhabitants wicked, except for Noah, and destroys the earth in a flood. When the waters subsides, God promises that he will not again destroy the world by water and permits humans to eat animal flesh. The authors of the P text note later (in Exodus 40) that all slaughter of animals must be done in the context of a sacrificial rite conducted by a priest.*

God blessed Noah and his sons, and said to them, "Be fertile and increase, and fill the earth. The fear and the dread of you shall be upon all the beasts of the earth and upon all the birds of the sky—everything with which the earth is astir—and upon all the fish of the sea; they are given into your hand. Every creature that lives shall be yours to eat; as with the green grasses, I give you all these. You must not, however, eat flesh with its life-blood in it. But for your own life-blood I will require a reckoning: I will require it of every beast; of man, too, will I require a reckoning for human life, of every man for that of his fellow man!

> Whoever sheds the blood of man,
> By man shall his blood be shed;
> For in His image
> Did God make man.

Be fertile, then, and increase; abound on the earth and increase on it."

And God said to Noah and to his sons with him, I now establish My covenant with you and your offspring to come, and with every living thing that is with you—birds, cattle, and every wild beast as well—all that have come out of the ark, every living thing on earth. I will maintain My covenant with you: never again shall all flesh be cut off by the waters of a flood, and never again shall there be a flood to destroy the earth."

God further said, "This is the sign that I set for the covenant between Me and you, and every living creature with you, for all ages to come. I have set My bow in the clouds, and it shall serve as a sign of the covenant between Me and the earth. When I bring clouds over the earth, and the bow appears in the clouds, I will remember My covenant between Me and you and every living creature among all flesh, so that the waters shall never again become a flood to destroy all flesh. When the bow is in the clouds, I will see it and remember the everlasting covenant between God and all living creatures, all flesh that is on earth. That," God said to Noah, "shall be the sign of the covenant that I have established between Me and all flesh that is on earth."

[Genesis 9:1–17]

COVENANT WITH ABRAHAM

The second great covenant of the Tanakh, *as appears in the P text, is between God and Abraham, where Abraham is selected by God to be father of a multitude. God indicates that he will inherit the land of Canaan and that circumcision is to be the sign of that covenant. Circumcision is a rite to be performed by priests.*

When Abram was ninety-nine years old, the Lord appeared to Abram and said to him, "I am El Shaddai [God heeds]. Walk in My ways and be blameless. I will establish My covenant between Me and you, and I will make you exceedingly numerous."

Abram threw himself on his face; and God spoke to him further, "As for Me, this is My covenant with you: You shall be the father of a multitude of nations. And you shall no longer be called Abram, but your name shall be Abraham, for I make you the father of a multitude of nations. I will make you exceedingly fertile, and make nations of you; and kings shall come forth from you. I will maintain My covenant between Me and you, and your offspring to come, as an everlasting covenant throughout the ages, to be God to you and to your offspring to come. I assign the land you sojourn in to you and your offspring to come, all the land of Canaan, as an everlasting holding. I will be their God."

God further said to Abraham, "As for you, you and your offspring to come throughout the ages shall keep My covenant. Such shall be the covenant between Me and you and your offspring to follow which you shall keep: every male among you shall be circumcised. You shall circumcise the flesh of your foreskin, and that shall be the sign of the covenant between Me and you. And throughout the generations, every male among you shall be circumcised at the age of eight days. As for the homeborn slave and the one bought from an outsider who is not of your offspring, they must be circumcised, homeborn and purchased alike. Thus shall My covenant be marked in your flesh as an everlasting pact. And if any male who is uncircumcised fails to circumcise the flesh of his foreskin, that person shall be cut off from his kin; he has broken My covenant."

And God said to Abraham, "As for your wife Sarai, you shall not call her Sarai, but her name shall be Sarah. I will bless her; indeed, I will give you a son by her. I will bless her so that she shall give rise to nations; rulers of peoples shall issue from her." Abraham threw himself on his face and laughed, as he said to himself, "Can a child be born to a man a hundred years old, or can Sarah bear a child at ninety? And Abraham said to

God, "O that Ishmael might live by Your favor!" God said, "Nevertheless, Sarah your wife shall bear you a son, and you shall name him Isaac; and I will maintain My covenant with him as an everlasting covenant for his offspring to come. As for Ishmael, I have heeded you. I hereby bless him. I will make him fertile and exceedingly numerous. He shall be the father of twelve chieftains, and I will make of him a great nation. But My covenant I will maintain with Isaac, whom Sarah shall bear to you at this season next year." And when He was done speaking with him, God was gone from Abraham.

[Genesis 17:1–22]

PASSOVER AND EXODUS

Abraham's descendants migrate to Egypt to avoid famine in Canaan and, within a few generations, their population dramatically increases. Intimidated by their numbers, the Pharaoh enslaves the Israelites and issues an edict that male infants are to be drowned. To save her child, one woman places her toddler, Moses, in a basket and floats it down the Nile, where it is discovered and he is adopted by the Pharaoh's daughter. When Moses grows up, God appears to him and instructs him to lead his people out of Egypt and into Canaan. To break the Pharaoh's resistance in releasing the Israelites, God kills the first born humans and cattle in Egypt. In preparation for the event, the Israelites are instructed to perform a series of activities as described below. Passover, one of Judaism's most sacred feasts, is in celebration of this event.

12. In the middle of the night the Lord struck down all the first-born in the land of Egypt, from the first-born of Pharaoh who sat on the throne to the first-born of the captive who was in the dungeon, and all the first-born of the cattle. And Pharaoh arose in the night, with all his courtiers and all the Egyptians—because there was a loud cry in Egypt; for there was no house where there was not someone dead. He summoned Moses and Aaron in the night and said, "Up, depart from among my people, you and the Israelites with you! Go, worship the Lord as you said! Take also your flocks and your herds, as you said, and be gone! And may you bring a blessing upon me also!"

    The Egyptians urged the people on, impatient to have them leave the country, for they said, "We shall all be dead." So the people took their dough before it was leavened, their kneading bowls wrapped in their cloaks upon their shoulders. The Israelites had done Moses' bidding and borrowed from the Egyptians objects of silver and gold, and clothing. And the Lord had disposed the Egyptians favorably toward the people, and they let them have their request; thus they stripped the Egyptians.

    The Israelites journeyed from Rameses to Succoth, about six hundred thousand men on foot, aside from children. Moreover, a mixed multitude went up with them, and very much livestock, both flocks and herds. And they baked unleavened cakes of the dough that they had taken out of Egypt, for it was not leavened, since they had been driven out of Egypt and could not delay; nor had they prepared any provisions for themselves.

The length of time that the Israelites lived in Egypt was four hundred and thirty years; at the end of the four hundred and thirtieth year, to the very day, all the ranks of the Lord departed from the land of Egypt. That was for the Lord a night of vigil to bring them out of the land of Egypt; that same night is the Lord's, one of vigil for all the children of Israel throughout the ages.

14. When the king of Egypt was told that the people had fled, Pharaoh and his courtiers had a change of heart about the people and said, "What is this we have done, releasing Israel from our service?" He ordered his chariot and took his men with him; he took six hundred of his picked chariots, and the rest of the chariots of Egypt, with officers in all of them. The Lord stiffened the heart of Pharaoh king of Egypt, and he gave chase to the Israelites. As the Israelites were departing defiantly, the Egyptians gave chase to them, and all the chariot horses of Pharaoh, his horsemen, and his warriors overtook them encamped by the sea, near Pihahiroth, before Baal-zephon.

As Pharaoh drew near, the Israelites caught sight of the Egyptians advancing upon them. Greatly frightened, the Israelites cried out to the Lord. And they said to Moses, "Was it for want of graves in Egypt that you brought us to die in the wilderness? What have you done to us, taking us out of Egypt? Is this not the very thing we told you in Egypt, saying, 'Let us be, and we will serve the Egyptians, for it is better for us to serve the Egyptians than to die in the wilderness'?" But Moses said to the people, "Have no fear! Stand by, and witness the deliverance which the Lord will work for you today; for the Egyptians whom you see today you will never see again. The Lord will battle for you; you hold your peace!"

Then the Lord said to Moses, "Why do you cry out to Me? Tell the Israelites to go forward. And you lift up your rod and hold out your arm over the sea and split it, so that the Israelites may march into the sea on dry ground. And I will stiffen the hearts of the Egyptians so that they go in after them; and I will gain glory through Pharaoh and all his warriors, his chariots and his horsemen. Let the Egyptians know that I am Lord, when I gain glory through Pharaoh, his chariots, and his horsemen."

The angel of God, who had been going ahead of the Israelite army, now moved and followed behind them; and the pillar of cloud shifted from in front of them and took up a place behind them, and it came between the army of the Egyptians and the army of Israel. Thus there was the cloud with the darkness, and it cast a spell upon the night, so that the one could not come near the other all through the night.

Then Moses held out his arm over the sea and the Lord drove back the sea with a strong east wind all that night, and turned the sea into dry ground. The waters were split, and the Israelites went into the sea on dry ground, the waters forming a wall for them on their right and on their left. The Egyptians came in pursuit after them into the sea, all of Pharaoh's horses, chariots, and horsemen. At the morning watch, the Lord looked down upon the Egyptian army from a pillar of fire and cloud, and threw the Egyptian army into a panic. He locked the wheels of their chariots so that they moved forward with difficulty. And the Egyptians said, "Let us flee from the Israelites, for the Lord is fighting for them against Egypt."

Then the Lord said to Moses, "Hold out your arm over the sea, that the waters may come back upon the Egyptians and upon their chariots and upon their horsemen." Moses held out his arm over the sea, and at daybreak the sea returned to its normal state, and the Egyptians fled at its approach. But the Lord hurled the Egyptians into the sea. The waters turned back and covered the chariots and the horsemen—Pharaoh's entire army that followed them into the sea; not one of them remained. But the Israelites had marched through the sea on dry ground, the waters forming a wall for them on their right and on their left.

[Exodus 12:29–41, 14:5–29]

MOSAIC COVENANT

The third great covenant in the Tanakh *text consists of God giving the Law to Moses at Mount Sinai, a means by which the Israelites could become a holy people. Mosaic Law is articulated throughout the books of Exodus, Leviticus, Numbers, and Deuteronomy, interspersed with narratives about the Israelites' 40 years of wandering. Exodus 19, a JE text, describes the people's preparation for receiving the Law from God. Exodus 20, which is possibly a reworked version of an ancient P text, presents the best known part of the Mosaic Law, the 10 Commandments.*

19. On the third new moon after the Israelites had gone forth from the land of Egypt, on that very day, they entered the wilderness of Sinai. Having journeyed from Rephidim, they entered the wilderness of Sinai and encamped in the wilderness. Israel encamped there in front of the mountain, and Moses went up to God. The Lord called to him from the mountain, saying, "Thus shall you say to the house of Jacob and declare to the children of Israel: 'You have seen what I did to the Egyptians, how I bore you on eagles' wings and brought you to Me. Now then, if you will obey Me faithfully and keep My covenant, you shall be My treasured possession among all the peoples. Indeed, all the earth is Mine, but you shall be to Me a kingdom of priests and a holy nation.' These are the words that you shall speak to the children of Israel."

Moses came and summoned the elders of the people and put before them all that the Lord had commanded him. All the people answered as one, saying, "All that the Lord has spoken we will do!" And Moses brought back the people's words to the Lord. And the Lord said to Moses, "I will come to you in a thick cloud, in order that the people may hear when I speak with you and so trust you ever after." Then Moses reported the people's words to the Lord, and the Lord said to Moses, "Go to the people and warn them to stay pure today and tomorrow. Let them wash their clothes. Let them be ready for the third day; for on the third day the Lord will come down, in the sight of all the people, on Mount Sinai. You shall set bounds for the people round about, saying, 'Beware of going up the mountain or touching the border of it. Whoever touches the mountain shall be put to death: no hand shall touch him, but he shall be either stoned or shot; beat or man, he shall not live.' When the ram's horn sounds a long blast, they may go up on the mountain."

Moses came down from the mountain to the people and warned the people to stay pure, and they washed their clothes. And he said to the people, "Be ready for the third day: do not go near a woman."

On the third day, as morning dawned, there was thunder, and lightening, and a dense cloud upon the mountain, and a very loud blast of the horn; and all the people who were in the camp trembled. Moses led the people out of the camp toward God, and they took their places at the foot of the mountain.

Now Mount Sinai was all in smoke, for the Lord had come down upon it in fire; the smoke rose like the smoke of a kiln, and the whole mountain trembled violently. The blare of the horn grew louder and louder. As Moses spoke, God answered him in thunder. The Lord came down upon Mount Sinai, on the top of the mountain, and the Lord called Moses to the top of the mountain and Moses went up. The lord said to Moses, Go down, warn the people not to break through to the Lord to gaze, lest many of them perish. The priests also, who come near the Lord, must stay pure, lest the Lord break out against them." But Moses said to the Lord, "The people cannot come up to the Mount Sinai, for You warned us saying, 'Set bounds about the mountain and sanctify it.'" So the Lord said to him, Go down, and come back together with Aaron; but let not the priests or the people break through to come up to the Lord, lest He break out against them." And Moses went down to the people and spoke to them.

20. God spoke all these words, saying:

I the Lord am your God who brought you out of the land of Egypt, the house of bondage: You shall have no other gods besides Me.

You shall not make for yourself a sculpted image, or any likeness of what is in the heavens above, or on the earth below, or in the waters under the earth. You shall not bow down to them or serve them for I the Lord your God am an impassioned God, visiting the guilt of the parents upon the children, upon the third and upon the fourth generations of those who reject Me, but showing kindness to the thousandth generation of those who love Me and keep My commandments.

You shall not swear falsely by the name of the Lord your God; for the Lord will not clear one who swears falsely by His name.

Remember the sabbath day and keep it holy. Six days you shall labor and do all your work, but the seventh day is a sabbath of the Lord your God: you shall not do any work—you, your son or daughter, your male or female slave, or your cattle, or the stranger who is within your settlements. For in six days the Lord made heaven and earth and sea, and all that is in them, and He rested on the seventh day; therefore the Lord blessed the sabbath day and hallowed it.

Honor your father and your mother, that you may long endure on the land that the Lord your God is assigned to you.

You shall not murder.

You shall not commit adultery.

You shall not steal.

You shall not bear false witness against your neighbor.

You shall not covet your neighbor's house; you shall not covet your neighbor's wife, or his male or female slave, or his ox or his ass, or anything that is your neighbor's.

All the people witnessed the thunder and lightening, the blare of the horn and the mountain smoking; and when the people saw it, they fell back and stood at a distance. "You speak to us," they said to Moses, "and we will obey; but let not God speak to us, lest we die." Moses answered the people, "Be not afraid; for God has come only in order to test you, and in order that the fear of Him may be ever with you, so that you do not go astray."

[Exodus 19, 20:1–17]

HOLINESS CODE

The Mosaic Law contains a series of codes on social, ethical, and religious topics, such as the Covenant Code (Exodus 21–23), the Purity Code (Leviticus 11–16), the Holiness Code (Leviticus 17–27), and the Law Code (Deuteronomy 12–26). The literary and legal style of these codes is frequently compared to other codes of the ancient near east, such as the Code of Hammurabi, king of Ur. For example, on the issue of kidnapping, the Hammurabi code states, "If a man has stolen the young son of a freeman, he shall be put to death." By comparison, the Covenant Code in Exodus 21:16 states, "He who kidnaps a man—whether he has sold him or is still holding him—shall be put to death." The following is from the Holiness Code, a P text in the Book of Leviticus.

19. The Lord spoke to Moses, saying, Speak to the whole Israelite community and say to them: You shall be holy, for I, the Lord your God, am holy.

You shall each revere his mother and his father, and keep My Sabbaths: I the Lord am your God.

Do not turn to idols or make molten gods for yourselves: I the Lord am your God.

When you sacrifice an offering of well-being to the Lord, sacrifice it so that it may be accepted on your behalf. It shall be eaten on the day you sacrifice it, or on the day following; but what is left by the third day must be consumed in fire. If it should be eaten on the third day, it is an offensive thing, it will not be acceptable. And he who eats of it shall bear his guilt, for he has profaned what is sacred to the Lord; that person shall be cut off from his kin.

When you reap the harvest of your land, you shall not reap all the way to the edges of your field, or gather the gleanings of your harvest. You shall not pick your vineyard bare, or gather the fallen fruit of your vineyard; you shall leave them for the poor and the stranger: I the Lord am your God.

You shall not steal; you shall not deal deceitfully or falsely with one another. You shall not swear falsely by My name, profaning the name of your God: I am the Lord.

You shall not defraud your fellow. You shall not commit robbery. The wages of a laborer shall not remain with you until morning.

You shall not insult the deaf, or place a stumbling block before the blind. You shall fear your God: I am the Lord.

You shall not render an unfair decision: do not favor the poor or show deference to the rich; judge your kinsman fairly. Do not deal basely with your countrymen. Do not profit by the blood of your fellow: I am the Lord.

You shall not hate your kinsfolk in your heart. Reprove your kinsman but incur no guilt because of him. You shall not take vengeance or bear a grudge against your countrymen. Love your fellow as yourself: I am the Lord.
You shall observe My laws.

You shall not let your cattle mate with a different kind; you shall not sow your field with two kinds of seed; you shall not put on cloth from a mixture of two kinds of material.

If a man has carnal relations with a woman who is a slave and has been designated for another man, but has not been redeemed or given her freedom, there shall be an indemnity; they shall not, however, be put to death, since she has not been freed. But he must bring to the entrance of the Tent of Meeting, as his guilt offering to the Lord, a ram of guilt offering. With the ram of guilt offering the priest shall make expiation for him before the Lord for the sin that he committed; and the sin that he committed will be forgiven.

When you enter the land and plant any tree for food, you shall regard its fruit as forbidden. Three years it shall be forbidden for you, not to be eaten. In the forth year all its fruit shall be set aside for jubilation before the Lord; and only in the fifth year may you use its fruit—that its yield to you may be increased: I the Lord am your God.

You shall not eat anything with its blood. You shall not practice divination or soothsaying. You shall not round off the side-growth on your head, or destroy the side-growth of your beard. You shall not make gashes in your flesh for the dead, or incise any marks on yourselves: I am the Lord.

Do not degrade your daughter and make her a harlot, lest the land fall into harlotry and the land be filled with depravity. You shall keep my Sabbaths and venerate My sanctuary: I am the Lord.

Do not turn to ghosts and do not inquire of familiar spirits, to be defiled by them: I the Lord am your God.

You shall rise before the aged and show deference to the old; you shall fear your God: I am the Lord.

When a stranger resides with you in your land, you shall not wrong him. The stranger who resides with you shall be to you as one of your citizens; you shall love him as yourself, for you were strangers in the land of Egypt: I the Lord am your God.

You shall not falsify measures of length, weight, or capacity. You shall have an honest balance, honest weights, an honest *ephah*, and an honest *hin*. I the Lord am your God who freed you from the land of Egypt. You shall faithfully observe all my laws and all my rules: I am the Lord.

[Leviticus 19:1–37]

ENTRY INTO CANAAN

After 40 years of wandering, the Israelites enter Canaan under the leadership of Joshua, Moses' successor. This account is part of a larger text sequence called the Deuteronomistic History, edited just before the Babylonian exile, and encompasses the books of Deuteronomy through second Kings. The story emphasizes Deuteronomist themes, such as the importance of the Ark of the Covenant as the focus of God's presence, and the command to annihilate the present occupants of Canaan as a means of assuring religious purity.

After the death of Moses the servant of the Lord, the Lord said to Joshua son of Nun, Moses' attendant:

"My servant Moses is dead. Prepare to cross the Jordan, together with all this people, into the land that I am giving to the Israelites. Every spot on which your foot treads I give to you, as I promised Moses. Your territory shall extend from the wilderness and the Lebanon to the Great River, the River Euphrates [on the east]—the whole Hittite country—and up to the Mediterranean Sea on the west. No one shall be able to resist you as long as you live. As I was with Moses, so I will be with you; I will not fail you or forsake you.

Be strong and resolute, for you shall apportion to this people the land that I swore to their fathers to assign to them. But you must be very strong and resolute to observe faithfully all the Teaching that My servant Moses enjoined upon you. Do not deviate from it to the right or to the left, that you may be successful wherever you go. Let not this Book of the Teaching cease from your lips, but recite it day and night, so that you may observe faithfully all that is written in it. Only then will you prosper in your undertakings and only then will you be successful.

I charge you: Be strong and resolute; do not be terrified or dismayed, for the Lord your God is with you wherever you go."

Joshua thereupon gave orders to the officials of the people: "Go through the camp and charge the people thus: Get provisions ready, for in three days' time you are to cross the Jordan, in order to enter and possess the land that the Lord your God is giving you as a possession."

Then Joshua said the to Reubenites, the Gadites, and the half-tribe of Manasseh, "Remember what Moses the servant of the Lord enjoined upon you, when he said: 'The Lord your God is granting you a haven; He has assigned this territory to you.' Let your wives, children, and livestock remain in the land that Moses assigned to you on this side of the Jordan; but every one of your fighting men shall go across armed in the van of your kinsmen. And you shall assist them until the Lord has given your kinsmen a haven, such as you have, and they too have gained possession of the land that the Lord your God has assigned to them. Then you may return to the land on the east side of the Jordan, which Moses the servant of the Lord assigned to you as your possession, and you may possess it."

They answered Joshua, "We will do everything you have commanded us and we will go wherever you send us. We will obey you just as we obeyed Moses; let but the Lord your God be with you as He was with Moses! Any man who flouts your commands and does not obey every order you give him shall be put to death. Only be strong and resolute!"

Early next morning, Joshua and all the Israelites set out from Shittim and marched to the Jordan. They did not cross immediately, but spent the night there. Three days later, the officials went through the camp and charged the people as follows: "When you see the Ark of the Covenant of the Lord your God being borne by the levitical priests, you shall move forward. Follow it—but keep a distance of some two thousand cubits from it, never coming any closer to it—so that you may know by what route to march, since it is a road you have not traveled before."

And Joshua said to the people, "Purify yourselves, for tomorrow the Lord will perform wonders in your midst."

Then Joshua ordered the priests, "Take up the Ark of the Covenant and advance to the head of the people." And they took up the Ark of the Covenant and advanced to the head of the people.

The Lord said to Joshua, "This day, for the first time, I will exalt you in the sight of all Israel, so that they shall know that I will be with you as I was with Moses. For you part, command the priests who carry the Ark of the Covenant as follows: When you reach the edge of the waters of the Jordan, make a halt in the Jordan."

And Joshua said to the Israelites, "Come closer and listen to the words of the Lord our God. By this," Joshua continued, "you shall know that a living God is among you, and that He will dispossess for you the Canaanites, Hittites, Hivites, Perizzites, Girgashites, Amorites, and Jebusites: the Ark of the Covenant of the Sovereign of all the earth is advancing before you into the Jordan. Now select twelve men from the tribes of Israel, one man from each tribe. When the feet of the priests bearing the Ark of the Lord, the Sovereign of all the earth, come to rest in the waters of the Jordan, the waters of the Jordan—-the water coming from upstream—will be cut off and will stand in a single heap."

When the people set out from their encampment to cross the Jordan, the priests bearing the Ark of the Covenant were at the head of the people. Now the Jordan keeps flowing over its entire bed throughout the harvest season. But as soon as the bearers of the Ark reached the Jordan, and the feet of the priests bearing the Ark dipped into the water at its edge, the waters coming down from upstream piled up in a single heap a great way off, at Adam, the town next to Zarethan; and those flowing away downstream to the Sea of the Arabah (the Dead Sea) ran out completely. So the people crossed near Jericho. The priests who bore the Ark of the Lord's Covenant stood on dry land exactly in the middle of the Jordan, while all Israel crossed over on dry land, until the entire nation had finished crossing the Jordan.

[Joshua 1, 3]

SONG OF DEBORAH

After entry into Canaan, the Israelites fight to dislodge the Canaanites. Israel is then governed by a series of legal and military Judges, including Deborah, one of a few women leaders in Jewish history. With the aid of the military leader Barak, Deborah and a small group defeat the army of Jabin, King of Canaan. The Canaanite army, headed by Sisera, has an initial advantage of 900 chariots. Due to a sudden divinely caused cloud burst and flash flood, the Israelites gain the advantage. The Song of Deborah, which commemorates this victory, is one of the oldest passages of the Tanakh. *Composed about 1100 B.C.E., it is similar in structure to Canaanite poems of the period. Historically it denotes the Israelites' successful habitation of the hillsides, overshadowing Canaanite occupation of the valley regions.*

> When locks go untrimmed in Israel,
> When people dedicate themselves—
> Bless the Lord
>
> Hear, O kings! Give ear, O potentates!
> I will sing, will sing to the Lord,
> Will hymn the Lord, the God of Israel.

O Lord, when you came forth from Seir,
Advanced from the country of Edom,
the earth trembled;
The heavens dripped,
Yea, the clouds dripped water,
The mountains quaked—
Before the Lord, Him of Sinai,
Before the Lord, God of Israel.

In the days of Shamgar son of Anath,
In the days of Jael, caravans ceased,
And wayfarers went
By Roundabout paths.
Deliverance ceased,
Ceased in Israel,
Till you arose, O Deborah,
Arose, O mother, in Israel!
When they chose new gods,
Was there a fighter then in the gates?
No shield or spear was seen
Among forty thousand in Israel!

My heart is with Israel's leaders,
With the dedicated of the people—
Bless the Lord!
You riders on tawny she-asses,
You who sit on saddle rugs,
And you wayfarers, declare it!
Louder than the sounds of archers,
There among the watering places
Let them chant the gracious acts of the Lord,
His gracious deliverance of Israel.
Then did the people of the Lord
March down to the gates!
Awake, awake, O Deborah!
Awake, awake, strike up the chant!
Arise, O Barak;
Take your captives, O son of Abinoam!

[Judges 5:2–12]

DAVIDIC COVENANT

In response to the need for a ruler who could unify the country against Philistine attacks, Saul is appointed the first king. The Deuteronomistic History relates how Saul's disobedience quickly puts him in disfavor with God, after which God selects David as Saul's more obedient successor. This reflects the most consistent theological theme throughout all seven books of the Deuteronomistic History: Obedience to God results in prosperity, disobedience results in hardship. The fourth and final great covenant in the Tanakh *is with King David, wherein a promise is given that David's house and kingship will be secure and his throne established forever.*

. . . Thus said the Lord of Hosts: I took you from the pasture, from following the flock, to be ruler of My people Israel, and I have been with you wherever you went, and have cut down all your enemies before you. Moreover, I will give you great renown like that of the greatest men on earth. I will establish a home for My people Israel and will plant them form, so that they shall dwell secure and shall tremble no more. Evil men shall not oppress them any more as in the past, ever since I appointed chieftains over my people Israel. I will give you safety from all your enemies.

The Lord declares to you that He, the Lord, will establish a house for you. When your days are done and you lie with your fathers, I will raise up your offspring after you, one of your own issue, and I will establish his kingship. He shall build a house for my name, and I will establish his royal throne forever. I will be a father to him, and he shall be a son to Me. When he does wrong, I will chastise him with the rod of men and the affliction of mortals; but I will never withdraw My favor from him as I withdrew it from Saul, whom I removed to make room for you. Your house and your kingship shall ever be secure before you; your throne shall be established forever.

[2 Samuel 7:8–16]

PSALMS ASCRIBED TO DAVID

The Book of Psalms is a collection of 150 songs and prayers written over a 600-year period, many after the Babylonian exile. The book may have taken its final form under the editorship of Ezra, and is sometimes referred to as the hymn book of the second temple. Although the authorship of most of the psalms is uncertain, 73 are ascribed in the text to David and are traditionally said to reflect happy or troubled periods of his life. The Psalms are classified as they relate to themes of deliverance, penitence, praise, pilgrimages, historical episodes, and messianic hope. The following is a selection of psalms of David.

8.

O Lord, our Lord,
    How majestic is Your name throughout the earth,
    You who have covered the heavens with Your splendor!
From the mouths of infants and sucklings
    You have founded strength on account of Your foes,
    to put an end to enemy and avenger.
When I behold Your heavens, the work of Your fingers,
    the moon and stars that You set in place,
    what is man that You have been mindful of him,
    mortal man that You have taken note of him,
    that You have made him little less than divine,
    and adorned him with glory and majesty;
    You have made him master over Your handiwork,
    lying the world at his feet,

sheep and oxen, all of them,
and wild beasts, too;
the birds of the heavens, the fish of the sea,
whatever travels the paths of the seas.
O Lord, our Lord, how majestic is Your name throughout the earth!

23.

The lord is my shepherd;
I lack nothing.
He makes me lie down in green pastures;
He leads me to a water in places of repose;
He renews my life;
He guides me in right paths
as befits His name.
Though I walk through a valley of deepest darkness,
I fear no harm, for You are with me;
Your rod and Your staff—they comfort me.
You spread a table for me in full view of my enemies;
You anoint my head with oil;
my drink is abundant.
Only goodness and steadfast love shall pursue me
all the days of my life,
and I shall dwell in the house of the Lord
For many long years.

27.

The lord is my light and my help;
whom would I fear?
The Lord is the stronghold of my life,
whom should I dread?
When evil men assail me
to devour my flesh—
it is they, my foes and my enemies,
who stumble and fall.
Should an army besiege me,
my heart would have no fear;
should war beset me,
still would I be confident.
One thing I ask of the Lord,
only that do I seek:
to live in the house of the Lord
all the days of my life,
to gaze upon the beauty of the Lord,
to frequent His temple.
He will shelter me in His pavilion
on an evil day,
grant me the protection of His tent,
raise me high upon a rock.
Now is my head high
over my enemies roundabout;

I sacrifice in His tent with shouts of joy,
  singing and chanting a hymn to the Lord.
Hear, O Lord, when I cry aloud;
  have mercy on me, answer me.
In Your behalf my heart says:
  seek My face!
O Lord, I seek Your face.
Do not hide Your face from me;
  do not thrust aside Your servant in anger;
  You have ever been my help.
Do not forsake me, do not abandon me,
  O God, my deliverer.
Though my father and mother abandon me,
  the Lord will take me in
Show me Your way, O Lord,
  and lead me on a level path
  because of my watchful foes.
Do not subject me to the will of my foes,
  for false witnesses and unjust accusers have appeared against me.
  Had I not the assurance that I would enjoy the goodness of the Lord in the
  land of the living . . .
Look to the Lord;
  be strong and of good courage!
O look to the Lord!

32.

Happy is he whose transgression is forgiven,
  whose sin is covered over.
Happy the man whom the Lord does not hold guilty,
  and in whose spirit there is no deceit.
As long as I said nothing,
  my limbs wasted away
  from my anguished roaring all day long.
For night and day
  Your hand lay heavy on me;
  my vigor waned
  as in the summer drought.
Then I acknowledge my sin to you;
  I did not cover up my guilt;
  I resolved, "I will confess my transgressions to the Lord,"
  and You forgave the guilt of my sin.
Therefore let every faithful man pray to You
  upon discovering [his sin]
  that the rushing mighty waters not overtake him
You are my shelter;
  You preserve me from distress;
  You surround me with the joyous shouts of deliverance.
Let me enlighten you
  and show you which way to go;
  let me offer counsel; my eye is on you

Be not like a senseless horse or mule
   whose movement must be curbed by bit and bridle,
   far be it from you!
Many are the torments of the wicked,
   but he who trusts in the Lord
   shall be surrounded with favor.
Rejoice in the Lord and exult, O you righteous;
   shout for joy, all upright men!

51.

Have mercy upon me, O God,
   as befits Your faithfulness;
   in keeping with Your abundant compassion,
   blot out my transgressions.
Wash me thoroughly of my iniquity,
   and purify me of my sin'
   for I recognize my transgressions,
   and am ever conscious of my sin.
Against You alone have I sinned,
   and done what is evil in Your sight;
   so You are just in Your sentence,
   and right in Your judgment.
Indeed I was born with iniquity;
   with sin my mother conceived me.
Indeed You desire truth about that which is hidden;
   teach me wisdom about secret things.
Purge me with hyssop till I am pure;
   wash me till I am whiter than snow.
Let me hear tidings of joy and gladness;
   let the bones You have crushed exult.
Hide Your face from my sins;
   blot out all my iniquities.
Fashion a pure heart for me, O God;
   create in me a steadfast spirit.
Do not cast me out of your presence,
   or take Your holy spirit away from me.
Let me again rejoice in Your help;
   let a vigorous spirit sustain me.
I will teach transgressors Your Ways,
   That sinners may return to you.
Save me from bloodguilt,
   O God, God, my deliverer,
   that I may sing forth Your beneficence.
O Lord, open my lips,
   and let my mouth declare Your praise.
You do not want me to bring sacrifices;
   you do not desire burnt offerings;
True sacrifice to God is a contrite spirit;
   God, You will not despise
   a contrite and crushed heart.

May it please You to make Zion prosper;
  rebuild the walls of Jerusalem
Then you will want sacrifices offered in righteousness,
  burnt and whole offerings;
  the bulls will be offered on Your altar.

[Psalms 8; 23; 27; 32; 51]

SOLOMON'S TEMPLE

Israel's glory peaked during the reign of King Solomon, David's son. Its borders extended further than they ever would again (though not as far as under David), and Israel was a key player in ancient near eastern politics. The jewel in the crown of Solomon's achievements was his temple, said to have taken 13 years to complete. According to the Deuteronomistic History, all sacrifices were to be performed only at the temple in Jerusalem; thus the temple became the focus of all religious activity in Israel. The following describes the extent and wealth of Solomon's kingdom, his wisdom, and his construction of the temple.

Judah and Israel were as numerous as the sands of the sea; they ate and drank and were content.

5. Solomon's rule extended over all the kingdoms of the Euphrates to the land of the Philistines and the boundary of Egypt. They brought Solomon tribute and were subject to him all his life. Solomon's daily provisions consisted of 30 *kors* of semolina, and 60 *kors* of [ordinary] flour, 10 fattened oxen, 20 pasture-fed oxen, and 100 sheep and goats, besides deer and gazelles, roebucks and fatted geese. For he controlled the whole region west of the Euphrates—all the kings west of the Euphrates, from Tiphsah to Gaza—and he had peace on all his borders roundabout. All the days of Solomon, Judah and Israel from Dan to Beer-sheba dwelt in safety, everyone under his own vine and under his own fig tree. Solomon had 40,000 stalls of horses for his chariotry and 12,000 horsemen.

All those prefects, each during his month, would furnish provisions for King Solomon and for all who were admitted to King Solomon's table; they did not fall short in anything. They would also, each in his turn, deliver barley and straw for the horses and the swift steeds to the places where they were stationed.

The lord endowed Solomon with wisdom and discernment in great measure, with understanding as vast as the sands on the seashore. Solomon's wisdom was greater than the wisdom of all the Kedemites and than all the wisdom of the Egyptians. He was the wisest of all men: [wiser] than Ethan the Ezrahite, and Heman, Chalkol, and Darda the sons of Mahol. His fame spread among all the surrounding nations. He composed three thousand proverbs, and his songs numbered one thousand and five. He discoursed about trees, from the cedar in Lebanon to the hyssop that grows out of the wall; and he discoursed about beasts, birds, creeping things, and fishes. Men of all peoples came to hear Solomon's wisdom, [sent] by all the kins of the earth who had heard of his wisdom.

King Hiram of Tyre sent his officials to Solomon when he heard that he had been anointed king in place of his father; for Hiram had always been a friend of David. Solomon sent this message to Hiram: "You know that my father David could not build a house for the name of the Lord his God because of the enemies that encompassed him, until the Lord had placed them under the soles of his feet. But now the Lord my God has given me respite all around; there is no adversary and not mischance. And so I propose to build a house for the name of the Lord my God, as the Lord promised my father David, saying, 'Your son, whom I will set on your throne in your place, shall build the house for My name.' Please, then, give orders for cedars to be cut for me in the Lebanon. My servants will work with yours, and I will pay you any wages you may ask for your servants; for as you know, there is none among us who knows how to cut timber like the Sidonians."

When Hiram heard Solomon's message, he was overjoyed. "Praised be the Lord this day," he said, "for granting David a wise son to govern this great people." So Hiram sent word to Solomon: "I have your message; I will supply all the cedar and cypress logs you require."

. . . King Solomon imposed forced labor on all Israel; the levy came to 30,000 men. He sent them to the Lebanon in shifts of 10,000 a month: they would spend one month in the Lebanon and two months at home. Adoniram was in charge of the forced labor. Solomon also had 70,000 porters and 80,000 quarriers in the hills, apart from Solomon's 3,300 officials who were in charge of the work and supervised the gangs doing the work.

The king ordered huge blocks of choice stone to be quarried, so that the foundations of the house might be laid with hewn stones. Solomon's masons, Hiram's masons, and the men of Gebal shaped them. Thus the timber and the stones for building the house were made ready.

. . . When Solomon had completed the construction of the House, he paneled the walls of the house on the inside with planks of cedar. He also overlaid the walls on the inside with wood, from the floor of the House to the ceiling. And he overlaid the floor of the House with planks of cypress. Twenty cubits from the rear of the House, he built [a partition] of cedar planks from the floor to the walls; he furnished its interior to serve as a shrine, as the Holy of Holies. The front part of the House,, that is, the Great Hall, measured 40 cubits. The cedar of the interior of the House had carvings of gourds and calyxes; It was all cedar, no stone was exposed. In the innermost part of the House, he fixed a shrine in which to place the Ark of the Lord's Covenant. The interior of the Shrine was 20 cubits long, 20 cubits wide, and 20 cubits high. He overlaid it with solid gold; he similarly overlaid [its] cedar altar. Solomon overlaid the interior of the House with solid gold; and he inserted golden chains into the door of the Shrine. He overlaid [the Shrine] with gold, so that the entire House was overlaid with gold; he even overlaid with gold the entire altar of the Shrine. And so the entire House was completed.

[1 Kings 4:20, 5:1–20, 27–33; 6:14–22]

PROVERBS ATTRIBUTED TO SOLOMON

In the above passage, Solomon is said to have been the wisest of all men and author of three thousand proverbs. The Book of Proverbs contains seven distinct collections of sayings, the first four of which are traditionally attributed to Solomon. Compiled during the time of Ezra, Proverbs contains sayings from throughout periods of the united and divided Kingdom, which are in the form of two-line sentences about an aspect of human experience, usually secular. Three literary styles are exhibited in the proverbs: synonymous parallelism, where the second line repeats the content of the first; antithetic parallelism, where good behavior in the first line is contrasted with bad behavior in the second line; and ascending parallelism, where the second line completes the train of thought in the first line. The following is from the second collection within Proverbs (thought to be the oldest part of the book) titled "The Proverbs of Solomon."

1. A gentle response allays wrath; A harsh word provokes anger.
2. The tongue of the wise produces much knowledge, But the mouth of dullards pours out folly.
3. The eyes of the Lord are everywhere, Observing the bad and the good.
4. A healing tongue is a tree of life, But a devious one makes for a broken spirit.
5. A fool spurns the discipline of his father, But one who heeds reproof becomes clever.
6. In the house of the righteous there is much treasure, But in the harvest of the wicked there is trouble.
7. The lips of the wise disseminate knowledge; Not so the minds of dullards.
8. The sacrifice of the wicked is an abomination to the Lord, But the prayer of the upright pleases Him.
9. The way of the wicked is an abomination to the Lord, But he loves him who pursues righteousness.
10. Discipline seems bad to him who forsakes the way; He who spurns reproof will die.
11. Sheol and Abaddon lie exposed to the Lord, How much more the minds of men!
12. The scoffer dislikes being reproved; He will not resort to the wise.
13. A joyful heart makes a cheerful face; A sad heart makes a despondent mood.
14. The mind of a prudent man seeks knowledge; The mouth of the dullard pursues folly.

15. All the days of a poor man are wretched, But contentment is a feast without end.
16. Better a little with fear of the Lord Than great wealth with confusion.
17. Better a meal of vegetables where there is love Than a fattened ox where there is hate.
18. A hot-tempered man provokes a quarrel; A patient man calms strife.
19. The way of a lazy man is like a hedge of thorns, But the path of the upright is paved.
20. A wise son makes his father happy; A fool of a man humiliates his mother.
21. Folly is joy to one devoid of sense; A prudent man walks a straight path.
22. Plans are foiled for want of counsel, But they succeed through many advisers.
23. A ready response is a joy to a man, And how good is a world rightly timed!
24. For an intelligent man the path of life leads upward, In order to avoid Sheol below.
25. The Lord will tear down the house of the proud, But he will establish the homestead of the widow.
26. Evil thoughts are an abomination to the Lord, But pleasant words are pure.
27. He who pursues ill-gotten gain makes trouble for his household; He who spurns gifts will live long.
28. The heart of the righteous man rehearses his answer, but the mouth of the wicked blurts out evil things.
29. The Lord is far from the wicked, But He hears the prayer of the righteous.
30. What brightens the eye gladdens the heart; Good news puts fat on the bones.
31. He whose ear heeds the discipline of life Lodges among the wise.
32. He who spurns discipline hates himself; He who heeds reproof gains understanding.
33. The fear of the Lord is the discipline of wisdom; Humility precedes honor.

[Proverbs 15]

ELIJAH VERSUS THE PRIESTS OF ASHERAH AND BAAL

After Solomon's reign, Israel divided into northern and southern kingdoms. The explanation given for this in the Deuteronomistic History is Solomon's continual worship of regional deities. Writers of the Tanakh condemn these worship practices and praise the Yahwist prophets and kings who challenge them. Israelite worship of the goddess Asherah is of particular interest. Asherah is the wife of the Canaanite high god, El, and in some popular Israelite religion may have been a consort of Yahweh. Worship rituals of Asherah center on sacred pillars, which in the Deuteronomistic History are strictly forbidden (Deuternonomy 16:21–22). The following story from the Deuteronomistic History dramatically presents a showdown between the prophets of Asherah and Baal on the one hand, and the prophet Elijah on the other hand. Elijah is the lone defender of Yahweh in the northern Kingdom at this time.

16. . . . Ahab son of Omri became king over Israel in the thirty-eighth year of King Asa of Judah, and Ahab son of Omri reigned over Israel in Samaria for twenty-two years. Ahab son of Omri did what was displeasing to the Lord, more than all who preceded him. Not content to follow the sins of Jeroboam son of Nebat, he took a wife Jezebel daughter of King Ethball of the Phoenicians, and he went and served Baal and worshipped him. He erected an alter to Baal in the temple of Baal which he built in Samaria. Ahab also made a sacred post. Ahab did more to vex the Lord, the God of Israel, than all the kings of Israel who preceded him.

17. Elijah the Tisbite, an inhabitant of Gilead, said to Ahab, "As the Lord lives, the God of Israel whom I serve, there will be no dew or rain except at my bidding." . . .

18. Much later, in the third year, a word of the Lord came to Elijah: "Go, appear before Ahab; then I will send rain upon the earth." Thereupon Elijah set out to appear before Ahab. . . .

    When Ahab caught sight of Elijah, Ahab said to him, "Is that you, you troubler of Israel?" He retorted, "It is not I who have brought trouble on Israel, but you and your father's House, by forsaking the commandments of the Lord and going after the Baalim. Now summon all Israel to join me at Mount Carmel, together with the four hundred and fifty prophets of Baal and the four hundred prophets of Asherah, who eat at Jezebel's table.

    Ahab sent orders to all the Israelites and gathered the prophets at Mount Carmel. Elijah approached all the people and said, "How long will you keep hopping between two opinions? If the Lord is God, follow Him; and if Baal, follow him!" But the people answered him not a word. Then Elijah said to the people, "I am the only prophet of the Lord left, while the prophets of Baal are four hundred and fifty men. Let two young bulls be given to us. Let them choose one bull, cut it up, and lay it on the wood, but let them not apply fire; I will prepare the other bull, and lay it on the wood, and will not apply fire. You will then invoke your god by name, and I will invoke the Lord by name; and let us agree: the god who responds with fire, that one is God." And all the people answered, "Very good!"

    Elijah said to the prophets of Baal, "Choose one bull and prepare it first, for you are the majority; invoke your god by name, but apply no fire." They took the bull that was given them; they prepared it, and invoked Baal by name from morning until noon, shouting, "O Baal, answer us!" But there was no sound, and none who responded; so they performed a hopping dance about the altar that had been set up. When noon came, Elijah mocked them, saying, "Shout louder! After all, he is a god. But he may be in conversation, he may be detained, or he may be on a journey, or perhaps he is asleep and will wake up." So they shouted louder, and gashed themselves with knives and spears, according to their practice, until the blood streamed over them. When noon passed, they kept raving until the hour of presenting the meal offering. Still there was no sound, and none who responded or heeded.

Then Elijah said to all the people, "Come closer to me"; and all the people came closer to him. He repaired the damaged altar of the Lord. Then Elijah took twelve stones, corresponding to the number of the tribes of the sons of Jacob—to whom the word of the Lord had come: "Israel shall be your name"—and with the stones he built an alter in the name of the Lord. Around the altar he made a trench large enough for two *seahs* of seed He laid out the wood, and he cut up the bull and laid it on the wood. And he said, "Fill four jars with water and pour it over the burnt offering and the wood." Then he said, "Do it a second time"; and they did it a second time. "Do it a third time," he said; and they did it a third time. The water ran down around the altar, and even the trench was filled with water.

When it was time to present the meal offering, the prophet Elijah came forward and said, "O Lord, God of Abraham, Isaac, and Israel! Let it be known today that You are God in Israel and that I am Your servant, and that I have done all these things at Your bidding. Answer me, O Lord, answer me, that this people may know that You, O Lord, are God; for You have turned their hearts backward."

Then fire from the Lord descended and consumed the burnt offering, the wood, the stones, and the earth; and it licked up the water that was in the trench. When they saw this, all the people flung themselves on thief faces and cried out: "The Lord alone is God, The Lord alone is God!"

[1 Kings 16:29–33; 17:1; 18:1–2, 17–40]

ISAIAH'S WARNING TO JUDAH

In 722 the northern Kingdom fell to the Mesopotamian superpower of the time, Assyria. Although the southern Kingdom of Judah survived Assyrian encroachment, it was embroiled in foreign political conflicts. The prophet Isaiah was an advisor to two Kings of the southern Kingdom at the time: Ahaz and his successor Hezekiah. Under the leadership of King Hezekiah, the Kingdom of Judah survived the Assyrian attack and continued for another 150 years. His advice to both kings was the same: do not participate in anti-Assyrian conspiracies, but trust in God for deliverance. The Book of Isaiah is an anthology of prophetic writings from Isaiah's time through the Babylonian exile. Of the book's 66 chapters, Isaiah's own words are confined to Chapters 1–11 and 28–32. Chapter 1 below expresses Isaiah's indictment against the people of Judah: They have forsaken God and risk being purged. Chapter 6 below is Isaiah's call to prophethood.

1. The prophecies of Isaiah son of Amoz, who prophesied concerning Judah and Jerusalem in the reigns of Uzziah, Jotham, Ahaz, and Hezekiah, kings of Judah.

> Hear, O heavens, and give ear, O earth,
> For the Lord has spoken:
> I reared children and brought them up—
> And they have rebelled against Me!
> An ox knows its owner,
> An ass its master's crib:
> Israel does not know,
> My people takes no thought.
>
> Ah, sinful nation!
> People laden with iniquity!
> Brood of evildoers!
> Depraved children!
> They have forsaken the Lord,
> Spurned the Holy One of Israel,
> Turned their backs [on Him].
>
> Why do you seek further beatings,
> That you continue to offend?
> Every head is ailing,
> And every heart is sick.
> From head to foot
> No spot is sound:
> All bruises, and welts,
> And festering sores—
> Not pressed out, not bound up,
> Not softened with oil.
> Your land is a waste,
> Your cities burnt down;
> Before your eyes, the yield of your soil
> Is consumed by strangers—
> A wasteland as overthrown by strangers!
> Fair Zion is left
> Like a booth in a vineyard,
> Like a hut in a cucumber field,
> Like a city beleaguered. Had not the Lord of Hosts
> Left us some survivors,
> We should be like Sodom,
> Another Gomorrah. . . .
>
> "Come, let us reach an understanding,—says the Lord.
> Be your sins like crimson,
> They can turn snow-white;
> Be they red as died wool,
> They can become like fleece."
> If, then, you agree and give heed,
> You will eat the good things of the earth;
> But if you refuse and disobey,

You will be devoured [by] the sword.
For it was the Lord who spoke.

6. In the year that King Uzziah died, I beheld my Lord seated on a high and lofty throne; and the skirts of His robe filled the Temple. Seraphs stood in attendance on Him. Each of them had six wings: with two he covered his face, with two he covered his legs, and with two he would fly.

> And one would call to the other,
> "Holy, holy, holy!
> The Lord of Hosts!
> His presence fills all the earth!"

The doorposts would shake at the sound of the one who called, and the House kept filling with smoke. I cried,

> "Woe is me; I am lost!
> For I am a man of unclean lips
> And I live among a people of unclean lips;
> Yet my own eyes have beheld
> The King Lord of Hosts."

Then one of the seraphs flew over to me with a live coal, which he had taken from the altar with a pair of tongs. He touched it to my lips and declared,

> Now that this has touched your lips,
> Your guilt shall depart
> And your sin be purged away.

Then I heard the voice of my Lord saying, "Whom shall I send? Who will go for us? And I said, "Here am I; send me." And He said, "Go say to that people:

> 'Hear, indeed, but do not understand;
> See, indeed, but do not grasp'
> Dull that people's mind,
> Stop its ears,
> And seal its eyes—
> Lest, seeing with its eyes
> And hearing with its ears,
> It also grasp with its mind,
> And repent and save itself."

I asked, "How long, my Lord?" And He replied:

> "Till towns lie waste without inhabitants
> And houses without people,
> And the ground lies waste and desolate—
> For the Lord will banish the population—
> And deserted sites are many
> In the midst of the land.

But while a tenth part yet remains in it, it shall repent. It shall be ravaged like the terebinth and the oak, of which stumps are left even when they are felled: its stump shall be a holy seed."

[Isaiah 1:1–9, 18–21; 6]

BABYLONIAN CONQUEST AND EXILE

Around 610 B.C.E. a group of Semites in Babylon, the Chaldeans, overthrew the Assyrians and formed a new Babylonian Empire. At first Judah's king paid tribute to the Empire, but later rebelled, thinking that Egypt would come to his defense if necessary. In retaliation, the Babylonian army marched into Judah, looted the temple and royal treasury, and exiled the royal family and upper class Israelites to Babylon. The Babylonians appointed Zedekiah as a puppet king but, when pressured by the Egyptians, he too rebelled. In 586 B.C.E., the Babylonian army again marched into Judah, this time destroying Jerusalem and the temple. The following recounts the tragedy of the exile.

24. . . . Jehoiachin was eighteen years old when he became king, and he reigned three months in Jerusalem; his mother's name was Nehushta daughter of Elnathan of Jerusalem. He did what was displeasing to the Lord, just as his father had done. At that time, the troops of King Nebuchadnezzar of Babylon marched against Jerusalem, and the city came under siege. King Nebuchadnezzar of Babylon advanced against the city while his troops were besieging it. Thereupon King Jehoiachin of Judah, along with his mother, and his courtiers, commanders, and officers, surrendered to the king of Babylon. The king of Babylon took him captive in the eighth year of his reign. He carried off from Jerusalem all the treasures of the House of the Lord and the treasures of the royal palace; he stripped off all the golden decorations in the Temple of the Lord—which King Solomon of Israel had made—as the Lord had warned. He exiled all of Jerusalem: all the commanders and all the warriors—ten thousand exiles—as well as all the craftsmen and smiths; only the poorest people in the land were left. He deported Jehoiachin to Babylon; and the king's mother and wives and officers and the notables of the land were brought as exiles from Jerusalem to Babylon. All the able men, to the number of seven thousand—all of them warriors, trained for battle—and a thousand craftsmen and smiths were brought to Babylon as exiles by the king of Babylon. And the king of Babylon appointed Mattaniah, Jehoiachin's uncle, king in his place, changing his name to Zedekiah.

Zedekiah was twenty-one years old when he became king, and he reigned eleven years in Jerusalem; his mother's name was Hamutal daughter of Jeremiah of Libnah. He did what was displeasing to the Lord, just as Jehoiakim had done. Indeed, Jerusalem and Judah were a cause of anger for the Lord, so that He cast them out of His presence.

25. Zedekiah rebelled against the king of Babylon. And in the ninth year of his reign, on the tenth day of the tenth month, Nebuchadnezzar moved against Jerusalem with his whole army. He besieged it; and they built towers against it all around. The city continued in a state of siege until the eleventh year of King Zedekiah. By the ninth day [of the fourth month] the famine had become acute in the city; there was no food left for the common people.

Then [the wall of] the city was breached. All the soldiers [left the city] by night through the gate between the double walls, which is near the king's garden—the Chaldeans were all around the city; and [the king] set out for the Arabah. But the Chaldean troops pursued the king, and they overtook him in the steppes of Jericho as his entire force left him and scattered. They captured the king and brought him before the king of Babylon at Riblah; and they put him on trial. They slaughtered Zedekiah's sons before his eyes; then Zedekiah's eyes were put out. He was chained in bronze fetters and he was brought to Babylon.

On the seventh day of the fifth month—that was the nineteenth year of King Nebuchadnezzar of Babylon—Nebuzaradan, the chief of the guards, an officer of the king of Babylon, came to Jerusalem. He burned the House of the Lord, the king's palace, and all the houses of Jerusalem; he burned down the house of every notable person. The entire Chaldean force that was with the chief of the guard tore down the walls of Jerusalem on every side. The remnant of the people that was left in the city, the defectors who had gone over to the king of Babylon—and the remnant of the population—were taken into exile by Nebuzaradan, the chief of the guards. But some of the poorest in the land were left by the chief of the guards, to be vinedressers and field hands.

The Chaldeans broke up the bronze columns of the House of the Lord, the stands, and the bronze tank that was in the House of the Lord; and they carried the bronze away to Babylon. They also took all the pails, scrapers, snuffers, ladles, and all the other bronze vessels used in the service. The chief of the guards took whatever was of gold and whatever was of silver: firepans and sprinkling bowls. The two columns, the one tank, and the stands that Solomon provided for the House of the Lord—all these objects contained bronze beyond weighing. The one column was eighteen cubits high. It had a bronze capital above it; the height of the capital was three cubits. and there was a meshwork [decorated] with pomegranates about the capital, all made of bronze. And the like was true of the other column with its meshwork.

[2 Kings 24:8–20; 25:1–17]

REMEMBERING ZION

Captive in Babylon, the psalmist in the following passage reflects nostalgically on the beauty of Zion, referring to the city of Jerusalem, possibly the Temple Mount.

By the rivers of Babylon,
   there we sat,
   sat and wept,
   as we thought of Zion.
There on the Poplars
   we hung up our lyres,
   for our captors asked us there for songs,
   our tormentors, for amusement,
   "Sing us one of the songs of Zion."
How can we sing a song of the Lord
   on alien soil?
If I forget you, O Jerusalem,
   let my right hand wither;
   let my tongue stick to my palate
   if I cease to think of you,
   if I do not keep Jerusalem in memory
   even at my happiest hour.
Remember, O Lord, against the Edomites
   the day of Jerusalem's fall;
   how they cried, "Strip her, strip her
   to her very foundations!"
Fair Babylon, you predator,
   a blessing on him who repays you in kind
   what you have inflicted on us;
   a blessing on him who seizes your babies
   and dashes them against the rocks!

[Psalms 137]

RETURN FROM EXILE AND RESTORATION

When Persian King Cyrus overthrew the Babylonian Empire in 539 B.C.E., he reversed the policy of exiling foreign captives as practiced by the Babylonians and, earlier, by the Assyrians. With his encouragement, 40,000 exiled Jews returned to their homeland. Cyrus encouraged the rebuilding of Jerusalem's temple and returned to the Jews the temple treasures which had been taken by the Babylonians.

1. In the first year of King Cyrus of Persia, when the word of the Lord spoken by Jeremiah was fulfilled, the Lord roused the spirit of King Cyrus of Persia to issue a proclamation throughout his realm by word of mouth and in writing as follows:
    "Thus said King Cyrus of Persia: The Lord God of Heaven has given me all the kingdoms of the earth and has charged me with building Him a house in Jerusalem, which is in Judah. Anyone of you of all His people—may his God be with him, and let him go up to Jerusalem that is in Judah and build the House of the Lord God of Israel, the God that is in Jerusalem; and all who stay behind, wherever he may be living, let the people of his place assist him with silver,

gold, goods, and livestock, besides the freewill offering to the House of God that is in Jerusalem."

So the chiefs of the clans of Judah and Benjamin, and the priests and Levites, all whose spirit had been roused by God, got ready to go up to build the House of the Lord that is in Jerusalem. All their neighbors supported them with silver vessels, with gold, with goods, with livestock, and with precious objects, besides what had been given as a freewill offering. King Cyrus of Persia released the vessels of the Lord's house which Nebuchadnezzar had taken away from Jerusalem and had put in the house of his God. The King Cyrus of Persia released through the office of Mithredath the treasurer, who gave an inventory of them to Sheshbazzar the prince of Judah. This is the inventory: 30 gold basins, 1,000 silver basins, 29 knives, 30 gold bowls, 410 silver doubled bowls, 1,000 other vessels, in all, 5,400 gold and silver vessels. Sheshbazzar brought all these back when the exiles came back from Babylon to Jerusalem.

3. When the seventh month arrived—the Israelites being settled in their towns—the entire people assembled as one man in Jerusalem. Then Jeshua son of Jozadak and his brother priests, and Zerubbabel son of Shealtiel and his brothers set to and built the altar of the God of Israel to offer burnt offerings upon it as is written in the Teaching of Moses, the man of God. They set up the Altar on its site because they were in fear of the peoples of the land, and they offered burnt offerings on it to the Lord, burnt offerings each morning and evening. Then they celebrated the festival of Tabernacles as is written, with its daily burnt offerings in the proper quantities, on each day as is prescribed for it, followed by the regular burnt offering and the offerings for the new moons and for all the sacred fixed times of the Lord, and whatever freewill offerings were made to the Lord. From the first day of the seventh month they began to make burnt offerings to the Lord, though the foundation of the Temple of the Lord had not been laid. They paid the hewers and craftsmen with money, and the Sidonians and Tyrians with food, drink , and oil to bring cedarwood from Lebanon by sea to Joppa, in accord with the authorization granted them by King Cyrus of Persia.

In the second year after their arrival at the House of God, at Jerusalem, in the second month, Zerubbabel son of Shealtiel and Jeshua son of Jozadak, and the rest of their brother priests and Levites, and all who had come from the captivity to Jerusalem, as their first step appointed Levites from the age of twenty and upward to supervise the work of the House of the Lord. Jeshua, his sons and brothers, Kadmiel and his sons, the sons of Judah, together were appointed in charge of those who did the work in the House of God; also the sons of Henadad, their sons and brother Levites.

When the builders had laid the foundation of the Temple of the Lord, priests in their vestments with trumpets, and Levites sons of Asaph with cymbals were stationed to give praise to the Lord, as King

David of Israel had ordained. They sang songs extolling and praising the Lord, "For He is good, His steadfast love for Israel is eternal." All the people raised a great shout extolling the Lord because the foundation of the House of the Lord had been laid. Many of the priests and Levites and the chiefs of the clans, the old men who had seen the first house, wept loudly at the sight of the founding of this house. Many others shouted joyously at the top of their voices. The people could not distinguish the shouts of joy from the people's weeping, for the people raised a great shout, the sound of which could be heard from afar.

[Ezra 1, 3]

ESTHER

The Book of Esther is one of two books of the Tanakh focusing on the life of a Jewish heroine (the book of Ruth is the other). Esther is queen to Persian King Ahasuerus (Xerxes I), one of Cyrus's successors, reigning from 486 to 465 B.C.E.. Unknown to the King, Esther is a Jew. When her cousin Mordecai refuses to bow to the King for religious reasons, Haman, a member of the court, is incensed and plots to have Mordicai, along with the rest of the Jews in the region, executed. The King sanctions Haman's plan. When Mordicai pleads with Esther to speak to the King on behalf of the Jews, she plans a banquet for the King during which she reveals Haman's plot at it. Haman is hanged on the very gallows he had prepared for Mordecai. The Jews are granted the right to defend themselves against their anti-Jewish enemies. The story of Esther is the basis for the Jewish feast Purim.

3. Some time afterward, King Ahasuerus promoted Haman son of Hammedatha the Agagite; he advanced him and seated him higher than any of his fellow officials. All the king's courtiers in the palace gate knelt and bowed low to Haman, for such was the king's order concerning him; but Mordecai would not kneel or bow low. Then the king's courtiers who were in the palace gate said to Mordecai, "Why do you disobey the king's order?" When they spoke to him day after day and he would not listen to them, they told Haman, in order to see whether Mordecai's resolve would prevail; for he had explained to them that he was a Jew. When Haman saw that Mordecai would not kneel or bow low to him, Haman was filled with rage. But he disdained to lay hands on Mordecai alone; having been told who Mordecai's people were, Haman plotted to do away with all the Jews, Mordecai's people, throughout the kingdom of Ahasuerus.

In the first month, that is, the month of Nisan, in the twelfth year of King Ahasuerus, *pur*—which means "the lot"—was cast before Haman concerning every day and every month, [until it fell on] the twelfth month, that is, the month of Adar. Haman then said to King Ahasuerus, "There is a certain people, scattered and dispersed among the other peoples in all the provinces of your realm, whose laws are different from those of any other people and who do not obey the king's laws; and it is not in Your Majesty's interest to tolerate them. If it pleases Your Majesty, let an edict be drawn for their destruction, and I will pay ten thousand talents of silver to the stewards for deposit in the royal treasury." Thereupon the king removed his signet ring from his hand and gave it to Haman son of Hammedatha the Agagite, the foe of the Jews. And the king said, "The money and the people are yours to do with as you see fit." . . .

7. So the king and Haman came to feast with Queen Esther. On the second day, the king again asked Esther at the wine feast, "What is your wish, Queen Esther? It shall be granted you. And what is your request? Even to half the kingdom, it shall be fulfilled." Queen Esther replied: "If Your Majesty will do me the favor, and if it pleases Your Majesty, let my life be granted me as my wish, and my people as my request. For we have been sold, my people and I, to be destroyed, massacred, and exterminated. Had we only been sold as bondmen and bondwomen, I would have kept silent; for the adversary is not worthy of the king's trouble."

Thereupon King Ahasuerus demanded of Queen Esther, "Who is he and where is he who dared to do this?" "The adversary and enemy," replied Esther, "is this evil Haman!" And Haman cringed in terror before the king and the queen. The king, in his fury, left the wine feast for the palace garden, while Haman remained to plead with Queen Esther for his life; for he saw that the king was resolved to destroy him. When the king returned from the palace garden to the banquet room, Haman was lying prostrate on the couch on which Esther reclined. "Does he mean," cried the king, "to ravish the queen in my own palace?" No sooner did these words leave the king's lips than Haman's face was covered. Then Harbonah, one of the eunuchs in attendance on the king, said, "What is more, a stake is standing at Haman's house, fifty cubits high, which Haman made for Mordecai— the man whose words saved the king" Impale him on it!" the king ordered. So they impaled Haman on the stake which he had put up for Mordecai, and the king's fury abated.

[Esther 3:7–11; 7]

EZRA AND THE LAW

The concluding events of the Tanakh *focus on the activities of Ezra and Nehemiah, found in the books which bear their names. Ezra was a Babylonian-born Jewish priest devoted to the Law of Moses. In 458 B.C.E., he petitioned Artaxerxes, the reigning King of the Persian Empire, to lead another migration of Jews back to their homeland. Artaxerxes agreed and empowered him to make political and religious reforms as Ezra saw fit. On arrival, he was distressed to see that the returning Jews before him had intermarried, and he proclaimed that 114 priests and laymen should have their*

*marriages annulled. Thirteen years after Ezra's return, Nehemiah, a Jewish cup-
bearer to the Persian King, was granted permission by the King to rebuild the walls
of Jerusalem, still in ruins from the Babylonian invasion. A gifted administrator, Nehemiah completed the project in 52 days, even in the face of opposition from neighboring provinces. Shortly after completion of the walls, the Jews celebrated a series of
feasts, during which Ezra publicly read and interpreted the scrolls of Moses. The following recounts Ezra's reading of the scrolls.*

When the seventh month arrived—the Israelites being [settled] in their
towns—the entire people assembled as one man in the square before the
Water Gate, and they asked Ezra the scribe to bring the scroll of the Teaching of Moses with which the Lord had charged Israel. On the first day of the
seventh month, Ezra the priest brought the Teaching before the congregation, men and women and all who could listen with understanding. He read
from it, facing the square before the Water Gate, from the first light until
midday, to the men and the women and those who could understand; the
ears of all the people were given to the scroll of the Teaching.

Ezra the scribe stood upon a wooden tower made for the purpose, and
beside him stood Mattithaih, Shema, Anaiah, Uriah, Hilkiah, and Maa-
seiah at his right, and at his left Pedaiah, Mishael, Malchijah, Hashum,
Hashbaddanah, Zechariah, Meshullam. Ezra opened the scroll in the sight
of all he people, for he was above all the people; as he opened it, all the
people stood up. Ezra blessed the Lord, the great God, and all the people
answered, "Amen, Amen," with hands upraised. Then they bowed their
heads and prostrated themselves before the Lord with their faces to the
ground. Jeshua, Bani, Sherebiah, Jamin, Akkub, Shabbethai, Hodiah, Maa-
seiah, Kelita, Azariah, Jozabad, Hanan, Pelaiah, and the Levites explained
the Teaching to the People, while the people stood in their places. They
read from the scroll of the Teaching of God, translating it and giving the
sense; so they understood the reading.

Nehemiah the Tirshatha, Ezra the priest and scribe, and the Levites
who were explaining to the people said to all the people, "This day is
holy to the Lord your God: you must not mourn or weep," for all the
people were weeping as they listened to the words of the Teaching. He
further said to them, "Go, eat choice foods and drink sweet drinks and
send portions to whoever has nothing prepared, for the day is holy to
our Lord. Do not be sad, for your rejoicing in the Lord is the source of
your strength." The Levites were quieting the people, saying, "Hush, for
the day is holy; do not be sad." Then all the people went to eat and drink
and send portions and make great merriment, for they understood the
things they were told.

On the second day, the heads of the clans of all the people and the
priests and Levites gathered to Ezra the scribe to study the words of the
Teaching. They found written in the Teaching that the Lord had commanded Moses that the Israelites must dwell in booths during the festival
of the seventh month, and that they must announce and proclaim throughout all their towns and Jerusalem as follows: "Go out to the mountains and

bring leafy branches of olive trees, pine trees, myrtles, palms and [other] leafy trees to make booths, as it is written." So the people went out and brought them, and made themselves booths on their roofs, in their court-yards, in the courtyards of the House of God, in the square of the Water Gate and in the square of the Ephraim Gate. The whole community that re-turned from the captivity made booths and dwelt in the booths—the Is-raelites had not done so from the days of Joshua son of Nun to that day—and there was very great rejoicing. He read from the scroll of the Teaching of God each day, from the first to the last day. They celebrated the festival seven days, and there was a solemn gathering on the eighth, as prescribed.

[Nehemiah 8]

SELECTIONS FROM POST-EXILIC SECTARIAN WRITINGS

GREEK RULE AND THE COMING OF THE MESSIAH

Although the final events reported in the Tanakh *take place around 430 B.C.E., the re-ligious drama of the Jewish people continues in post-exilic sectarian writings, consid-ered scriptural in many Jewish circles at the time. The extreme Hellenizing policies of Selucid King Antiochus Epiphanes created a crisis for traditional Jews, intensified fur-ther by the advocacy of these policies by Jewish High Priests themselves. Loyal Jewish writers sought a divine explanation for this crisis, which threatened their very exis-tence. They wrote apocalyptic texts reporting visionlike revelations about a Messianic deliverer, a cataclysmic end to the empires of their oppressors, topped by final divine judgment. The Book of Daniel in the* Tanakh *is thought to be an apocalyptic work from this period. The following is from the First Book of Enoch, one of the most well known apocalyptic texts of the Pseudepigrapha. The work, written by several authors between 200 B.C.E. and 100 C.E., reflects traditional apocalyptic themes.*[4]

46. At the place, I saw the one to whom belongs the time before time. And his head was white like wool, and there was with him another indi-vidual, whose face was like that of a human being. His countenance was full of grace like that of one among the holy angels. And I asked the one—from among the angels—who was going with me, and who had revealed to me all the secrets regarding the One who was born of human beings. "Who is this, and from whence is he who is going as the prototype of the Before-Time [i.e., Ancient of Days]? And he an-swered me and said to me, "This is the Son of Man, to whom belongs righteousness, and with whom righteousness dwells. And he will open all the hidden storerooms; for the Lord of the Spirits has chosen him, and he is destined to be victorious before the Lord of the Spirits in eternal uprightness. This Son of Man whom you have seen is the One who would remove the kings and the mighty ones from their comfortable seats and the strong ones from their thrones. He shall loosen the reins of the strong and crush the teeth of the sinners. He

shall depose the kings from their thrones and kingdoms. For they do not extol and glorify him, and neither do they obey him, the source of their kingship. The faces of the strong will be slapped and be filled with shame and gloom. Their dwelling places and their beds will be worms. They shall have no hope to rise from their beds, for they do not extol the name of the Lord of the Spirits. And they have become the judges of the stars of heaven; they raise their hands (to reach) the Most High while walking upon the earth and dwelling in her. They manifest all their deeds in oppression. Their power (depends) upon their wealth. And their devotion is to the gods which they have fashioned with their own hands. But they deny the name of the Lord of the Spirits. Yet they like to congregate in his houses and (with) the faithful ones who cling to the Lord of the Spirits.

48. **The Son of Man: The Antecedent of Time: His Judgment.** Furthermore, in that place I saw the fountain of righteousness, which does not become depleted and is surrounded completely by numerous fountains of wisdom. All the thirsty ones drink (of the water) and become filled with wisdom. (Then) their dwelling places become with the holy, righteous, and elect ones. At that hour, that Son of Man was given a name, in the presence of the Lord of the Spirits, the Before-Time, even before the creation of the sun and the moon, before the creation of the stars, he was given a name in the presence of the Lord of the Spirits. He will become a staff for the righteous ones in order that they may lean on him and not fall. He is the light of the gentiles and he will become the hope of those who are sick in their hearts. All those who dwell upon the earth shall fall and worship before him; they shall glorify, bless, and sing the name of the Lord of the Spirits. For this purpose he became the Chosen One; he was concealed in the presence of (the Lord of the Spirits) prior to the creation of the world, and for eternity. And he has revealed the wisdom of the lord of the Spirits to the righteous and the holy ones, for he has preserved the portion of the righteous because they have hated and despised this world of oppression (together with) all its ways of life and its habits in the name of the Lord of the Spirits; and because they will be saved in his name and it is his good pleasure that they have life. In those days, the kings of the earth and the mighty landowners shall be humiliated on account of the deeds of their hands. Therefore, on the day of their misery and weariness, they will not be able to save themselves. I shall deliver them into the hands of my elect ones like grass in the fire and like lead in the water, so they shall burn before the face of the holy ones and sink before their sight, and a place will be found for them. On the day of their weariness, there shall be an obstacle on the earth and they shall fall on their faces; and they shall not rise up (again), nor anyone (be found) who will take them with his hands and raise them up. For they have denied the Lord of the Spirits and his Messiah. Blessed be the name of the Lord of the Spirits!

51. **Resurrection of the Dead.** In those days, Sheol will return all the deposits which she had received and hell will give back all that which it owes. And he shall choose the righteous and the holy ones from among (the risen dead), for the day when they shall be selected and saved has arrived. In those days, (the Elect One) shall sit on my throne, and from the conscience of his mouth shall come out all the secrets of wisdom, for the Lord of the Spirits has given them to him and glorified him. In those days, mountains shall dance like rams; and the hills shall leap the kids satiated with milk. And the faces of all the angels in heaven shall glow with joy, because on that day the Elect One has arisen. And the earth shall rejoice; and the righteous ones shall dwell upon her and the elect shall walk upon her.

55. **The Scene of Judgment.** My eyes saw there a deep valley with a wide mouth. And all those who dwell upon the earth, the sea, and the islands shall bring to it gifts, presents, and tributes; yet this deep valley shall not become full. They shall fulfill the criminal deeds of their hands and eat all the produce of crime which the sinners toil for. Sinners shall be destroyed from before the face of the Lord of the Spirits— they shall perish eternally, standing before the face of the earth. So I saw all the angels of plague cooperating and preparing all the chains of Satan. And I asked the angel of peace, who was going with me, "For whom are they preparing these chains?" And he answered me, saying, "They are preparing these for the kings and the potentates of this earth in order that they may be destroyed thereby. And this, the Righteous and Elect One will reveal the house of his congregation. From that time, they shall not be hindered in the name of the Lord of the Spirits. And these mountains shall become (flat) like earth in the presence of his righteousness, and the hills shall become like a fountain of water. And the righteous ones shall have rest from the oppression of sinners."

[First Enoch, 46, 48, 51, 53]

MACCABEAN REVOLT

The Book of Maccabees chronicles the clash between Hellenistic and Jewish culture, and culminates in the Maccabean revolt and rise to power. The Book of Maccabees, written about 100 B.C.E. and included in the Septuagint, is the primary source of information for this period of Jewish history. The following describes the Hellenizing policies of Antiochus Epiphanes and the initial revolt launched by Mattathias.[5]

1. After Alexander the Macedonian, Philip's son, who came from the land of Kittim, had defeated Darius, king of the Persians and Medes, he became king in his place, having first ruled in Greece. He fought many campaigns, captured fortresses, and put kings to death. He advanced to the ends of the earth, gathering plunder from many nations; the earth fell silent before him, and his heart became proud and arrogant.

He collected a very strong army and conquered provinces, nations, and rulers, and they became his tributaries. But after all this he took to his bed, realizing that he was going to die. He therefore summoned his officers, the nobles, who had been brought up with him from his youth, to divide his kingdom among them while he was still alive. Alexander had reigned twelve years when he died.

So his officers took over his kingdom, each in his own territory, and after his death they all put on royal crowns, and so did their sons after them for many years, causing much distress over the earth.

There sprang from these a sinful offshoot, Antiochus Epiphanes, son of King Antiochus, once a hostage at Rome. He became king in the year one hundred and thirty-seven of the kingdom of the Greeks.

In those days there appeared in Israel men who were breakers of the law, and they seduced many people, saying: "Let us go and make an alliance with the Gentiles all around us; since we separated from them, many evils have come upon us." The proposal was agreeable; some from among the people promptly went to the king, and he authorized them to introduce the way of living of the Gentiles. Thereupon they built a gymnasium in Jerusalem according to the Gentile custom. They covered over the mark of their circumcision and abandoned the holy covenant; they allied themselves with the Gentiles and sold themselves to wrongdoing.

When his kingdom seemed secure, Antiochus proposed to become king of Egypt, so as to rule over both kingdoms. He invaded Egypt with a strong force, with chariots and elephants, and with a large fleet, to make war on Ptolemy, king of Egypt. Ptolemy was frightened at his presence and fled, leaving many casualties. The fortified cities in the land of Egypt were captured, and Antiochus plundered the land of Egypt.

After Antiochus had defeated Egypt in the year one hundred and forty-three, he returned and went up to Israel and to Jerusalem with a strong force. He insolently invaded the sanctuary and took away the golden altar, the lampstand for the light with all its fixtures, the offering table, the cups and the bowls, the olden censers, the curtain, the crowns, and the golden ornament on the facade of the temple. He stripped off everything, and took away the gold and silver and the precious vessels; he also took all the hidden treasures he could find. Taking all this, he went back to his own country, after he had spoken with great arrogance and shed much blood. . . .

Two years later, the king sent the Mysian commander to the cities of Judah, and he came to Jerusalem with a strong force. He spoke to them deceitfully in peaceful terms, and won their trust. Then he attacked the city suddenly, in a great onslaught, and destroyed many of the people in Israel. He plundered the city and set fire to it, demolished its houses and its surrounding walls, took captive the women and children, and seized the cattle. Then they built up the City of

David with a high, massive wall and strong towers, and it became their citadel. There they installed a sinful race, perverse men, who fortified themselves inside it, storing up weapons and provisions, and depositing there the plunder they had collected from Jerusalem. And they became a great threat. . . .

Then the king wrote to his whole kingdom that all should be one people, each abandoning his particular customs. All the Gentiles conformed to the command of the king, and many Israelites were in favor of his religion; they sacrificed to idols and profaned the Sabbath.

The king sent messengers with letters to Jerusalem and to the cities of Judah, ordering them to follow customs foreign to their land: to prohibit holocausts, sacrifices, and libations in the sanctuary, to profane the sabbaths and feast days, to desecrate the sanctuary and the sacred ministers, to build pagan altars and temples and shrines, to sacrifice swine and unclean animals, to leave their sons uncircumcised, and to let themselves be defiled with every kind of impurity and abomination, so that they might forget the law and change all their observances. Whoever refused to act according to the command of the king should be put to death.

Such were the orders he published throughout his kingdom. He appointed inspectors over all the people, and he ordered the cities of Judah to offer sacrifices, each city in turn. Many of the people, those who abandoned the law, joined them and committed evil in the land. Israel was driven into hiding, wherever places of refuge could be found.

On the fifteenth day of the month Chislev, in the year one hundred and forty-five, the king erected the horrible abomination upon the altar of holocausts, and in the surrounding cities of Judah they built pagan altars. They also burnt incense at the doors of houses and in the streets. Any scrolls of the law which they found they tore up and burnt. Whoever was found with a scroll of the covenant, and whoever observed the law, was condemned to death by royal decree. So they used their power against Israel, against those who were caught, each month, in the cities. On the twenty-fifth day of each month they sacrificed on the altar erected over the altar of holocausts. Women who had had their children circumcised were put to death, in keeping with the decree, with the babies hung from their necks; their families also and those who had circumcised them were killed. But many in Israel were determined and resolved in their hearts not to eat anything unclean; they preferred to die rather than to be defiled with unclean food or to profane the holy covenant; and they did die. Terrible affliction was upon Israel.

2. In those days Mattathias, son of John, son of Simeon, a priest of the family of Joarib, left Jerusalem and settled in Modein. He had five sons: John, who was called Gaddi; Simon, who was called Thassi; Judas, who was called Maccabeus; Eleazar, who was called Avaran; and Jonathan, who was called Apphus. When he saw the sacrileges

that were being committed in Judah and in Jerusalem, he said: "Woe is me! Why was I born to see the ruin of my people and the ruin of the holy city, and to sit idle while it is given into the hands of enemies, and the sanctuary into the hands of strangers? . . ."

Then Mattathias and his sons tore their garments, put on sackcloth, and mourned bitterly.

The officers of the king in charge of enforcing the apostasy came to the city of Modein to organize the sacrifices. Many of Israel joined them, but Mattathias and his sons gathered in a group apart. Then the officers of the king addressed Mattathias: "You are a leader, an honorable and great man in this city, supported by sons and kinsmen. Come now, be the first to obey the king's command, as all the Gentiles and the men of Judah and those who are left in Jerusalem have done. Then you and your sons shall be numbered among the King's Friends, and shall be enriched with silver and gold and many gifts" But Mattathias answered in a loud voice: "Although all the Gentiles in the king's realm obey him, so that each forsakes the religion of his fathers and consents to the king's orders, yet I and my sons and my kinsmen will keep to the covenant of our fathers. God forbid that we should forsake the law and the commandments. We will not obey the words of the king nor depart from our religion in the slightest degree."

As he finished saying these words, a certain Jew came forward in the sight of all to offer sacrifice on the altar in Modein according to the king's order. When Mattathias saw him, he was filled with zeal; his heart was moved and his just fury was aroused; he sprang forward and killed him upon the altar. At the same time, he also killed the messenger of the king who was forcing them to sacrifice, and he tore down the altar. Thus he showed his zeal for the law, just as Phinehas did with Zimri, son of Salu.

Then Mattathias went through the city shouting, "Let everyone who is zealous for the law and who stands by the covenant follow after me!" Thereupon he fled to the mountains with his sons, leaving behind in the city all their possessions.

[First Maccabees 1:1–24, 29–35, 41–63; 2:1–7, 14–28]

QUMRAN *COMMUNITY RULE*

Isolating themselves from despotic foreign rulers and politically driven religious leaders, the desert community of Qumran believed it was preparing for a final battle between good and evil. The following, from the Qumran's Community Rule, *describes our dual human nature as consisting of a spirit of truth and a spirit of error, the sources of proper and improper conduct, respectively. Reminiscent of Zoroastrianism, God has "established the two spirits in equal measure until the last period." Followers of truth, the Sons of Light, will ultimately wage a victorious war over followers of error, the Sons of Darkness.[6]*

The Master shall instruct all the sons of light and shall teach them the nature of all the children of men according to the kind of spirit which they possess, the signs identifying their works during their lifetime, their visitation for chastisement, and the time of their reward.

From the God of knowledge comes all that is and shall be. Before ever they existed He established their whole design, and when, as ordained for them, they come into being, it is in accord with His glorious design that they accomplish their task without change. The laws of all things are in His hand and He provides them with all their needs.

He has created man to govern the world, and has appointed for him two spirits in which to walk until the time of His visitation: the spirits of truth and falsehood. Those born of truth spring from a fountain of light, but those born of falsehood spring from a source of darkness. All the children of righteousness are ruled by the Prince of Light and walk in the ways of light, but all the children of falsehood are ruled by the Angel of Darkness and walk in the ways of darkness.

The Angel of Darkness leads all the children of righteousness astray, and until his end, all their sin, iniquities, wickedness, and all their unlawful deeds are caused by his dominion in accordance with the mysteries of God. Every one of their chastisements, and every one of the seasons of their distress, shall be brought about by the rule of his persecution; for all his allotted spirits seek the overthrow of the sons of light.

But the God of Israel and His Angel of Truth will succor all the sons of light. For it is He who created the spirits of Light and Darkness and founded every action upon them and established every deed [upon] their [ways]. And He loves the one everlastingly and delights in its works for ever; but the counsel of the other He loathes and for ever hates its ways.

These are their ways in the world for the enlightenment of the heart of man, and that all the paths of true righteousness may be made straight before him, and that the fear of the laws of God may be instilled in his heart: a spirit of humility, patience, abundant charity, unending goodness, understanding, and intelligence; (a spirit of) mighty wisdom which trusts in all the deeds of God and leans on His great lovingkindness; a spirit of discernment in every purpose, of zeal for just laws, of holy intent with steadfastness of heart, of great charity towards all the sons of truth, of admirable purity which detests all unclean idols, of humble conduct sprung from an understanding of all things, and of faithful concealment of the mysteries of truth. These are the counsels of the spirit to the sons of truth in this world.

And as for the visitation of all who walk in this spirit, it shall be healing, great peace in a long life, and fruitfulness, together with every everlasting blessing and eternal joy in life without end, a crown of glory and a garment of majesty in unending light.

But the ways of the spirit of falsehood are these: greed, and slackness in the search for righteousness, wickedness and lies, haughtiness and pride, falseness and deceit, cruelty and abundant evil, ill-temper and much folly and brazen insolence, abominable deeds (committed) in a spirit of lust, and ways of lewdness in the service of uncleanness, a blaspheming tongue, blindness of eye and dullness of ear, stiffness of neck and heaviness of heart, so that man walks in all the ways of darkness and guile.

And the visitation of all who walk in the spirit shall be a multitude of plagues by the hand of all the destroying angels, everlasting damnation by the avenging wrath of the fury of God, eternal torment and endless disgrace together with shameful extinction in the fire of the dark regions. The times of all their generations shall be spent in sorrowful mourning and in bitter misery and in calamities of darkness until they are destroyed without remnant or survivor.

The nature of all the children of the men is ruled by these (two spirits), and during their life all the hosts of men have a portion of their divisions and walk in (both) their ways. And the whole whether each man's portion in their two divisions is great or small. For God has established the spirits in equal measure until the final age, and has set everlasting hatred between their divisions. Truth abhors the works of falsehood, and falsehood hates all the ways of truth. And their struggle is fierce in all their arguments for they do not walk together.

But in the mysteries of His understanding, and in His glorious wisdom, God has ordained an end for falsehood, and at the time of the visitation he will destroy it for ever. Then truth, which has wallowed in the ways of wickedness during the dominion of falsehood until the appointed time of judgment, shall arise in the world for ever. God will then purify every deed of man with his truth; He will refine for Himself the human frame by rooting out all spirit of falsehood from the bounds of his flesh. He will cleanse him of all wicked deeds with the spirit of holiness; like purifying waters He will shed upon him the spirit of truth (to cleanse him) of all abomination and falsehood. And he shall be plunged into the spirit of purification that he may instruct the upright in the knowledge of the Most High and teach the wisdom of the sons of heaven to the perfect of way. For God has chosen them for an everlasting Covenant and all the glory of Adam shall be theirs. There shall be no more lies and all the works of falsehood shall be put to shame.

Until now the spirits of truth and falsehood struggle in the hearts of men and they walk in both wisdom and folly. According to his portion of truth so does a man hate falsehood, and according to his inheritance in the realm of falsehood so is he wicked and so hates truth. For God has established the two spirits in equal measure until the determined end, and until the Renewal, and He knows the reward of their deeds from all eternity. He has allotted them to the children of men that they may know good [and evil, and] that the destiny of all the living may be according to the spirit within [them at the time] of the visitation.

["The Community Rule," Cave 1 Copy, Column 3:13–4:26]

SIBYLLINE ORACLE ON THE DESTRUCTION
OF THE TEMPLE

The destruction of the Jerusalem Temple in 70 C.E. by the Romans was another land-mark tragedy upon which sectarian writers focused. The selection below is an apoca-lyptic vision of this event from the pseudepigraphic Sibylline Oracles. *In Greek mythology, the Sibyl is an aged prophetess who predicts disaster while in an ecstatic state. The oldest Greek myths recount a single Sibyl, but by the Middle Ages writers postulated ten, each residing in a distinct Mediterranean area, foretelling tragedy at different periods of time. In Jewish tradition, the* Sibylline Oracles *are a complex patchwork of apocalyptic oracles written between 200 B.C.E. and 600 C.E. that were pseudepigraphically attributed to the various Sibyl. The following selection was writ-ten about 80 C.E.*[7]

The Rise of Rome. Nor will the power of Macedonia survive, but from the west a great Italian war will bloom under with the world will serve, bear-ing the yoke of slavery for the Italians. You also, miserable Corinth, will one day behold your capture. Carthage, your tower will also bend the knee to the ground. Wretched Laodicea, at some time an earthquake will throw you headlong and spread you flat, but you will be founded again as a city, and stand. Beautiful Myra of Lycia, the shuddering earth will no longer support you, but falling down headlong on the earth, you will pray to flee to another land as an exile when the Lord spreads out the dark water of the sea with thunderings and earthquakes because of the impi-eties of Patara. Armenia, the compulsion of slavery awaits you also.

The Destruction of Jerusalem. An evil storm of war will also come upon Jerusalem from Italy, and it will sack the great Temple of God, whenever they put their trust in folly and cast off piety and commit repul-sive murders in front of the Temple. Then a great king will flee from Italy like a runaway slave unseen and unheard over the channel of the Eu-phrates, when he dares to incur a maternal curse for repulsive murder and many other things, confidently, with wicked hand. A leader of Rome will come to Syria who will burn the Temple of Jerusalem with fire, at the same time slaughter many men and destroy the great land of the Jews with its broad roads. Then indeed an earthquake will destroy at once Salamis and Paphos when the dark water overwhelms Cyprus, which is washed by many waves.

Impiety of the Last Times. But when faith in piety perishes from among men, and justice is hidden in the world, untrustworthy men, living for unholy deeds, will commit outrage, wicked and evil deeds. No one will take account of the pious, but they will even destroy them all, by fool-ishness, very infantile people, rejoicing in outrages and applying their hands to blood. Even then know that God is no longer benign but gnash-ing his teeth in wrath and destroying the entire race of men at once by a great conflagration.

[*Sibylline Oracles*, Book 4:101–129, 151–160]

SELECTIONS FROM RABBINIC WRITINGS

WISDOM OF THE FATHERS FROM THE *MISHNAH*

The best known section of the Mishnah *is* Abot *(literally fathers), also called Wisdom of the Fathers. This section was considered so important that medieval copies of the* Talmud *have* Abot *as the conclusion of each of its six key divisions. The typical style of the* Mishnah *is a give-and-take legal debate between the* Tannaim. Abot *is different in that it is a collection of proverbs by the* Tannaim *that are not debated. The first two divisions of* Abot, *presented below, begin by listing the transmitters of the oral law from Moses to the* Tannaim *themselves.*[8]

1. Moses received the Torah at Sinai. Hey conveyed it to Joshua; Joshua to the elders; the elders to the prophets; and the prophets transmitted it to the men of the Great Assembly. The latter emphasized three principles: Be deliberate in judgment; raise up may disciples; and make a fence to safeguard the Torah.
2. Simeon the Just was of the last survivors of the Great Assembly. He used to say: The world rests on three foundations: the Torah; the divine service; and the practices of lovingkindness between man and man.
3. Antigonus of Soho received the tradition from him. He was accustomed to say: Be not like servants who serve their master because of the expected reward, but be like those who serve a master without expecting a reward; and let the fear of God be upon you.
4. Yose ben Yoezer of Zeredah and Yose ben Yohanan of Jerusalem received the tradition from them. Yose ben Yoezer of Zeredah said: Let your house be a gathering place for wise men; sit attentively at their feet, and drink of their words of wisdom with eagerness.
5. Yose ben Yohanan of Jerusalem said: Let your home be a place of hospitality to strangers; and make the poor welcome in your household; and do not indulge in gossip with women. This applies even with one's own wife, and surely so with another man's wife. The sages generalized from this: He who engages in profuse gossiping with women causes evil for himself and neglects the study of the Torah, and he will bring upon himself retributions in the hereafter.
6. Joshua ben Perahya and Nittai the Arbelite received the tradition from them. Joshua ben Perahya said: Get yourself a teacher; and acquire for yourself a companion; and judge all people favorably.
7. Nittai the Arbelite said: Avoid an evil neighbor; do not associate with the wicked; and do not surrender your faith in divine retribution.
8. Judah ben Tabbai and Simeon ben Shatah received the traditions from them. Judah ben Tabbai said: Let not the judge play the part of the counselor; when they leave after submitting to the court's decree, regard them both as guiltless.
9. Simeon ben Shatah said: Search the witnesses thoroughly and be cautious with your own words lest you give them an opening to false testimony.

10. Shemaya and Abtalyon received the traditions from them. Shemaya said: love work; hate domineering over others; and do not seek the intimacy of public officials.
11. Abtalyon said: Sages, be precise in your teachings. you may suffer exile to a place where heresy is rampant, and your inexact language may lead your disciples astray, and they will lose their faith, thus leading to a desecration of the divine name.
12. Hillel and Shammai received the tradition from them. Hillel said: Be of the disciples of Aaron. Love peace and pursue peace; love your fellow creatures and bring them near to the Torah.
13. He also said: He who strives to exalt his name will in the end destroy his name; he who does not increase his knowledge decreases it; he who does not study has undermined his right to life; and he who makes unworthy use of the crown of the Torah will perish.
14. He also said: If I am not for myself who will be? But if I am for myself only, what am I? And if not now, when?
15. Shammai said: Set a fixed time for the study of the Torah; say little and do much; and greet every person with a cheerful countenance.
16. Rabban Gamaliel said: Provide yourself with a teacher, and extricate yourself from doubt; and do not habitually contribute your tithes by rough estimates.
17. Simeon his son said: All my life I was raised among scholars and I found that no virtue becomes a man more than silence; what is more essential is not study but practice; and in the wake of many words is sin.
18. Rabban Simeon ben Gamaliel said: The world rests on three foundations: truth, justice, and peace. As it is written (Zech 8:16): "You shall administer truth, justice and peace within your gates."

[Mishnah, Abot, ch. 1]

THE *TALMUD* ON RABBINIC AUTHORITY

The chief theological paradox of the Talmud *is how collected opinions of early Rabbis can count as divine law. Although Judaism traces its oral law back to Moses, the* Mishnah *and* Talmud *are, quite obviously, only collected sayings of the* Tannaim *and* Amoraim. *Early Rabbis themselves were aware of this paradox and provide an answer. In this selection from* Baba Mezia *(one of the most famous sections of the* Talmud*), they explain that the majority position held by the carriers of oral law becomes the law. At that time, the sages of the* Talmud *were the carriers.[9]*

We studied in the Mishnah (Eduyot 7:7) that if a pottery stove was cut into tiles, and cemented over with sand placed between the tiles, R. Eliezer declared it unsusceptible to ritual uncleanliness, while the other Sages declared it susceptible. This was the Akhnai Stove.[10]

Why was it called Akhnai? Said R. Judah in the name of Samuel. They surrounded it with arguments as a snake winds its body around an object, and declared it unclean. It has been taught: On that day R. Eliezer marshaled every conceivable argument, but they did not accept them. Then he said: If the law is according to my views, let this carob tree prove it. Thereupon the carob tree was thrust to a distance of a hundred cubits from its place, and some say four hundred. They replied to him: We adduce no evidence from a carob tree. Again he said to them: If the law is in accordance with my views, let the stream of water prove it, and at once the stream of water flowed in the opposite direction. But they said: We adduce no evidence from a stream of water. Again he said to them: If the law agrees with my views, let the walls of the academy prove it, and the walls of the academy began to bend and were about to fall. R. Joshua rebuked them, saying: If scholars argue on a point of law, what business is it of yours? The walls did not fall out of respect for R. Joshua, but they did not become straight again out of respect for R. Eliezer.

Thereupon he said: If the law is in accordance with my views, let them prove it from heaven. A heavenly voice came forth, saying: What have you against R. Eliezer? The law is as he propounds it in all instances. R. Joshua then stood up and quoted: "It is not in the heavens" (Dt 30:12). What did he mean by quoting: "It is not in the heavens?" Said R. Jeremiah: That the Torah has already been given at Sinai, and we pay no attention to heavenly voices, for You have written at Sinai in the Torah: "Incline after the majority" (Ex 23:2).

R. Nathan met the prophet Elijah and he asked him: What did the Holy One, praised be He, do at that time? He replied: He laughed, and He said: My children have won over me, my chlordane have won over me!

[*Talmud*, Baba Mezia 59a–59b]

THE *TALMUD* ON MARRIAGE

Typical of the times, women did not have equal religious status under Talmudic law. Although Rabbinic sages considered women "a nation apart" rather than inferior, women were nevertheless excluded from certain ceremonial rituals and from studying the Torah. Further, during menstruation and childbirth, women were considered unclean and were required to follow rituals of seclusion and purification. In other important ways the Talmud *bucks trends of the day by acknowledging equal status for women under civil and criminal law, and insisting on monogamous marriages. The following from the* Talmud *tractate* Yebamot *discusses reasons for marriage and procreation. A principal reason for marriage is that Adam, the original human, was created both male and female, and only later was separated into male and female bodies.*[11]

A person should not abstain from carrying out the obligation to "be fruitful and multiply" (Gn 1:28) unless he already has two chlordane. The Beit Shammai ruled: This means two sons, and the Beit Hillel ruled: A son and a daughter, because it is written: "Male and female He created them" (Gn 5:2). The duty of procreation applies to a man, but not to a woman. R. Yohanan b.

Beroka said: Concerning both it is written: "And God blessed them and said to them: Be fruitful and multiply" (Gn 1:28). *Mishnah* 6:6

This means that if he has children he may abstain from the duty of procreation but he may not abstain from the duty of living with a wife. This supports the view of R. Nahman who reported a ruling in the name of Samuel, that even though a person has many children, he may not remain without a wife, as it is written: "It is not good for a man to be alone" (Gn 2:18). Others held the view that if he had children, he may abstain from the duty of procreation and he may also abstain from the duty of living with a wife. Shall we say that this contradicts what was reported by R. Nahman in the name of Samuel? No. if he has no children, he is to marry a woman capable of having a child, but if he already has children, he may marry a woman who is incapable of having children.

Elsewhere it was taught: R. Nathan said: According to the Beit Shammai, a person satisfies the obligation to "be fruitful and multiply" if he has a son and a daughter, and according to the Beit Hillel if he has a son or a daughter. Said Rava: what is the reason for the view of the Beit Hillel? It is written: "He created it not to be a waste, He formed it to be inhabited" (Is 45:18), and [by having a son or a daughter] he has already contributed to making it a place of habitation.

It was stated: If a person had children while he was an idolater, and was later converted [to Judaism], R. Yohanan said that he has already fulfilled the duty of procreation but Resh Lakish said that he has not fulfilled it, because when a person is converted he is like a born-again child.

The Mishnah does not agree with the view of R. Joshua, for it was taught that R. Joshua stated: if a person married in his youth he is also to marry in his old age; if he had children in his youth, he is also to have children in his old age, for it is written: "Sow your seed in the morning and do not withdraw your hand in the evening, for you do not know which will prosper, this or that, or whether both alike will be good" (Eccl 11:6).

Said R. Tanhum in the name of R. Hanilai: A person who is without a wife is without joy, without blessing, without good. Without joy—as it is written: "You shall rejoice, you and your household" (Dt 14:26); without blessing—as it is written: "That a blessing may rest on your house" (Ez 44:30) ["house" in such a context has generally been interpreted to mean one's wife]; without good—as it is written: "It is not good for a man to be alone" (Gn 2:18). In Palestine they said: He is without Torah, and without protection [from the ravages of life]. Without Torah—as it is written: "In truth, I have no one to help me [a wife], and sound wisdom [Torah] is driven from me" (Jb 6:13); without protection—as it is written: "A woman protects a man" (Jer 31:22). R. b. Ila said: He is without peace—as it is written: "And you shall know that your tent [when presided over by one's wife] is at peace, and you will visit your habitation and you will not sin" (Jb 5:24)

Said R. Joshua b. Levi: A person who knows his wife to be a God-fearing woman and he does not have marital relations with her is a sinner, as it is written: "And you shall visit your habitation [a euphemism for having relations with one's wife] and you will not sin."

The Rabbis taught: When one loves his wife as himself, and honors her more than himself, and trains his sons and daughters in the right path and arranges for their marriage at a young age—concerning such a person does the verse say: "And you shall know that your tent is at peace."

Said R. Eleazar: A man without a wife is not a complete man, as it is written: "Male and female created He them, and he called their name *adam*, 'man'" (Gn 5:2).

Turn away your eyes from the charms of another man's wife, lest you be trapped in her net. Do not join in fellowship with her husband, to drink with him wine and strong drink, for through the appearance of a beautiful woman have many been destroyed, and a mighty host are all her slain.

[*Talmud*, Yebamot 61b–64a]

SELECTIONS FROM MYSTICAL WRITINGS

THE ZOHAR ON CREATION

The key doctrine of early Kabbala as expressed in the Zohar *is that of the* Sefirot, *which are ten emanations of God's personality. These attributes of the divinity permeate all of creation, including our personal lives. The* Zohar *does not systematically discusses the* Sefirot *and typically does not refer to them by their formal names. Instead, it relies heavily on metaphors, leaving it to the reader to make the association. The following is the* Zohar's *account of creation, presented as a* midrash *on the first clause of the Book of Genesis, "In the beginning . . ." The passage describes how God,* eyn sof, *or the Infinite, created two primary* Sefirot. *The first is* Hokhmah *(wisdom), described below as* point *and* Beginning, *and is the primal point of God's emanation. The second is* Binah *(derivative wisdom), described below as* palace, *the prime mother who receives seed from* Hokhmah, *and gives birth to seven lower* Sefirot.[12]

"In the beginning" [Gen. 1:1]—when the will of the King began to take effect, he engraved signs into the heavenly sphere [that surrounded him]. Within the most hidden recess a dark flame issued from the mystery of *eyn sof*, the Infinite, like a fog forming in the unformed—enclosed in the ring of that sphere, neither white nor black, neither red nor green, of no color whatever. Only after this flame began to assume size and dimension, did it produce radiant colors. From the innermost center of the flame sprang forth a well out of which colors issued and spread upon everything beneath, hidden in the mysterious hiddenness of *eyn sof*.

The well broke through and yet did not break through the ether [of the sphere]. It could not be recognized at all until a hidden, supernal point shone forth under the impact of the final breaking through.

Beyond this point nothing can be known. Therefore it is called *reshit*, beginning—the first word [out of the ten] by means of which the universe has been created. When King Solomon "penetrated into the depths of the nut garden," as it is written, "I descended into the garden of nuts" [Cant. 6:11], he took up a nut shell and studying it, he saw an analogy in its layers with the spirits which motivate the sensual desires of humans, as it is written, "and the delights of the sons of men [are from] male and female demons" [Eccles. 2:8]

The Holy One, be blessed, saw that it was necessary to put into the world all of these things so as to make sure of permanence, and of having, so to speak, a brain surrounded by numerous membranes. The whole world, upper and lower, is organized on this principle, from the primary mystic center to the very outermost of all the layers. All are coverings, the one to the other, brain within brain, spirit inside of spirit, shell within shell.

The primal center is the innermost light, of translucence, subtlety, and purity beyond comprehension. That inner point extended becomes a "palace" which acts as an enclosure for the center, and is also of a radiance translucent beyond the power to know it.

The "palace" vestment for the incognizable inner point, while it is an unknowable radiance in itself, is nevertheless of a lesser subtlety and translucency than the primal point. The "palace" extends into a vestment for itself, the primal light. From then outward, there is extension upon extension, each constituting a vesture to the one before, as a membrane to the brain. Though membrane first, each extension becomes brain to the next extension.

Likewise does the process go on below; and after this design, man in the world combines brain and membrane, spirit and body, all to the more perfect ordering of the world. When the moon was conjoined with the sun, she was luminous, but when she went apart from the sun and was given governance of her own hosts, her status and her light were reduced, and shell after shell as fashioned for investing the brain, and all was for its good.

[*Zohar*, 1:49b]

MYSTICAL TALES BY NAHMAN OF BRATSLAV

The Hasidic movement was founded by Baal Shem Tov (1700–1760) as a mystical response to disillusionment in both Messianic hope (brought on by messianic pretenders of the previous century) and in Rabbinic legalism. Followers of Baal Shem Tov were preachers, rather than theologians, and thus communicated orally rather than in writing. Their homilies were eventually put in writing by their sons or disciples. The Hasids describe God panthiestically, and maintain that God can be directly accessed. Another genre of writing also emerged from the Hasidic movement: the tale. These parable-like stories draw from events in peasant life and describe God more anthropomorphically, rather than pantheistically. The most distinguished of these are by the Ukrainian Rabbi Nahman of Bratslav (1772–1810). The following selection is from his most well known and cryptic tale, "The Seven Beggars." The story surrounds a wedding ceremony that is attended by six deformed beggars who each present tales explaining his respective deformity (a seventh beggar remained in the forest). Their stories emphasize the illusory nature of the world in which we live.[13]

. . . Today I present you a wedding gift that you should be as I am. Do you think my neck is twisted? My neck is not twisted at all. In fact, I have a straight neck, a very handsome neck. Only that there are worldly vanities (empty breaths) which are so numerous that I do not want to exhale the last breath. . . . But I really have a handsome neck, a wonderful neck because I have such a wonderful voice. I can imitate with my voice every speechless sound. . . . And I have an affidavit to that effect from a certain country.

For there is a country where everyone is skilled in the art of music. Everyone practices these arts, even little children. . . . The youngest in that country would be the wisest in another country in the art of music. And the wise men, and the king of that country and the musicians are experts in the art of music.

Once, the country's wise men sat and boasted of their expertise in the art of music. One boasted that he could play on one instrument; another, on another; and still another, on all instruments. This one boasted that he could imitate with his voice the sound of one instrument, and another boasted that he could imitate with his voice yet another instrument. . . . Another one boasted that with his voice he could make the sound of cannon firing.

I, too, was there, so I declared saying, "My Voice is better than all of yours. And here is the proof. If you are such wise men in music, see if you can save these two countries. There are two countries one thousand miles apart from each other where no one can sleep when night falls. As soon as night falls, everyone begins to wail with such anguish—men, women, and children—because they hear a certain wailing sound of mourning. Stones would melt because of this wail. . . . So if you are all so very wise in music, let us see if you can save these two countries, or at least imitate the sounds of the laments heard there."

And they all arose to go there. They left and reached one of those two countries. When they arrived, and night fell, as usual, everyone began to wail and the wise men also wailed. And so they saw that they were of no help at all to the two countries. And I said to the wise men: "Can you, at least, tell me where the sound of the wailing comes from?" They asked: "Do you know?" And I answered: "Of course I know. There are two birds, a male and a female. There was only one pair of these species on earth. The female was lost and the male roamed about seeking her. She was also seeking him. They searched for each other for such a long time that they lost their ways and realized they could no longer find one another. They remained where they were and made nests. . . . And when night fell, each one of this pair of birds began to lament with a very great wail. Each wailed for its mate. This is the wailing that is heard in these two countries, and because of the sound, everyone must wail and no one can sleep." . . .

The wise man said to me: "and you set it right?" I answered: "Yes, I can set it right, since I can imitate all the sounds of the world. I can also throw my voice, so that in the place from where I throw my voice, nobody hears, but it is heard far, far away. . . ."

But who could believe me? So I led them into a forest. They heard somebody open a door, and shut it, and lock it with a bolt. Then I shot a gun and sent my dog to retrieve what I had shot. And the dog struggled in the snow. These wise men heard it all and looked around, but they saw absolutely nothing. They heard no sound from me . . . so they understood that I could imitate all the sounds and could throw my voice and thus could set everything right.

[Selections from "The Seven Beggars"]

GLOSSARY

Amoraim   Rabbinic sages from 200–500 C.E. whose comments on the *Mishnah* are in the *Talmud.*

Diaspora   dispersion of the Jews outside of Israel.

Deuteronomistic History   the historical sequence of books in the *Tanakh* from Deuteronomy through Chronicles, connected in terms of authorship and theology.

Elohim   Hebrew for *God.*

Israelite   people of Israel until the return from the Babylonian exile.

Jew   descendants of the Israelites from the return from the Babylonian exile to the present. *Jew* is from the Hebrew *jehudi,* meaning a descendant of Jacob's son Judah.

Judea   the name for the land of the Jews from the post-exilic period to the early Roman period.

Kabbala   (literally *Tradition*) the largest school of Jewish mysticism, from the 12th century C.E. to the present.

Midrash   a verse-by-verse style of commentary on the *Tanakh,* especially as used by early Rabbis.

Mishnah   the written expression of the oral law, compiled in 200 C.E. by Rabbi Judah ha-Nasi.

Saboraim   Rabbinic sages from 500-700 whose comments on the *Mishnah* were added to those of the Amoraim in the *Talmud.*

Sefirot   the ten emanations of God, as described in early Kabbalist theology.

Talmud   an extensive collection of commentaries on the *Mishnah* compiled from the sayings of Rabbis from 200–500 C.E..

Tanakh   the Hebrew Bible. The term comes from the initials of its three divisions: Torah (law), Neviim (prophets), Ketuvim (writings).

Torah   Hebrew for *law, teaching,* or *instruction.* In the broad sense "Torah" refers to the law of Moses, both written and oral. In the narrow sense it refers to first five books of the *Tanakh,* traditionally called the Books of Moses.

Tannaim   Rabbinic sages of the first two centuries C.E. whose sayings are compiled in the *Mishnah.*

Yahweh   the personal name of God in Judaism.

SUGGESTIONS FOR FURTHER READING

AGUS, JACOB. *The Jewish Quest* (1983).

ALEXANDER, PHILLIP S. *Textual Sources for the Study of Judaism* Totowa, NJ: Barnes and Noble, 1986.

BAECK, LEO. *The Essence of Judaism,* rev. ed. (1987).

BLAU, JOSEPH L. *Modern Varieties of Judaism* (1966).

BLECH, B. *Understanding Judaism* (1991).

FACKENHEIM, E. L. *What Is Judaism?* (1988).

GLAZER, NATHAN. *American Judaism,* 2d ed. (1973).

GOLDBERG, D., AND RAYNER, J. *The Jewish People* (1987).

HOLTZ, BARRY. *Back to the Sources: Reading the Classic Jewish Texts.* New York: Touchstone, 1984.

MEYER, MICHAEL. *Ideas of Jewish History* (1987).

NEUSNER, JACOB. *The Life of the Torah: Readings in the Jewish Religious Experience* (1974)

SANDMEL, SAMUEL. *The Hebrew Scriptures.* Oxford: University Press, 1978.

SILVER, D., AND MARTIN, B. *A History of Judaism,* 2 vols. (1974).

STEINSALTZ, ADIN. *The Essential Talmud.* San Francisco: Harper Collins, 1976.

WIGODER, G. *Encyclopedia of Judaism* (1989).

Christianity

Christianity is founded on the life and teachings of Jesus, a first century C.E. Jew who was executed by the Roman authorities for subversion. During its first few decades Christianity was a sect within Judaism, but quickly expanded beyond its Palestinian borders and Jewish framework, becoming an independent religion. Two elements of Christian doctrine are essentially Jewish. First, Jesus is the messiah, or anointed king, who is spoken of in Jewish prophetic writings. The term *christ* is a Greek translation of the Hebrew word *messiah*, and so Jesus is referred to as the Christ. Second, the message of Jesus is the kingdom of God. Keeping with Jewish apocalyptic notions of the messiah, early Christians expected that the kingdom would be established by cataclysmic events. A third element of Christianity departs from its Jewish heritage, namely, that Jesus is God in human form. Building on this, a fourth element is that, by his work, teachings, death, and resurrection, Jesus became the savior of the world.

THE HISTORY OF CHRISTIANITY

The Life of Jesus

Jesus left no writings, and the knowledge we have of his life and teachings comes almost exclusively from the gospels of Matthew, Mark, and Luke. These narratives are traditionally ascribed to his disciples, but were probably written and compiled anonymously between 40 and 60 years after his death. They were also written by believers for believers, blending historical memories with early church teaching. Reconstructing an accurate picture of Jesus, then, is difficult, and, according to some theologians, impossible.

Jesus was born about 4 B.C.E. and raised in Nazareth, an insignificant agricultural city in the Galilee region. Little is known about Jesus until he began his ministry at about age 30. Jewish territories at that time were under especially oppressive Roman rule, which caused widespread unrest. Since the times of the independent Jewish monarchies hundreds of years earlier, 90 percent of the Jewish population consisted of agrarian peasants who supported the ruling priestly elite through taxes on their harvest. Additional taxes were imposed by the Romans, and still more to support local building projects, such as those of

King Herod. By the time of Jesus, peasant taxes totaled about 40 percent of their harvest, which forced many into debt or sale of family land. Unemployment was also high. As the Romans reduced the size of Jewish territories, Jews from surrounding areas flooded into Judea and Galilee, the two principle territories of Jewish settlement. Occasional famine made economic times worse and intensified the rift between peasants and the ruling class, which supported the Romans.

Desperate peasants rallied around charismatic leaders who offered hope.[1] Some supported social bandits who systematically robbed rich Jewish landowners and shared the wealth with the peasants. Others found comfort in the company of prophets who, in the tradition of the old Jewish prophets, pronounced apocalyptic judgment against the Romans and called the people to repentance. Still others took refuge in the leadership of messiahs, that is, anointed kings. The concept of a messiah in Jewish literature did not become fixed until Rabbinic discussions after the revolt of 66. Prior to that, written discussions refer to a Davidic king, a prophet like Moses or a perfect priest, although the actual term *messiah* is rarely used. The notion of messiah in the minds of the illiterate peasants was somewhat different from that which appeared in the writings of the ruling elite. Although they retained the idea of kingship, they saw the anointing of this king as a revolutionary act of popular election. The messiah was to be a flesh-and-blood military leader, not just an apocalyptic figure waging spiritual war.

Jesus began his ministry during his association with John the Baptist, an apocalyptic prophet, who proclaimed impending doom. John baptized Jesus, and shortly after was executed by the ruler of Galilee, who feared that John's enthusiastic followers might provoke a rebellion. Jesus attracted his own followers in Galilee, who initially saw him as a popular prophet, rather more like John the Baptist than a political messiah. Of his large following of both men and women, later Christian tradition honored 12 as having special authority (although there is disagreement on who exactly the 12 were). With his disciples, Jesus traveled around Galilee teaching, befriending outcasts, healing people, and performing exorcisms. He taught to both small gatherings in synagogues and to large peasant crowds in open-air places. His ministry lasted only a couple of years until he was executed on a Roman cross. The precise reasons for his execution may never be known. For John the Baptist, attracting large crowds in a revolutionary environment was enough to cost him his life. To the extent that Jesus appeared to be another popular prophet, Jewish and Roman leaders had reason for concern.

The Teaching of Jesus

Like the events of his life, Jesus' teachings in the gospels also blend his words with early church doctrine. Some scholars argue that less than 20 percent of the sayings attributed to Jesus in the Gospels were spoken by him.[2] The dominant message that emerges, though, is the kingdom of God. The "kingdom" is never defined, but is the final state of affairs in which the world runs according to God's will. Paradoxically, some teachings proclaim that the kingdom will arrive in the near future, while others maintain that the kingdom has already begun. Although the concepts of both a future and present kingdom of God can be found in Jewish apocalyptic literature, Jesus is unique in making the doctrine of the kingdom the basis of ethical behavior. Moral acts of repentance, love, charity, and nonviolence are God's requirements for acceptance into the kingdom. Because of the urgency in preparing for the kingdom, uncompromising behavior is required. Jesus did not see himself as the messianic ruler of the kingdom he proclaimed, especially in view of the military implications of the popular messiahs.

Along with its content, the style of Jesus' teaching is also important: the parable. Most broadly, a parable is a statement, story, or dialogue that has a metaphorical or figurative meaning. It can be as short as a single sentence, such as "It is easier for a camel to pass through the eye of a needle than for a rich man to enter the kingdom of God" (Mark 10:25), or paragraphs long. Understood this way, almost everything attributed to Jesus in the synoptic gospels is in the form of a parable. More narrowly, parables are extended metaphorical narratives, or figurative stories, about 30 of which appear in the first three Gospels and the Gospel of Thomas (see below). In view of their figurative nature, the parables require interpretation, and sometimes an early Christian explanation is presented within the Gospel text itself. The interpretation of virtually all of the parables, though, relates to some challenging aspect of the kingdom. Like much of Old Testament literature, Jesus' parables follow specific literary structures. For example, Luke 11:9–10 follows step parallelism:

> A   Ask, and it will be given you
>   B   Seek, and you will find
>   C   Knock, and it will be opened to you
> A'   For everyone who asks receives
>   B'   And he who seeks finds
>   C'   And to him who knocks it will be opened

Even the longest narrative parables follow a combination of various parallel structures.[3]

The Early Church

After his execution, strong leaders and apostles emerged within the Jesus movement, keeping its spirit alive and recruiting even more followers. Jesus was quickly seen as the crucified and risen messiah who would return from heaven at any moment and begin an apocalyptic (as opposed to military) reign. Old testament messianic prophecies were applied to him, bolstering the interpretation that Jesus was the Christ. Some followers sold their possessions and waited his arrival. Others, such as Paul, a former Pharisee, effectively recruited believers from among non-Jews. Early interpretations of Jesus and his message varied greatly among the new followers, and the Christian tradition we inherit was defined in reaction to and in competition with early alternatives. The New Testament canon and early church hierarchy are products of the winning tradition, whereas the losing traditions were branded as heresies along the way. An early losing interpretation was that of Judaizers who believed that Christianity was the messianic fulfillment of Judaism, and not a different religion. Thus, Christians were still bound by traditional Jewish laws, such as circumcision and food rituals. However, the Judaizers' narrow notion of Christianity did not fit the broader vision of other early church leaders.

Another unsuccessful early interpretation of Christianity was offered by Gnosticism, a diverse religious movement that flourished throughout the Near East from 100 to 400 C.E. The aim of the Gnostic religion in general was to free one's spirit from the illusions of the evil, material world and reascend to heaven. Release was to be accomplished by acquiring special knowledge (*gnosis*). In Christian Gnosticism, the material world was created by an evil demigod, and Jesus' teachings provide the knowledge that redeems us from worldly illusion. Church leaders reacted vehemently to the Gnostic interpretation, penning many polemics against it.

While theologians battled over doctrine, churches were established throughout the Roman Empire, and bishops—reputedly successors of the original Apostles—officiated in key regions. At first Roman rulers did not distinguish between Christians and Jews. But the rapid advance of Christianity soon made the distinction apparent, and, from their perspective, threatened the unity of the Empire. Christianity was outlawed and, throughout the first three centuries C.E., several emperors systematically persecuted Christians, some bent on their extinction. A decisive turning point came when the Christian emperor Constantine took the throne, and in 313 C.E. he proclaimed complete religious liberty for Christians. He sponsored a world church council, at Nicea, which determined that Christ was not subordinate to God, but substantively identical with God. The council also established the bishops of Rome, Antioch, and Alexandria as the primary officiators of the Church; later the bishop of Constantinople was added to the list. In 392 C.E. Emperor Theodosius declared Christianity the only allowable religion throughout the empire.

Christian Denominations

During the fourth century C.E., the vast Roman Empire became too difficult to manage from a single location, so it was regionally divided, with the western territory governed by Rome and the eastern territory governed by Constantinople. Now inseparably tied to empire politics, the Church too established parallel jurisdictions. The western jurisdiction, later designated *catholic*, was led by Rome's bishop, or *Pope*, and the eastern (or *orthodox*) jurisdiction, looked, less formally, to Constantinople's bishop, or *Patriarch*. Differences of worship and authority further divided the regions, such as the east's use of icons, rejection of Papal authority, and emphasis on Christ's divinity above his humanity. The rift was complete in 1054 when Rome's Pope Leo IX and Constantinople's Patriarch Michael Cerularius mutually excommunicated each other. Since the great catholic-orthodox schism, the three original eastern church jurisdictions (Antioch, Alexandria, and Constantinople) have multiplied to over 20, each with its own Patriarch. Although the Orthodox jurisdictions govern independently, they are unified by shared liturgy and doctrine.

After the fall of the western Roman empire from barbarian invasions in the fifth century, missionary journeys spread Christianity throughout northern Europe. The Pope was on a par with emperors of new and primitive European states, and Christian monasteries were the default centers of learning. By the 15th century, growing discontentment with Catholic hierarchy erupted in the Protestant Reformation, led by the German priest Martin Luther. Luther stressed that the Bible is Christianity's exclusive authority, not the Pope, and not church traditions. Salvation, Luther declared, is achieved through God's grace, not through human achievement, and is available to all who ask. Luther was particularly successful in convincing German nobility of the benefits of breaking ties with Rome. As surrounding European countries soon followed the reformer's lead, Luther believed that the protesters would remain theologically unified because God would guide each person toward the same interpretation of the Bible. This was not to be, and five centuries later, hundreds of Protestant denominations have emerged from disputes over doctrine. The largest Protestant denominations are the Baptists, Lutherans, Presbyterians, Methodists, and Episcopalians. The large denominations are often doctrinally divided among themselves; the more conservative emphasize evangelism and Biblical inerrency, whereas the more liberal stress social concerns and metaphorical interpretations of the Bible. Pentecostal churches are part of a movement, rather than a single denomination, and stress spiritual gifts, such as prophecy and speaking in tongues.

CHRISTIAN SACRED TEXTS

Christian sacred texts may be classed into four main divisions: (1) the Bible, (2) early sectarian writings, (3) mystical writings, and (4) recent sectarian writings. Christians consider only the Bible to be sacred, although the other groups of texts are thought to be authoritative in many circles.

The Bible

The primary body of scriptures in the Christian tradition is the Bible, containing an Old and New Testament. The Old Testament is the Jewish *Tanakh*, which makes the Christian Bible unique among world scriptures by including the canon of a different religion. The Christian Old Testament was initially based on the Septuagint, the Greek translation of the Jewish canon from 100 B.C.E. Accordingly, the Old Testament retains the book arrangement of the Septuagint. Catholic and Orthodox Christians also accept the apocryphal books from the Septuagint, although Protestants reject these, opting for what they believe are the older books as appear in the Jewish *Tanakh*. The term *Old Testament* was coined by Paul, who used it in reference to the writings of the Mosaic covenant (2 Cor. 3:14).

By the fourth century C.E., the term *New Testament* was commonly used to refer to a collection of 27 early Christian texts composed in Greek. Traditionally they are thought to be written by the original Apostles who were Jesus' followers. Historically, though, all of the texts are now thought to be written by second- and third-generation Christians from 50–150 C.E. For the first few centuries, there was no fixed New Testament canon, and manuscripts of hundreds of individual Christian texts circulated independently among the early churches. Early church fathers made recommendations as to which of these were authoritative. The first known list containing the present 27 books appears as a side comment in St. Athanasias' Easter letter of 367 C.E.

As Latin became the spoken language of the Roman Empire, Latin translations of the Old Testament and various Christian texts circulated. In 382 the Pope commissioned Jerome, a priest and scholar, to bring order to the chaotic collection of Latin texts. Returning to Hebrew and Greek language texts, Jerome produced a new Latin translation of the Old and New Testaments, referred to as the Vulgate, which, after some resistance, was accepted as definitive. Even with a more fixed canon, early theologians questioned the authority of several Old and New Testament texts and introduced a distinction between protocanonical and deuterocanonical texts: canonical writings with either a primary or secondary status. In the 13th century the traditional chapter divisions were added to each book of the Bible by a cardinal who was preparing a biblical index. The Vulgate continued to be the official text of the Bible until the Protestant Reformation, when several modern language translations appeared, many of which removed the books of the Old Testament Apocrypha, or at least relegated them to an appendix. Verse divisions were also added at this time. As scholars today discover older manuscript copies of biblical books, passages are revised or deleted to reflect the earliest sources. For example, the well-known story from John 9 of the stoning of the adulterous woman ("Let him who is without sin cast the first stone") is now removed from modern editions of the Bible.

The texts of the New Testament fall into five categories:

Gospels: Matthew, Mark, Luke, John

Book of Acts

Letters of Paul: Romans, 1 and 2 Corinthians, Galatians, Ephesians, Philippians, Colossians, 1 and 2 Thessalonians, 1 and 2 Timothy, Titus, Philemon, Hebrews

General letters: Letter of James, 1 and 2 Letters of Peter, 1, 2, and 3 Letters of John, Letter of Jude

Book of Revelation

The Gospels, which contain accounts of Jesus, have always been considered the most primary of all Christian texts. Scholars believe that for a few decades after Jesus' execution, the recollections of his immediate followers were transmitted orally. The first written accounts, from perhaps 50 C.E., were simply lists of his sayings with no stories. None of these have survived intact. The book of Mark appeared around 70 C.E., based on oral traditions of Jesus' life and teachings. Matthew and Luke then appeared around 85 C.E., both using information from Mark and an earlier lost list of sayings called *Quelle* (German for *source*). Matthew and Luke also contain unique stories and sayings, based on either oral traditions or earlier lost lists of sayings. Mark, Matthew, and Luke are referred to as the *synoptic gospels*, since they give very similar accounts of Jesus' life and teachings. Finally, the Gospel of John appeared in 90 C.E.. Initially considered heretical by some early church fathers, it presents an account that is 90 percent different in content. All four Gospels first circulated anonymously, and were only ascribed to the apostles during the middle second century.

The Book of Acts is a continuation of Luke, penned by the same author, and discusses the spread of early Christianity immediately after Jesus. Of particular concern is the relationship of Christianity to Judaism in view of the large numbers of non-Jewish converts. More than half of Acts chronicles the conversion and missionary journeys of Paul. Of the 14 letters ascribed to Paul, only 7 are confidently traced to him (Romans, 1 and 2 Corinthians, Galatians, Philippians, 1 Thessalonians, and Philemon). His letters, composed between 50 and 60 C.E., contain encouragement and instructions to the churches he helped establish, but they did not gain a wide readership until the end of the first century. The general letters were written at the close of the first century as tracts or sermons addressing problems in early church communities. Finally, the Book of Revelation, also written at the close of the first century, describes a series of apocalyptic visions that contain instructions for Christians to remain faithful in the face of Roman persecution.

Early Sectarian Writings

Early sectarian Christian writings fall into three groups: the Apostolic Fathers, the New Testament Apocrypha, and Gnostic texts.

The term *Apostolic Fathers* was coined in the 17th century in reference to a collection of writings attributed to followers of the original apostles. The 14 texts now included under this label were not only popular in the early church, but some were included in scripture lists by early church fathers. Of particular interest in this collection is the Didache, or Teaching of the Twelve, which gives instructions on baptism, fasting, prayer, and the Eucharist.

The expression *New Testament Apocrypha* is applied loosely to a range of early Christian texts, mostly from the second century, that are not included in the New Testament. Many of these were considered sacred by early churches and are the source of Christian beliefs, such as the assumption of Mary. Frequently they aim to fill gaps in the chronologies of Jesus' life and the early church. Paralleling the genres of New Testament texts, the writings fall into the categories of gospels, acts, epistles, and apocalypses. They are of particular value as a possible source of stray sayings of Jesus that continued to circulate into the second century.

The early sectarian writings that have recently attracted the most scholarly attention are the Gnostic texts discovered in 1945 in Nag Hammadi, Egypt. The 45 texts are fourth- and fifth-century Coptic translations of Greek manuscripts, although the originals go back much earlier. Representing both Christian and non-Christian Gnostic ideas, they are thought to be the library of an early Gnostic Christian monastery, which buried the documents in containers for protection. The texts suggest that early Christianity was much more theologically diverse than initially believed, and that the lasting tradition was only one among several viable alternatives. Many texts emphasize a divine Mother, whereas by 200 C.E. feminine imagery of God disappeared from the emerging mainstream tradition. Most important among the texts is the Gnostic Gospel of Thomas, a list of 114 sayings of Jesus. The list is based on an earlier compilation of sayings, predating the New Testament gospels, and thus, like Q, represents the earliest strata of sayings attributed to Jesus.

Mystical Writings

Since the early middle ages, the Bible was seen as the only scripture for mainstream Christian denominations. However, other sacred texts have emerged in various Christian traditions, particularly among medieval mystics and within modern American movements. Four mystical essays by an unknown fifth-century author named Pseudo-Dionysius the Areopagite were greatly valued among mystics, especially the *Mystical Theology*, which maintains that the highest knowledge of God is attained by way of negation. The *Ladder of Divine Ascent*, by John Climacus (580–650), abbot of the monastery at Mount Sinai, describes 30 rungs stretching from earth to heaven, symbolizing transition to the contemplative life.

Eastern Orthodox mystics in particular view as sacred a collection of more than 30 mystical texts written between the 4th and 14th centuries and known as the *Philokalia*. The texts, part of the monastic libraries of Mt. Athos, Greece, were written by ascetic monks as guidebooks for other monks on successful ascetic living. First published in 1782, the collection went through several translations, and a greatly expanded five-volume Russian edition appeared between 1867 and 1890. Many of the texts are how-to guides for overcoming the bodily and mental distractions that Satan creates in order to deter mystics. Others explain various techniques for contemplation and direct encounter with God. The texts of the *Philokalia* were not only cherished by the medieval ascetics who followed their practices but, since their publication, also by lay orthodox mystics.

Catholicism has a long mystical tradition that produced hundreds of texts, only a few of which can be mentioned here. Prior to the 12th century, comments on mystical practices were scattered and informal. Twelfth-century writers such as Bernard of Clairvaux (1090–1153), Hugh of St. Victor (d. 1141), and William of St. Thierry (d. 1148) systematized mystical doctrine and established key elements for later mystics. Foremost was the interiorized experience, affective piety, and patterns of "contemplation" (the term they used for what we now call "mysticism"). The German women's movement of the next century produced several mystics, including Hildegard of Bingen, Mechthild of Magdeburg, and Elizabeth of Schonau. Fourteenth-century mystics include Julian of Norwich (1342–1413), a Benedictine nun who lived isolated in a small cell, and Meister Eckhart (1260–1327), a German Dominican monk, whose more pantheistic writings were pronounced heretical after papal investigation. The greatest work of fifteenth-century mysticism is the *Imitation of Christ*, attributed to Thomas à Kempis (1379–1471), and that of the 16th century is *The Interior Castle* by Spanish Carmelite nun Teresa of Avila (1515–1582).

Recent Sectarian Writings

Keeping with the religious freedom and pioneering spirit of 19th-century America, various Christian movements produced sacred texts. The distinct beliefs of the Church of Latter-Day Saints are founded on the *Book of Mormon*, a text produced by founder Joseph Smith (1805–1844). Mormons believe that Smith translated the text from gold plates buried during a previous age, the location of which was revealed to Smith in an angelic vision. Smith also translated a lost text of Abraham, made a series of prophesies, and was supposedly divinely inspired with a new version of the Bible. These are included in the church's two other sacred writings: the *Doctrine and Covenants*, and the *Pearl of Great Price*. The Christian Science movement reveres *Science and Health* (1875) by founder Mary Baker Eddy (1821–1910), which emphasizes the healing aspect of Christianity. According to Eddy, the material world and all illness associated with it are unreal and illusory. Healing comes after prayer when God simply removes the afflicted person's false belief in the illusion. Associated with the New Age movement, American pastor Levi H. Dowling (1844–1911) produced the *Aquarian Gospel* in 1907 via automatic typewriting, which recounts 18 lost years of Jesus as he traveled to India, Tibet, Egypt, Persia, and Greece.

SELECTIONS FROM THE BIBLE

ISAIAH'S PRINCE OF PEACE AND SUFFERING SERVANT

The principal value of the Old Testament for Christianity is that Christ is the ultimate fulfillment of its covenants and messianic prophesies. Nowhere is that seen more clearly than in the following two selections from Isaiah on the birth of the prince of peace and the suffering servant. For Christians, these are allusions to Jesus' birth and his suffering on the cross.[4]

9.

For to us a child is born, to us a son is given, and the government will be on his shoulders. And he will be called Wonderful Counselor, Mighty God, Everlasting Father, Prince of Peace. Of the increase of his government and peace there will be no end. He will reign on David's throne and over his kingdom, establishing and upholding it with justice and righteousness from that time on and forever. The zeal of the Lord Almighty will accomplish this.

53.

He grew up before him like a tender shoot, and like a root out of dry ground. He had no beauty or majesty to attract us to him, nothing in his appearance that we should desire him. He was despised and rejected by men, a man of sorrows, and familiar with suffering. Like one from whom men hide their faces he was despised, and we esteemed him not. Surely he took up our infirmities and carried our sorrows, yet we considered him stricken by God, smitten by him, and afflicted. But he was pierced for our transgressions, he was crushed for our iniquities; the punishment that brought us peace was upon him, and by his wounds we are healed. We all, like sheep, have gone astray, each of us has turned to his own way; and the Lord has laid on him the iniquity of us all.

He was oppressed and afflicted, yet he did not open his mouth; he was lead like a lamb to the slaughter, and as a sheep before her shearers is silent, so he did not open his mouth. By oppression and judgment he was taken away. And who can speak of his descendants? For he was cut off from the land of the living; for the transgression of my people he was stricken. He was assigned a grave with the wicked, and with the rich in his death, though he had done no violence, nor was any deceit in his mouth.

Yet it was the Lord's will to crush him and cause him to suffer, and though the Lord makes his life a guilt offering, he will see his offspring and prolong his days, and the will of the Lord will prosper in his hand. After the suffering of his soul, he will see the light [of life) and be satisfied; by his knowledge my righteous servant will justify many, and he will bear their iniquities.

[Isaiah 9:6–7, 53:2–11]

BIRTH OF JESUS

Two of the four canonical gospels give accounts of the birth of Jesus, each slightly different. The following is Luke's version. The author of Luke was an educated non-Jewish Christian and, thus, his gospel reflects the broader non-Jewish implications of both Jesus' life and the Christian church. Unlike Matthew, Luke begins by placing the birth story in the context of Roman emperor Augustus' reign.[5]

In those days it so happened that a decree was issued by Emperor Augustus that a census be taken of the whole civilized world. This first census was taken while Quirinius was governor of Syria. Everybody had to travel to their ancestral city to be counted in the census. So Joseph too went up from Galilee, from the town of Nazareth, to Judea, to the town of David called Bethlehem, because he was a descendant of David, to be counted in the census with Mary, to whom he was engaged; Mary was pregnant. It so happened while they were there that the time came for her to give birth; and she gave birth to a son, her firstborn. She wrapped him in strips of cloth and laid him in a feeding trough, because the travelers' shelter was no place for that.

Now in the same area there were shepherds living outdoors. They were keeping watch over their sheep at night, when a messenger of the Lord stood near them and the glory of the Lord shone around them. They became terrified. But the messenger said to them, "Don't be afraid: I bring you good news of a great joy, which is to benefit the whole nation; today in the city of David, the Savior was born to you—he is the Anointed, the Lord. And this will be a sign for you: you will find a baby wrapped in strips of cloth and lying in a feeding trough."

And suddenly there appeared with the messenger a whole troop of the heavenly army praising God:

> Glory to God in the highest,
> and on earth peace to people whom he has favored!

It so happened when the messengers left and returned to heaven that the shepherds said to one another, "Come on! Let's go over to Bethlehem and see what has happened, the event the Lord has told us about." And they hurried away, and found Mary, Joseph, and the baby lying in a feeding trough. And when they saw it they reported what they had been told about this child. Everyone who listened was astonished at what the shepherds told them. But Mary took all this in and reflected on it. And the shepherds returned, glorifying and praising God for all they had heard and seen; everything turned out just as they had been told.

Now eight days later, when the time came to circumcise him, they gave him the name Jesus, the name assigned him by the heavenly messenger before he was conceived in the womb.

Now when the time came for their purification according to the Law of Moses, they brought him up to Jerusalem to present him to the Lord—as it is written in the Law of the Lord, "Every male that opens the womb is to be considered holy to the lord"—and to offer sacrifice according to what is dictated in the Law of the Lord: "A pair of turtledoves or two young pigeons." . . .

And when they had carried out everything required by the Law of the Lord, they returned to Galilee, to Nazareth, their own city. And the boy grew up and became strong, and was filled with wisdom; and God regarded him favorably.

[Luke 2:1–24, 39, 40]

JESUS' BAPTISM, TEMPTATION, AND FIRST DISCIPLES

The first canonical gospel to appear was Mark. Mark focuses more on activities in the life of Jesus than on teachings. His narrative is concise, matter of fact, and probably written for a non-Jewish audience in Rome about 70 C.E. Since virtually the entire content of Mark's account is included in the longer gospels of Matthew and Luke (which use Mark as one of several sources), Mark's gospel was typically not the most popular. However, as modern scholars try to identify the earliest recorded accounts of Jesus, preference is now given to Mark's narrative. The following selection, from the opening chapter of Mark, describes Jesus' baptism by John the Baptist. This initiated his ministry, his temptation in the desert where he confronted Satan, and his acquiring of his first followers. Some scholars believe that after Jesus' death early Christians had to explain why the Jewish populace did not recognize Jesus as the messiah. Mark has an explanation which both Matthew and Luke adopt: Jesus purposefully kept word of his messiahship from circulating in order to minimize conflict with officials. Referred to as the messianic secret, *this explanation appears twice in the following passage.*

The good news of Jesus the Anointed begins with something Isaiah the prophet wrote:

> Here is my messenger,
> whom I send on ahead of you
> to prepare your way!
> A voice of someone shouting in the wilderness:
> "Make ready the way of the Lord,
> make his paths straight."

So, John the Baptizer appeared in the wilderness calling for baptism and a change of heart that lead to forgiveness of sins. And everyone from the Judean countryside and all the residents of Jerusalem streamed out to him and got baptized by him in the Jordan river, admitting their sins. And John wore a mantel made of camel hair and had a leather belt around his waist and lived on locust and raw honey. And he began his proclamation by saying:

"Someone more powerful than I will succeed me, whose sandal straps I am not fit to bend down and untie. I have been baptizing you with water, but he'll baptize you with holy spirit."

During the same period Jesus came from Nazareth, Galilee, and was baptized in the Jordan by John. And just as he got up out of the water, he saw the skies torn open and the spirit coming down toward him like a dove. There was also a voice from the skies: "You are my favored son—I fully approve of you."

And right away the spirit drives him out into the wilderness, where he remained for forty days, being put to the test by Satan. While he was living there among the wild animals, the heavenly messengers looked after him.

After John was locked up, Jesus came to Galilee proclaiming God's good news. His message went:

"The time is up: God's imperial rule is closing in. Change your ways, and put your trust in the good news!"

As he was walking along by the Sea of Galilee, he spotted Simon and Andrew, Simon's brother, casting [their nets] into the sea—since they were fishermen—and Jesus said to them: "Become my followers and I'll have you fishing for people!"

And right then and there they abandoned their nets and followed him.

When he had gone a little farther, he caught sight of James, son of Zebedee, and his brother John mending their nets in the boat. Right then and there he called out to them as well, and they left their father Zebedee behind in the boat with the hired hands and accompanied him.

Then they come to Capernaum, and on the sabbath day he went right to the synagogue and started teaching. They were astonished at his teaching, since he would teach them on his own authority, unlike the scholars.

Now right there in their synagogue was a person possessed by an unclean spirit, which shouted, "Jesus! What do you want with us, you Nazarene? Have you come to get rid of us? I know you, who you are: God's holy man!"

But Jesus yelled at it, "Shut up and get out of him!"

Then the unclean spirit threw the man into convulsions, and letting out a loud shriek it came out of him. And they were all so amazed that they asked themselves, "What's this? A new kind of teaching backed by authority! He gives orders even to unclean spirits and they obey him!"

So his fame spread rapidly everywhere throughout Galilee and even beyond.

They left the synagogue right away and entered the house of Simon and Andrew along with James and John. Simon's mother-in-law was in bed with a fever, and they told him about her right away. He went up to her, took hold of her hand, raised her up, and the fever disappeared. Then she started looking after them.

In the evening, at sundown, they would bring all the sick and demon possessed to him. And the whole town would crowd around the door. On such occasions he cured many people afflicted with various diseases and drove out many demons. He would never let the demons speak, because they realized who he was.

And rising early, while it was still very dark, he went outside and stole away to an isolated place, where he started praying. Then Simon and those with him hunted him down. When they had found him they say to him, "They're all looking for you."

But he replies: "Let's go somewhere else, to the neighboring villages, so I can speak there too, since that's what I came for."

So he went all around Galilee speaking in their synagogues and driving out demons.

Then a leper comes up to him, pleads with him, falls down on his knees, and says to him, "If you want to, you can make me clean."

Although Jesus was indignant, he stretched out his hand, touched him, and says to him, "Okay—you're clean!"

And right away the leprosy disappeared, and he was made clean. And Jesus snapped at him, and dismissed him curtly with this warning: "See that you don't tell anyone anything, but go, have a priest examine [your skin]. Then offer for your cleansing what Moses commanded, as evidence [of your cure].

But after he went out, he started telling everyone and spreading the story, so that [Jesus] could no longer enter a town openly, but had to stay out in the countryside. Yet they continued to come to him from everywhere.

[Mark 1]

SERMON ON THE MOUNT

Matthew's Gospel was written for a Jewish audience, and it continually draws parallels from the Old Testament. He incorporates Jesus' sayings into five distinct discourses, possibly representing the five books of Moses, to symbolize a new Torah. The Sermon on the Mount is the first of these and, again, the mountain motif here parallels the story of Moses receiving the Law at Mount Sinai. Many of the teachings in Matthew overlap those in Luke, suggesting that they independently drew their information from a third source (called Q by contemporary scholars). Thus, sayings in the Sermon on the Mount also appear in Luke in a section often called the Sermon on the Plain (6:20–49). Matthew's discourse opens with a description of how the kingdom of God will involve a dramatic reversal of conditions for the oppressed and faithful. Citizens of the kingdom must distinguish themselves through obedience to a new law, principally one of love for others, forgiveness, and trust in God.

5. Taking note of the crowds, he climbed up the mountain, and when he had sat down, his disciples came to him. He then began to speak, and this is what he would teach them:

> Congratulations to the poor in spirit!
> Heaven's domain belongs to them.
> Congratulations to those who grieve!
> They will be consoled.
> Congratulations to the gentle!
> They will inherit the earth.
> Congratulations to those who hunger and thirst for justice!
> They will have a feast.
> Congratulations to the merciful!
> They will receive mercy.
> Congratulations to those with undefiled hearts!
> They will see God.
> Congratulations to those who work for peace!
> They will be known as God's children.
> Congratulations to those who have suffered persecution for the sake of justice!
> Heaven's domain belongs to them.

"Congratulations to you when they denounce you and persecute you and spread malicious gossip about you because of me. Rejoice and be glad! In heaven you will be more than compensated. Remember, this is how they persecuted the prophets who preceded you.

"You are the salt of the earth. But if salt loses its zing, how will it be made salty? It then has no further use than to be thrown out and stomped on. You are the light of the world. A city sitting on top of a mountain can't be concealed. Nor do people light a lamp and put it under a bushel basket but rather on a lampstand, where it sheds light for everyone in the house. That's how your light is to shine in the presence of others, so they can see your good deeds and acclaim your Father in the heavens.

"Don't imagine that I have come to annul the Law or the Prophets. I have come not to annul but to fulfill. I swear to you, before the world disappears, not one iota, not one serif, will disappear from the Law, until that happens. Whoever ignores one of the most trivial of these regulations, and teaches others to do so, will be called trivial in Heaven's domain. But whoever acts on [these regulations] and teaches [others to do so], will be called great in Heaven's domain. Let me tell you: unless your religion goes beyond that of the scholars and Pharisees, you won't set foot in Heaven's domain.

"As you know, our ancestors were told, 'You must not kill' and 'Whoever kills will be subject to judgment.' But I tell you: those who are angry with a companion will be brought before a tribunal. And those who say to a companion, 'You moron,' will be subject to the sentence of the court. And whoever says, 'You idiot,' deserves the fires of Gehenna. So, even if you happen to be offering your gift at the altar and recall that your friend has some claim against you, leave your gift there at the altar. First go and be reconciled with your friend, and only then return and offer your gift. You should come to terms quickly with your opponent while you are both on the way [to court], or else your opponent will hand you over to the judge, and the judge [will turn you over] to the bailiff, and you are thrown in jail. I swear to you, you'll never get out of there until you've paid the last dime.

As you know, we once were told, 'You are not to commit adultery.' But I tell you: Those who leer at a woman and desire her have already committed adultery with her in their hearts. And if your right eye gets you into trouble, rip it out and throw it away! You would be better off to lose a part of your body, than to have your whole body thrown into Gehenna. And if your right hand gets you into trouble, cut it off and throw it away! You would be better off to lose a part of your body, than to have your whole body wind up in Gehenna.

We once were told, 'Whoever divorces his wife should give her a bill of divorce.' But I tell you: Everyone who divorces his wife (except in the case of infidelity) makes her the victim of adultery; and whoever marries a divorced woman commits adultery.

Again, as you know, our ancestors were told, 'You must not break an oath,' and 'Oaths sworn in the name of God must be kept.' But I tell you: Don't swear at all. Don't invoke heaven, because it is the throne of God, and don't earth, because it is God's footstool, and don't invoke Jerusalem, because it is the city of the great king. You shouldn't swear by your head either, since you aren't able to turn a single hair either white or black. Rather, your responses should be simply 'Yes' and 'No.' Anything that goes beyond this is inspired by the evil one.

As you know, we once were told, 'An eye for an eye' and 'A tooth for a tooth.' But I tell you: Don't react violently against the one who is evil: when someone slaps you on the right cheek, turn the other as well. If someone is determined to sue you for your shirt, let that person have your coat along with it. Further, when anyone conscripts you for one mile, go along an extra mile. Give to the one who begs from you; and don't turn away the one who tries to borrow from you.

As you know, we once were told, 'You are to love your neighbor' and 'You are to have your enemy.' But I tell you: Love your enemies and pray for your persecutors. You'll then become children of your Father in the heavens. [God] causes the sun to rise on both the bad and the good, and sends rain on both the just and the unjust. Tell me, if you love those who love you, why should you be condemned for that? Even the toll collectors do as much, don't they? And if you greet only your friends, what have you done that is exceptional! Even the pagans do as much, don't they? To sum up, you are to be as liberal in your love as your heavenly Father is."

6. "Take care that you don't flaunt your religion in public to be noticed by others. Otherwise, you will have no recognition from your Father in the heavens. For example, when you give to charity, don't bother to toot your own horn as some phony pietists do in houses of worship and on the street. They are seeking human recognition. I swear to you, their grandstanding is its own reward. Instead, when you give to charity, don't let your left hand in on what your right hand is up to, so your acts of charity may remain hidden. And your Father, who has an eye for the hidden, will applaud you.

"And when you pray, don't act like phonies. They love to stand up and pray in houses of worship and on street corners, so they can show off in public. I swear to you, their prayers have been answered! When you pray, go into a room by yourself and shut the door behind you. Then pray to your Father, the hidden one. And your Father, with his eye for the hidden, will applaud you. And when you pray, you should not babble on as the pagans do. They imagine that the length of their prayers will command attention. So don't imitate them. After all, your Father knows what you need before you ask. Instead, you should pray like this:

> Our Father in the heavens,
> your name be revered.
> Impose your imperial rule,
> enact your will on earth as you have in heaven.
> Provide us with the bread we need for the day.
> Forgive our debts
> to the extent that we have forgiven those in debt to us.
> And please don't subject us to test after test,
> but rescue us from the evil one.

"For if your forgive others their failures and offenses, your heavenly Father will also forgive yours. And if you don't forgive the failures and mistakes of others, your Father won't forgive yours.

"When you fast, don't make a spectacle of your remorse as the pretenders do. As you know, they make their faces unrecognizable so their fasting may be publicly recognized. I swear to you, they have been paid in full. When you fast, comb your hair and wash your face, so your fasting may go unrecognized in public. But it will be recognized by your Father, the hidden one, and your Father, who has an eye for the hidden, will applaud you.

"Don't acquire possessions here on earth, where moths and insects eat away and where robbers break in and steal. Instead, gather your nest egg in heaven, where neither moths nor insects eat away and where no robbers break in or steal. As you know, what you treasure is your heart's true measure.

"The eye is the body's lamp. If follows that if your eye is clear, your whole body will be flooded with light. If your eye is clouded, your whole body will be shrouded in darkness. If, then, the light within you is darkness, how dark that can be!

"No one can be a slave to two masters. No doubt that slave will either hate one and love the other, or be devoted to one and disdain the other. You can't be enslaved to both God and a bank account!

"That's why I tell you: Don't fret about your life—what you're going to eat and drink—or about your body—what you're going to wear. There is more to living than food and clothing, isn't there? Take a look at the birds of the sky: they don't plant or harvest, or gather into barns. Yet your heavenly Father feeds them. You're worth more than they, aren't you? Can any of you add one hour to life by fretting about it? Why worry about clothes? Notice how the wild lilies grow: they don't slave and they never spin. Yet let me tell you, even Solomon at the height of his glory was never decked out like one of them. If God dresses up the grass in the field, which is here today and tomorrow is thrown into an oven, won't [God care for] you even more, you who don't take anything for granted? So don't fret. Don't say, 'What am I going to eat?' or 'What am I going to drink?' or 'What am I going to wear?' These are all things pagans seek. After all, our heavenly Father is aware that you need them. You are to seek [God's] domain, and his justice first, and all these things will come to you as a bonus. So don't fret about tomorrow. Let tomorrow fret about itself. The troubles that the day brings are enough.

7. "Don't pass judgment, so you won't be judged. Don't forget, the judgment you hand out will be the judgment you get back. And the standard you apply will be the standard applied to you. Why do you notice the sliver in your friend's eye, but overlook the timber in your own? How can you say to your friend, 'Let me get the sliver out of your eye,' when there is that timber in your own? You phony, first take the timber out of your own eye and then you'll see well enough to remove the sliver from your friend's eye.

"Don't offer to dogs what is sacred, and don't throw your pearls to pigs, or they'll trample them underfoot and turn and tear you to shreds.

"Ask—it'll be given to you; seek—you'll find; knock—it'll be opened for you. Rest assured: everyone who asks receives; everyone who seeks finds; and for the one who knocks it is opened. Who among you would hand a son a stone when it's bread he's asking for? Again, who would hand him a snake when it's fish he's asking for? Of course no one would! So if you, worthless as you are, know how to give your children good gifts, isn't it much more likely that your Father in the heavens will give good things to those who ask him?

"Consider this: Treat people in ways you want them to treat you. This sums up the whole of the Law and the Prophets.

Try to get in through the narrow gate. Wide and smooth is the road that leads to destruction. The majority are taking that route. Narrow and rough is the road that leads to life. Only a minority discover it.

Be on the lookout for phony prophets, who make their pitch disguised as sheep; inside they are really voracious wolves. You'll know who they are by what they produce. Since when do people pick grapes from thorns or figs from thistles? Every healthy tree produces choice fruit, but the rotten tree produces spoiled fruit. A healthy tree cannot produce spoiled fruit, any more than a rotten tree can produce choice fruit. Every tree that does not produce choice fruit gets cut down and tossed on the fire. Remember, you'll know who they are by what they produce.

Not everyone who addresses me as 'Master, master,' will get into Heaven's domain—only those who carry out the will of my Father in heaven. On that day many will address me: 'Master, master, didn't we use your name when we prophesied? Didn't we use your name when we exorcised demons? Didn't we use your name when we performed all those miracles? Then I will tell them honestly: 'I never knew you; get away from me, you subverters of the Law!'

"Everyone who pays attention to these words of mine and acts on them will be like a shrewd builder who erected a house on bedrock. Later the rain fell, and the torrents came, and the winds blew and pounded that house, yet it did not collapse, since its foundation rested on bedrock. Everyone who listens to these words of mine and doesn't act on them will be like a careless builder, who erected a house on the sand. When the rain fell, and the torrents came, and the winds blew and pounded that house, it collapsed. Its collapse was colossal."

And so, when Jesus had finished this discourse, the crowds were astonished at his teaching, since he had been teaching them on his own authority, unlike their [own] scholars.

[Matthew 5–7]

PARABLES OF THE GOOD SAMARITAN
AND PRODIGAL SON

Of the approximately 30 parables of Jesus, the two most famous appear only in Luke: the good Samaritan and the prodigal son. Luke sets both parables in a larger narra-

tive context. The good Samaritan parable is introduced in a dialogue between Jesus and a lawyer (adapted from Mark 12:28–34) on loving one's neighbor. Jesus then explains that the notion of one's neighbor crosses religious and social boundaries, just as a Samaritan aids a battered Jew, in spite of enmity between their two ethnic groups. The prodigal son parable is one of three which Jesus gives in response to criticisms that he associates with sinners. The parable's message is one of forgiveness. The father (representing God) forgives the younger son (representing non-Jews) who squanders his inheritance, while the dutiful older brother (representing Jews) protests.

10. On one occasion, a legal expert stood up to put him to the test with a question: "Teacher, what do I have to do to inherit eternal life?"

     He said to him, "How do you read what is written in the Law?"

     And he answered, "You are to love the Lord your God with all your heart, with all your soul, with all your energy, and with all your mind; and your neighbor as yourself."

     Jesus said to him, "You have given the correct answer; do this and you will have life."

     But with a view to justifying himself, he said to Jesus, "But who is my neighbor?"

     Jesus replied:

     This fellow was on his way from Jerusalem down to Jericho when he fell into the hands of robbers. They stripped him, beat him up, and went off, leaving him half dead. Now by coincidence a priest was going down that road; when he caught sight of him, he went out of his way to avoid him. In the same way, when a Levite came to the place, he took one look at him and crossed the road to avoid him. But this Samaritan who was traveling that way came to where he was and was moved to pity at the sight of him. He went up to him and bandaged his wounds, pouring olive oil and wine on them. He hoisted him onto his own animal, brought him to an inn, and looked after him. The next day he took out two silver coins, which he gave to the innkeeper, and said, "Look after him, and on my way back I'll reimburse you for any extra expenses you have had."

     "Which of these three, in your opinion, acted like a neighbor to the man who fell into the hands of the robbers?"

     He said, "The one who showed him compassion."

     Jesus said to him, "Then go and do the same yourself."

15. Now the toll collectors and sinners kept crowding around Jesus so they could hear him. But the Pharisees and the scholars would complain to each other: "This fellow welcomes sinners and eats with them."

     So he told them this parable: . . .

     Once there was this man who had two sons. The younger of them said to his father, "Father give me the share of the property that's coming to me." So he divided his resources between them.

     Not too many days later, the younger son got all his things together and left home for a faraway country, where he squandered his property by living extravagantly. Just when he had spent it all, a serious famine swept through that country, and he began to do without. So he went and hired himself out to one of the citizens of that country, who sent him out to his farm to feed the pigs. He longed to satisfy his hunger with the carob pods, which the pigs usually ate; but no one offered him anything. Coming to his senses he said, "Lots of my father's hired hands have more than enough to eat, while here I am dying of starvation! I'll get up and go to my father and I'll say to him, 'Father, I have sinned against heaven and affronted you; I don't deserve to be called a son of yours any longer; treat me like one of your hired hands.'" And he got up and returned to his father.

But while he was still a long way off, his father caught sight of him and was moved to compassion. He went running out to him, threw his arms around his neck, and kissed him. And the son said to him, "Father, I have sinned against heaven and affronted you; I don't deserve to be called a son of yours any longer."

But the father said to his slaves, "Quick! Bring out the finest robe and put it on him; put a ring on his finger and sandals on his feet. Fetch the fat calf and slaughter it; let's have a feast and celebrate, because this son of mine was dead and has come back to life; he was lost and now is found." And they started celebrating.

Now his elder son was out in the field; and as he got closer to the house, he heard music and dancing. He called one of the servant-boys over and asked what was going on.

He said to him, "Your brother has come home and your father has slaughtered the fat calf, because he has him back safe and sound."

But he was angry and refused to go in. So his father came out and began to plead with him. But he answered his father, "See here, all these years I have slaved for you. I never once disobeyed any of your orders; yet you never once provided me with a kid goat so I could celebrate with my friends. But when this son of yours shows up, the one who has squandered your estate with prostitutes—for him you slaughter the fat calf."

But [the father] said to him, "My child, you are always at my side. Everything that's mine is yours. But we just had to celebrate and rejoice, because this brother of yours was dead, and has come back to life; he was lost, and now is found."

[Luke 10:25–37; 15:1–3, 11–32]

PETER RECEIVES THE KEYS

Early Christian traditions typically traced their lineage back to an original follower of Jesus. Early Gnostics viewed Jesus' brothers, James and Thomas, as their founders. For Ethiopians, the founder is the eunuch of Acts 8. For the Orthodox of Constantinople, he is Andrew the Apostle. The Catholic church, though, considers its foundation to be Peter, the first supreme Pope. The concept of the Petrine Papacy is based on two doctrines. First, the doctrine of apostolic succession maintains that the original Apostles had authority over specific regional churches, which they passed on to their suc-

cessors. Peter established the church of Rome and, at his death, authority was passed to Linus. Second, the doctrine of the primacy of Peter, forged in the third through fifth centuries, maintains that Peter was given supreme authority over all church congregations. The argument for this latter claim is based on the following passage from Matthew. Drawing from a scene in Mark 8:27 in which Peter identifies Jesus as the Messiah, Matthew then recounts that Jesus rewarded Peter with keys to the kingdom of God. Although the language is metaphorical, Peter is clearly given sweeping authority, thus indicating Matthew's allegiance to the Petrine tradition. Matthew continues by foreshadowing Jesus' fate.

When Jesus came to the region of Caesarea Philippi, he started questioning his disciples, asking, "What are people saying about the son of Adam?"

They said, "Some [say, 'He is] John the Baptist,' but others, 'Elijah,' and others, 'Jeremiah or one of the prophets.'"

He says to them, "What about you, who do you say I am?"

And Simon Peter responded, "You are the Anointed, the son of the living God!"

And in response Jesus said to him, "You are to be congratulated, Simon son of Jonah, because flesh and blood did not reveal this to you but my Father who is in heaven. Let me tell you, you are Peter, 'the Rock,' and on this very rock I will build my congregation, and the gates of Hades will not be able to overpower it. I shall give you the keys of Heaven's domain, and whatever you bind on earth will be considered bound in heaven, and whatever you release on earth will be considered released in heaven."

Then he ordered the disciples to tell no one that he was the Anointed.

From that time on Jesus started to make it clear to his disciples that he was destined to go to Jerusalem, and suffer a great deal at the hands of the elders and ranking priests and scholars, and be killed and, on the third day, be raised.

And Peter took him aside and began to lecture him, saying, "May God spare you, master; this surely can't happen to you."

But he turned and said to Peter, "Get out of my sight, you Satan, you. You are dangerous to me because you are not thinking in God's terms, but in human terms."

Then Jesus said to his disciples, "If any of you wants to come after me you should deny yourself, pick up your cross, and follow me!

"Remember by trying to save your own life, you are going to lose it, but by losing your own life for my sake, you are going to find it. After all, what good will it do if you acquire the whole world but forfeit your life? Or what will you give in exchange for your life?

Remember, the son of Adam is going to come in the glory of his father with his messengers, and then he will reward everyone according to their deeds. I swear to you: Some of those standing here won't ever taste death before they see the son of Adam's imperial rule arriving."

[Matthew 16:13–28]

LAZARUS RAISED FROM THE DEAD

The Gospel of John presents an account of Jesus that is almost entirely different from that of the synoptic gospels. In John, Jesus' ministry is three years, as opposed to one year; the subject of eternal life is emphasized, and not the kingdom of God; Jesus performs no exorcisms, refers to himself as the son of God, is the subject of his own teachings, and says little about the poor. Although Jesus performs miracles in both John and the synoptics, the purpose is different. In John, they are intentionally performed as signs indicating his divine role, whereas in the synoptics, such signs are shunned and miracles are depicted mainly as acts of compassion. In the following passage, Jesus performs his most dramatic miracle by raising a dead man to life. For John, as well as the synoptics, Jesus' supernatural powers were seen by the Jewish leaders as a threat to social and religious stability, inciting them to plot against him.

Now someone named Lazarus had fallen ill; he was from Bethany, the village of Mary and her sister Martha. (This was the Mary who anointed the Master with oil and wiped his feet with her hair; it was her brother Lazarus who was sick.) So the sisters sent for [Jesus]: "Master, the one you love is sick."

But when Jesus heard this he said, "This illness is not fatal; it is to show God's majesty, so God's son also will be honored by it."

Jesus loved Martha and her sister and Lazarus. When he heard that [Lazarus] was sick, he lingered two more days where he was; then he says to the disciples, "Let's go to Judea again."

The disciples say to him, "Rabbi, just now the Judeans were looking for the opportunity to stone you; are you really going back there?"

"Aren't there twelve hours in the day?" Jesus responded. "Those who walk during the day won't stumble; they can see by this world's light. But those who walk at night are going to stumble, because they have no light to go by."

He made these remarks, and then he tells them, "Our friend Lazarus has fallen asleep, but I am going to wake him up."

"Master, if he's only fallen asleep," said the disciples, "he'll revive." (Jesus had been speaking of death but they thought that he meant [he was] only asleep.)

Then Jesus told them plainly, "Lazarus is dead; and I'm happy for you that I wasn't there, so you can believe. Now let's go to him."

Then Thomas, called "the Twin," said to his fellow disciples, "Let's go along too, so we can die with him."

When Jesus arrived, he found that [Lazarus] had been buried four days earlier. Bethany was near Jerusalem, about two miles away, and many of the Judeans had come to Martha and Mary to console them about their brother. When Martha heard that Jesus was coming, she went to meet him; Mary stayed at home. "Master," said Martha, "if you'd been here, my brother wouldn't have died. Still I know that whatever you ask of God, God will grant you."

Jesus says to her, "Your brother will be resurrected."

Martha responds, "I know he'll be raised in the resurrection on the last day."

Jesus said to her, "I am resurrection and life; those who believe in me, even if they die, will live; but everyone who is alive and believes in me will never die. Do you believe this?"

"Yes, Master," she says, "I believe that you are the Anointed, God's son, who is to come to earth."

At this point she went to call her sister Mary, telling her privately, "The Teacher is here and is asking for you." When she heard that, she got up quickly and went to him.

Jesus hadn't yet arrived at the village; he was still where Martha had met him.

When the Judeans, who hovered about her in the house to console her, saw Mary get up and go out quickly, they followed her, thinking she was going to the tomb to grieve there. When Mary got to where Jesus was and saw him, she fell down at his feet. "Master," she said, "if you'd been here, my brother wouldn't have died."

When Jesus saw her crying, and the Judeans who accompanied her crying too, he was agitated and deeply disturbed; he said, "Where have you put him?"

"Master," they say, "come and see."

Then Jesus cried.

So the Judeans observed, "Look how much he loved him." But some wondered: "He opened the blind man's eyes; couldn't he have kept this man from dying?"

Again greatly agitated, Jesus arrives at the tomb; it was a cave, and a stone lay up against the opening. Jesus says, "Take the stone away."

Martha, sister of the dead man, replies, "But Master, by this time the body will stink; it's been four days."

Jesus says to her, "Didn't I tell you, if you believed you'll see God's majesty?" So they took the stone away, and Jesus looked upwards and said, "Father, thank you for hearing me. I know you always hear me, but I say this because of the people standing here, so they'll believe that you sent me." The he shouted at the top of his voice, "Lazarus, come out!" The dead man came out, his hands and feet bound in strips of burying cloth, and his face covered with a cloth. Jesus says to them, "Free him [from the burying cloth] and let him go."

As a result, many of the Judeans who had come to Mary and observed what Jesus had done came to believe in him. But some of them went to the Pharisees and reported what Jesus had done.

So the ranking priests and Pharisees called the Council together and posed this question to them: "What are we going to do now that this fellow performs many miracles? If we let him go on like this, everybody will come to believe in him. Then the Romans will come and destroy our [holy] place and our nation."

Then one of them, Caiaphas, that year's high priest, addressed them as follows: "Don't you know anything? Don't you realize that it's to your advantage to have one person die for the people and not have the whole nation wiped out?"

(He didn't say this on his own authority, but since he was that year's high priest he could foresee that Jesus would die for the nation. In fact, [he would die] not only for the nation, but to gather together all God's dispersed children and make them one [people].)

[John 11:1–54]

LAST SUPPER

Jesus' final days took place in Jerusalem during the Jewish holiday of Passover. The four Gospels depict Jesus and his disciples gathering for a meal, known as the "Last Supper" (Luke describes this as the traditional meal of the passover festival). At this meal, according to the synoptic gospels, Jesus performed symbolic acts with the bread and wine. This event is the basis of the Christian sacrament of the Eucharist. In Christian doctrine, a sacrament is a visible religious rite that confers special grace. The number of sacraments has varied throughout Christian history; 12th-century theologian Hugo of St. Victor listed 30. Baptism and the Eucharist have always been the most important.

Now it was two days until Passover and the feast of Unleavened Bread. And the ranking priests and the scholars were looking for some way to arrest him by trickery and kill him. For their slogan was "Not during the festival, otherwise the people will riot."

When he was in Bethany at the house of Simon the leper, he was just reclining there, and a woman came in carrying an alabaster jar of myrrh, of pure and expensive nard. She broke the jar and poured [the myrrh] on his head.

Now some were annoyed [and thought] to themselves: "What good purpose is served by this waste of myrrh? For she could have sold the myrrh for more than three hundred silver coins and given [the money] to the poor." And they were angry with her.

Then Jesus said, "Let her alone! Why are you bothering her? She has done me a courtesy. Remember, there will always be poor around, and whenever you want you can do good for them, but I won't always be around. She did what she could—she anticipates in anointing my body for burial. So help me, wherever the good news is announced in all the world, what she has done will also be told in memory of her!"

And Judas Iscariot, one of the twelve, went off to the ranking priests to turn him over to them. When they heard, they were delighted, and promised to pay him in silver. And he started looking for some way to turn him in at the right moment.

On the first day of Unleavened Bread, when they would sacrifice the Passover lamb, his disciples say to him, "Where do you want us to go and get things ready for you to celebrate Passover?"

He sends two of his disciples and says to them, "Go into the city, and someone carrying a waterpot will meet you. Follow him, and whatever place he enters say to the head of the house, 'The teacher asks, "Where is my guest room where I can celebrate Passover with my disciples?"' And he'll show you a large upstairs room that has been arranged. That's the place you're to get ready for us."

And the disciples left, went into the city, and found it exactly as he had told them; and they got things ready for Passover.

When evening comes, he arrives with the twelve. And as they reclined at tables and were eating, Jesus said, "So help me, one of you eating with me is going to turn me in!"

They began to fret and to say to him one after another, "I'm not the one, am I?"

But he said to them, "It's one of the twelve, the one who is dipping into the bowl with me. The son of Adam departs just as the scriptures predict, but damn the one responsible for turning the son of Adam in! It would be better for that man had he never been born!"

And as they were eating, he took a loaf, gave a blessing, broke it into pieces and offered it to them. And he said, "Take some; this is my body!" He also took a cup, gave thanks and offered it to them, and they all drank from it. And he said to them: "This is my blood of the covenant, which has been poured out for many! So help me, I certainly won't drink it for the first time in God's domain!"

[Mark 14:1–25]

FATHER, SON, AND HOLY SPIRIT

In John's account of the last supper, Jesus gives a farewell discourse, presented below. Unlike the synoptic gospels, in which Jesus speaks in short, crisp sayings and parables, in John Jesus speaks in extended discourses. The discourse topic here is the relation between God the Father and Jesus the Son. The doctrine of the Trinity, central to Christianity, holds that God is a unity of three persons: the Father, Son, and Holy Spirit. Although the term "Trinity" and its technical meaning were developed by early church fathers, passages that associate the Father, Son, and Holy Spirit are the scriptural basis of the doctrine. The following is particularly important in this regard. The Holy Spirit is only briefly mentioned at the end of this passage. In the Old Testament occasional references are made to a spirit of God, but John and other New Testament writers expand on this notion and see the Holy Spirit both as a divine presence and as an agent of guidance for the church.

"Don't give in to your distress. You believe in God, then believe in me too. There are plenty of places to stay in my Father's house. If it weren't true,

I would have told you; I'm on my way to make a place ready for you. And if I go to make a place ready for you, I'll return and embrace you. So where I am you can be too. You know where I'm going and you know the way."

Thomas says to him, "Master, we don't know where you're going. How can we possibly know the way?"

"I am the way, and I am truth, and I am life," replies Jesus. "No one gets to the Father unless it is through me. If you do recognize me, you will recognize my Father also. From this moment on you know him and you've even seen him."

"Let us see the Father," Philip says to him, "and we'll be satisfied."

"I've been around you all this time," Jesus replies, "and you still don't know me, do you, Philip? Anyone who has seen me has seen the Father. So how can you say, 'Let us see the Father'? Don't you believe that I'm in the Father and the Father is in me? I don't say what I say on my own. The Father is with me constantly, and I perform his labors. You ought to believe that I'm in the Father and the Father is in me. If not, at least you ought to believe these labors in and of themselves. I swear to God, anyone who believes in me will perform the works I perform and will be able to perform even greater feats, because I'm on my way to the Father. In addition, I'll do whatever you request in my name, so the Father can be honored by means of the son. If you request anything using my name, I'll do it."

"If you love me, you'll obey my instructions. At my request the Father will provide you with yet another advocate, the authentic spirit, who will be with you forever. The world is unable to accept [this spirit] because it neither perceives nor recognizes it. You recognize it because it dwells in you and will remain in you.

"I won't abandon you as orphans; I'll come to you. In a little while the world won't see me any longer, but you'll see me because I'm alive as you will be alive. At the time you will come to know that I'm in my Father and that you're in me and I'm in you. Those who accept my instructions and obey them—they love me. And those who love me will be loved by my Father; moreover, I will love them and make myself known to them."

Judas (not Iscariot) says to him, "Master, what has happened that you are about to make yourself known to us but not to the world?"

Jesus replied to him, "Those who love me will heed what I tell them, and my Father will love them, and we'll come to them and make our home there. Those who don't love me won't follow my instructions. Of course, the things you heard me say are not mine but come from the Father who sent me.

"I have told you these things while I am still here with you. Yet the advocate, the holy spirit the Father will send in my stead, will teach you everything and remind you of everything I told you. Peace is what I leave behind for you; my peace is what I give you. What I give you is not a worldly gift. Don't give in to your distress or be overcome by terror. You heard me tell you, 'I'm going away and I'm going to return to you.' If you loved me, you'd be glad that I'm going to the Father, because the Father is greater than I am. So I have now told you all this ahead of time so you will believe when it happens.

"Time does not permit me to tell you much more; you see, the ruler of this world is already on the way. However, so the world may know I love the Father, I act exactly as my Father instructed me. Come on, let's get out of here."

[John 14:1–26]

TRIAL, CRUCIFIXION, RESURRECTION

After the last supper, Jesus went with his disciples to a hillside graveyard to pray. There he was arrested, brought before the Jewish legal council, and accused of blasphemy. Not empowered to perform criminal executions, the council brought Jesus to the Roman governor Pilate, where they made a case for treason based on Jesus' messianic claims. Pilate pronounced the desired verdict and sentence. All four Gospels place responsibility on the Jews, first the priests and then an angry mob, although the ultimate decision rested with the governor. Jesus was then executed on a cross, in classic Roman fashion, and placed in the rock-hewn tomb of a wealthy follower. Mark's Gospel reports that after a few days the tomb was found empty, and a young man present at the tomb announced that Jesus was resurrected. The other Gospels report appearances of the resurrected Jesus.

14. And right away, while he was still speaking, Judas, one of the twelve, shows up, and with him a crowd, dispatched by the ranking priests and the scholars and the elders, wielding swords and clubs. Now the one who was to turn him in had arranged a signal with them, saying, "The one I'm going to kiss is the one you want. Arrest him and escort him safely away!" And right away he arrives, comes up to him, and says, "Rabbi," and kisses him.

And they seized him and held him fast. One of those standing around drew his sword and struck the high priest's slave and cut off his ear. In response Jesus said to them, "Have you come out to take me with swords and clubs as though you were apprehending a rebel? I was with you in the temple area day after day teaching and you didn't lift a hand against me. But the scriptures must come true!"

And they all deserted him and ran away. And a young man was following him, wearing a shroud over his nude body, and they grab him. But he dropped the shroud and ran away naked.

And they brought Jesus before the high priest, and all the ranking priests and elders and scholars assemble.

Peter followed him at a distance until he was inside the courtyard of the high priest, and was sitting with the attendants and keeping warm by the fire.

The ranking priests and the whole Council were looking for evidence against Jesus in order to issue a death sentence, but they couldn't find any. Although many gave false evidence against him, their stories didn't agree. And some people stood up and testified falsely against him: "We have heard him saying, 'I'll destroy this temple made with hands and in three days I'll build another, not made with hands!'" Yet even then their stories did not agree.

And the high priest got up and questioned Jesus: "Don't you have some answer to give? Why do these people testify against you?"

But he was silent and refused to answer.

Once again the high priest questioned him and says to him, "Are you the Anointed, the son of the Blessed One?"

Jesus replied, "I am! And you will see the son of Adam sitting at the right hand of Power and coming with the clouds of the sky!"

Then the high priest tore his vestments and says, "Why do we still need witnesses? You have heard the blasphemy! What do you think?" And they all concurred in the death penalty.

And some began to spit on him, and to put a blindfold on him, and punch him, and say to him, "Prophesy!" And the guards abused him as they took him into custody.

And while Peter was below in the courtyard, one of the high priest's slave women comes over, and sees Peter warming himself; she looks at him closely, then speaks up: "You too were with that Nazarene, Jesus!"

But he denied it, saying, "I haven't the slightest idea what you're talking about!" And he went outside into the forecourt.

And when the slave woman saw him, she once again began to say to those standing nearby, "This fellow is one of them!"

But once again he denied it.

And a little later, those standing nearby would again say to Peter, "You really are one of them, since you also are a Galilean!"

But he began to curse and swear, "I don't know the fellow you're talking about!" And just then a rooster crowed a second time, and Peter remembered what Jesus had told him: "Before a rooster crows twice you will disown me three times!" And he broke down and started to cry.

15. And right away, at daybreak, the ranking priests, after consulting with the elders and scholars and the whole Council, bound Jesus and led him away and turned him over to Pilate. And Pilate questioned him: *You* are 'the King of the Judeans'?"

And in response he says to him, "If you say so."

And the ranking priests started a long list of accusations against him. Again Pilate tried questioning him: "Don't you have some answer to give? You see what a long list of charges they bring against you!"

But Jesus still did not respond, so Pilate was baffled.

At each festival it was the custom for him to set one prisoner free for them, whichever one they requested. And one called Barabbas was being held with the insurgents who had committed murder during the uprising. And when the crowd arrived, they began to demand that he do what he usually did for them.

And in response Pilate said to them, "Do you want me to set 'the King of the Judeans' free for you? After all, he realized that the ranking priests had turned him over out of envy.

But the ranking priests incited the crowd to get Barabbas set free for them instead.

But in response [to their request] Pilate would again say to them, "What do you want me to do with the fellow you call 'the King of the Judeans'?"

And they in turn shouted, "Crucify him!"

Pilate kept saying to them, "Why? What has he done wrong?"

But they shouted all the louder, "Crucify him!" And because Pilate was always looking to satisfy the crowd, he set Barabbas free for them, had Jesus flogged, and then turned him over to be crucified.

And the soldiers led him away to the courtyard of the governor's residence, and they called the whole company together. And they dressed him in purple and crowned him with a garland woven of thorns. And they began to salute him: "Greetings, 'King of the Judean'!" And they kept striking him on the head with a staff, and spitting on him; and they would get down on their knees and bow down to him. And when they had made fun of him, they stripped off the purple and put his own clothes back on him. And they lead him out to crucify him.

And they conscript someone named Simon of Cyrene, who was coming in from the country, the father of Alexander and Rufus, to carry his cross.

And they bring him to the place Golgotha (which means "Place of the Skull"). And they tried to give him wine mixed with myrrh, but he didn't take it. And they crucify him, and they divide up his garments, casting lots to see who would get what. It was 9 o'clock in the morning when they crucified him. And the inscription, which identified his crime, read, 'The King of the Judeans.' And with him they crucify two rebels, one on his right and one on his left.

Those passing by kept taunting him, wagging their heads, and saying, "Ha! You who would destroy the temple and rebuild it in three days, save yourself and come down from the cross!"

Likewise the ranking priests had made fun of him to one another, along with the scholars; they would say, "He saved others, but he can't save himself! 'The Anointed,' 'the King of Israel,' should come down from the cross here and now, so that we can see and trust for ourselves!"

Even those being crucified along with him would abuse him.

And when noon came, darkness blanketed the whole land until mid-afternoon. And at 3 o'clock in the afternoon Jesus shouted at the top of his voice, *"Eloi, Eloi, lema sabachthani"* (which means "My God, my God, why did you abandon me?").

And when some of those standing nearby heard, they would say, "Listen, he's calling Elijah!" And someone ran and filled a sponge with sour wine, stuck it on a pole, and offered him a drink, saying, Let's see if Elijah comes to rescue him!"

But Jesus let out a great shout and breathed his last.

And the curtain of the temple was torn in two from top to bottom! When the Roman officer standing opposite him saw that he had died like this, he said, "This man really was God's son!"

Now some women were observing this from a distance, among whom were Mary of Magdala, and Mary the mother of James the younger and Joses, and Salome. [These women] had regularly followed and assisted him when he was in Galilee, along with many other women who had come up to Jerusalem in his company.

And when it had already grown dark, since it was preparation day (the day before the sabbath), Joseph of Arimathea, a respected council member, who himself was anticipating God's imperial rule, appeared on the scene, and dared to go to Pilate to request the body of Jesus. And Pilate was surprised that he had died so soon. He summoned the Roman officer and asked him whether he had been dead for long. And when he had been briefed by the Roman officer, he granted the body to Joseph. And he brought a shroud and took him down and wrapped him in the shroud, and placed him in a tomb that had been hewn out of rock, and rolled a stone up against the opening of the tomb. And Mary of Magdala and Mary the mother of Joses noted where he had been laid to rest.

16. And when the sabbath day was over, Mary of Magdala and Mary the mother of James and Salome brought spices so they could go and embalm him. And very early on Sunday they got to the tomb just as the sun was coming up. And they had been asking themselves, "Who will help us roll the stone away from the opening of the tomb?" Then they look up and discover that the stone has been rolled away! (For in fact the stone was very large.)

And when they went into the tomb, the saw a young man sitting on the right, wearing a white robe, and they grew apprehensive.

He says to them, "Don't be alarmed! You are looking for Jesus the Nazarene who was crucified. He was raised, he is not here! Look at the spot where they put him! But go and tell his disciples, including 'Rock,' "He is going ahead of you to Galilee! There you will see him, just as he told you."

And once they got outside, they ran away from the tomb, because great fear and excitement got the better of them. And they didn't breathe a word of it to anyone: talk about terrified. . . .

[Mark, 14:43–16:8]

ASCENSION, PENTECOST

The book of the Acts of the Apostles, written about 85 c.e., chronicles the events of the early Church after Jesus' resurrection. The book is sometimes termed the Gospel of the Holy Spirit, since the author depicts the expansion of the early church as being guided by the Holy Spirit. The opening of Acts, appearing below, recounts Jesus' Ascension into heaven and the arrival of the holy spirit a few days later, during the Jewish agricultural festival of Pentecost. The believers are directly affected by the presence of the Holy Spirit, as evidenced by their speaking in foreign tongues. Peter emerges as the leader of the Church, and thousands of believers are baptized.[6]

1. After his suffering, he showed himself to these men [i.e., the Apostles] and gave many convincing proofs that he was alive. He appeared to them over a period of forty days and spoke about the kingdom of God. On one occasion, while he was eating with them, he gave them this command: "Do not leave Jerusalem, but wait for the gift my Father promised, which you have heard me speak about. For John baptized with water, but in a few days you will be baptized with the Holy Spirit."

   So when they met together, they asked him, "Lord, are you at this time going to restore the kingdom to Israel?"

   He said to them: "It is not for you to know the times or dates the Father has set by his own authority. Bt you will receive power when the Holy Spirit comes on you; and you will be my witnesses in Jerusalem, and in all Judea and Samaria, and to the ends of the earth."

   After he said this, he was taken up before their very eyes, and a cloud hid him from their sight.

   They were looking intently up into the sky as he was going, when suddenly two men dressed in white stood beside them. "Men of Galilee," they said, "why do you stand here looking into the sky? This same Jesus, who has been taken from you into heaven, will come back in the same way you have seen him go into heaven."

2. When the day of Pentecost came, they were all together in one place. Suddenly a sound like the blowing of a violent wind came from heaven and filled the whole house where they were sitting. They saw what seemed to be tongues of fire that separated and came to rest on each of them. All of them were filled with the Holy Spirit and began to speak in other tongues as the Spirit enabled them.

   Now there were staying in Jerusalem God-fearing Jews from every nation under heaven. When they heard this sound, a crowd came together in bewilderment, because each one heard them speaking in his own language. Utterly amazed, they asked: "Are not all these men who are speaking Galileans? Then how is it that each of us hears them in his own native language? Pathians, Medes and Elamites; residents of Mesopotamia, Judea and Cappadocia, Pontus and Asia, Phrygia and Pamphylia, Egypt and the parts of Libya near Cyrene; visitors from Rome (both Jews and converts to Judaism); Cretans and Arabs—we hear them declaring the wonders of God in our own tongues!" Amazed and perplexed, they asked one another, "What does this mean?"

Some, however, made fun of them and said, "They have had too much wine."

Then Peter stood up with the Eleven, raised his voice and addressed the crowd: "Fellow Jews and all of you who live in Jerusalem, let me explain this to you; listen carefully to what I say. These men are not drunk, as you suppose. It's only nine in the morning! No, this is what was spoken by the prophet Joel:

> In the last days, God says, I will pour out my Spirit on all people. Your sons and daughters will prophesy, your young men will see visions, your old men will dream dreams. Even on my servants, both men and women, I will pour out my Spirit in those days, and they will prophesy. I will show wonders in the heaven above and signs on the earth below, blood and fire and billows of smoke. The sun will be turned to darkness and the moon to blood before the coming of the great and glorious day of the Lord. And everyone who calls on the name of the Lord will be saved.

"Men of Israel, listen to this: Jesus of Nazareth was a man accredited by God to you by miracles, wonders, and signs, which God did among you through him, as you yourselves know. This man was handed over to you by God's set purpose and foreknowledge; and you, with the help of wicked men, put him to death by nailing him to the cross. But God raised him from the dead, freeing him from the agony of death, because it was impossible for death to keep its hold on him. . . .

With many other words he warned them; and he pleaded with them, "Save yourselves from this corrupt generation." Those who accepted his message were baptized, and about three thousand were added to their number that day.

They devoted themselves to the apostles' teaching and to the fellowship, to the breaking of bread and to prayer. Everyone was filled with awe, and many wonders and miraculous signs were done by the apostles. All the believers were together and had everything in common. Selling their possessions and goods, they gave to anyone as he had need. Every day they continued to meet together in the temple courts. They broke bread in their homes and ate together with glad and sincere hearts, praising God and enjoying the favor of all the people. And the Lord added to their number daily those who were being saved.

[Acts 1:3–11, 2:1–24, 40–47]

PAUL ON THE DISTINCTION BETWEEN CHRISTIANITY AND JUDAISM

After a dramatic conversion experience and a period of indoctrination, Paul soon rose in the leadership to the status of an Apostle. During three missionary journeys in non-Jewish territories throughout the Mediterranean region, he established dozens of churches and corresponded with many of them. Written about 55 c.e., Paul's letter to the church of Galatia is a pivotal text in the development of early Christianity. Shortly after his visit, church members in Galatia were persuaded by Christian Judaizers that adherence to Jewish law was a prerequisite for becoming a Christian. Paul argues vehemently that obedience to Jewish law will not absolve our sins. Justification/righteousness comes about only through faith in Christ, and this is open to Jews and non-Jews alike. The larger issue in the debate was whether Christianity was merely a Jewish sect or a distinct religion; in the first two chapters presented below, Paul describes his efforts to set Christianity apart from its Jewish framework. His account is important for its autobiographical content, and also because it is the earliest written discussion of first-century church politics.

1. I am astonished that you are so quickly deserting the one who called you by the grace of Christ and are turning to a different gospel— which is really no gospel at all. Evidently some people are throwing you into confusion and are tying to pervert the gospel of Christ. But even if we or an angel from heaven should preach a gospel other than the one we preached to you, let him be eternally condemned! As we have already said, so now I say again: If anybody is preaching to you a gospel other than what you accepted, let him be eternally condemned!

   Am I now trying to win the approval of men, or of God? Or am I trying to please men? If I were still trying to please men, I would not be a servant of Christ.

   I want you to know, brothers, that the gospel I preached is not something that man made up. I did not receive it from any man, nor was I taught it; rather, I received it by revelation from Jesus Christ.

   For you have heard of my previous way of life in Judaism, how intensely I persecuted the church of God and tried to destroy it. I was advancing in Judaism beyond many Jews of my own age and was extremely zealous for the traditions of my fathers. But when God, who set me apart from birth and called me by his grace, was pleased to reveal his Son in me so that I might preach him among the Gentiles, I did not consult any man, nor did I go up to Jerusalem to see those who were apostles before I was, but I went immediately into Arabia and later returned to Damascus.

   Then after three years, I went up to Jerusalem to get acquainted with Peter and stayed with him fifteen days. I saw none of the other apostles—only James, the Lord's brother. I assure you before God that what I am writing you is no lie. Later I went to Syria and Cilicia. I was personally unknown to the churches of Judea that are in Christ. They only heard the report: "The man who formerly persecuted us is now preaching the faith he once tried to destroy."

2. Fourteen years later I went up again to Jerusalem, this time with Barnabas. I took Titus along also. I went in response to a revelation

and set before them the gospel that I preach among the Gentiles. But I did this privately to those who seemed to be leaders, for fear that I was running or had run my race in vain. Yet not even Titus, who was with me, was compelled to be circumcised, even though he was a Greek. [This matter arose] because some false brothers had infiltrated our ranks to spy on the freedom we have in Christ Jesus and to make us slaves. We did not give in to them for a moment, so that the truth of the gospel might remain with you.

As for those who seemed to be important—whatever they were makes no difference to me; God does not judge by external appearance—those men added nothing to my message. On the contrary, they saw that I had been entrusted with the task of preaching the gospel to the Gentiles, just as Peter had been to the Jews. For God, who was at work in the ministry of Peter as an apostle to the Jews, was also at work in my ministry as an apostle to the Gentiles. James, Peter and John, those reputed to be pillars, gave me and Barnabas the right hand of fellowship when they recognized the grace given to me. They agreed that we should go to the Gentiles, and they to the Jews. All they asked was that we should continue to remember the poor, the very thing I was eager to do.

When Peter came to Antioch, I opposed him to his face, because he was clearly in the wrong. Before certain men came from James, he used to eat with the Gentiles. But when they arrived, he began to draw back and separate himself from the Gentiles because he was afraid of those who belonged to the circumcision group. The other Jews joined him in his hypocrisy, so that by their hypocrisy even Barnabas was led astray.

When I saw that they were not acting in line with the truth of the gospel, I said to Peter in front of them all, "You are a Jew, yet you live like a Gentile and not like a Jew. How is it, then, that you force Gentiles to follow Jewish customs?

"We who are Jews by birth and not 'Gentile sinners' know that a man is not justified by observing the law, but by faith in Jesus Christ. So we, too, have put our faith in Christ Jesus that we may be justified by faith in Christ and not by observing the law, because by observing the law no one will be justified.

"If, while we seek to be justified in Christ, it becomes evident that we ourselves are sinners, does that mean that Christ promotes sin? Absolutely not! If I rebuild what I destroyed, I prove that I am a lawbreaker. For through the law I died to the law so that I might live for God. I have been crucified with Christ and I no longer live, but Christ lives in me. The life I live in the body, I live by faith in the Son of God, who loved me and gave himself for me. I do not set aside the grace of God, for if righteousness could be gained through the law, Christ died for nothing!"

[Galatians 1:6–23, 2:1–21]

PAUL ON LIFE AFTER DEATH

An immediate theological difficulty faced by Paul was the question of how Jesus could be divine despite his criminal execution. Paul's solution was to see Jesus' death on the cross and subsequent resurrection as the end of the old Jewish law and the beginning of a new era of divine grace. Through baptism, Christians symbolically participate in the cross by dying to their old lives and reemerging anew. The crucifixion and resurrection are so central to Paul's teaching that they are the only features of the life of Jesus with which he is concerned. In the following discussion from Paul's first letter to the church of Corinth, written about 55 C.E., life after death is also linked to the resurrection: Because Christ resurrected, we are assured that we too will be. Unlike Greek writers, who construe life after death as the continuation of a bodiless, immortal soul, Christian doctrine holds to the bodily resurrection of the dead as found in post-exilic Jewish writings. Paul teaches that our new bodies will be heavenly and imperishable in nature, rather than earthly and perishable, and that all those who belong to Christ will be simultaneously resurrected when he returns.

15. But if it is preached that Christ has been raised from the dead, how can some of you say that there is no resurrection of the dead? If there is no resurrection of the dead, then not even Christ has been raised. And if Christ has not been raised, our preaching is useless and so is your faith. More than that, we are then found to be false witnesses about God, for we have testified about God that he raised Christ from the dead. But he did not raise him if in fact the dead are not raised. For if the dead are not raised, then Christ has not been raised either. And if Christ has not been raised, your faith is futile; you are still in your sins. Then those also who have fallen asleep in Christ are lost. If only for this life we have hope in Christ, we are to be pitied more than all men.

    But Christ has indeed been raised from the dead, the firstfruits of those who have fallen asleep. For since death came through a man, the resurrection of the dead comes also through a man. For as in Adam all die, so in Christ all will be made alive. But each in his own turn: Christ; the firstfruits; then, when he comes, those who belong to him. Then the end will come, when he hands over the kingdom to God the Father after he has destroyed all dominion, authority and power. For he must reign until he has put all his enemies under his feet. The last enemy to be destroyed is death. For he "has put everything under his feet." Now when it says that "everything" has been put under him, it is clear that this does not include God himself, who put everything under Christ. When he has done this, then the Son himself will be made subject to him who put everything under him, so that God may be all in all.

    But someone may ask, "How are the dead raised? With what kind of body will they come?" How foolish! What you sow does not come to life unless it dies. When you sow, you do not plant the body that will be, but just a seed, perhaps of wheat or of something else. But God gives it a body as he has determined, and to each kind of seed he gives its own body. All flesh is not the same: Men have one kind of flesh, animals have another, birds another and fish another. There are also heavenly bodies and there are earthly bodies; but the splendor of the heavenly bodies is one kind, and the splendor of the earthly bodies is another. The sun has one kind of splendor, the moon another and the star another; and star differs from star in splendor.

So will it be with the resurrection of the dead. The body that is sown is perishable, it is raised imperishable; it is sown in dishonor, it is raised in glory; it is sown in weakness, it is raised in power; it is sown a natural body, it is raised a spiritual body. If there is a natural body, there is also a spiritual body.

So it is written: "The first man Adam became a living being"; the last Adam, a life-giving spirit. The spiritual did not come first, but the natural, and after that the spiritual. The first man was of the dust of the earth, the second man from heaven. As was the earthly man, so are those who are of the earth; and as is the man from heaven, so also are those who are of heaven. And just as we have borne the likeness of the earthly man, so shall we bear the likeness of the man from heaven.

I declare to you, brothers, that flesh and blood cannot inherit the kingdom of God, nor does the perishable inherit the imperishable. Listen, I tell you a mystery: We will not all sleep, but we will all be changed—in a flash, in the twinkling of an eye, at the last trumpet. For the trumpet will sound, the dead will be raised imperishable, and we will be changed. For the perishable must clothe itself with the imperishable, and the mortal with immortality. When the perishable has been clothed with the imperishable, and the mortal with immortality, then the saying that is written will come true: "Death has been swallowed up in victory."

"Where, O death, is your victory?

Where, O death, is your sting?"

The sting of death is sin, and the power of sin is the law. But thanks to God! He gives us the victory through our Lord Jesus Christ.

[1 Corinthians 15:12–28, 35–57]

SELECTIONS FROM EARLY SECTARIAN WRITINGS

DIDACHE ON BAPTISM, PRAYER, AND THE EUCHARIST

Discovered in 1873, the Didache *is a manual of early church doctrine from the Syrian church of Antioch. Eusibius, a fourth century bishop, notes the high value placed on the* Didache *by early churches. Although the original date of the work is disputed, scholars believe that some parts are of first-century origin and contemporaneous with the Gospels. The brief work can be divided into four parts. The opening lists a series of moral injunctions culled from various parts of the Bible. Instructions concerning food, baptism, fasting, and prayer ritual follow. Next, instructions are given on receiving new prophets, apostles, and Christians. Finally, a warning is given concerning the return of Jesus. The following are the instructions on ritual from the second division.*[7]

6. Concerning eating, follow the traditions that you are able to follow. But by all means you should abstain from meat sacrificed to idols since it is the worship of dead gods.

7. Now concerning baptism, you should baptize as follows. Having first recited all these things, baptize in the name of the Father and of the Son and of the Holy Spirit in running water. But if you do not have running water, then baptize in other available water. And if you are not able to do it in cold, then use warm. But if you have neither, then pour water on the head three times in the name of the Father and of the Son and of the Holy Spirit. But before the baptism let him that baptizes and him who is baptized fast, and any others also who can. And you should order him who is baptized to fast a day or two before.

8. But do not allow your fasts to be on the same days as the hypocrites who fast on the second and the fifth day of the week. Instead, you should keep your fast on the fourth and the sixth day. Neither should you pray as the hypocrites, but instead pray as the Lord commanded in his Gospel. So you should pray,

> Our Father in heaven, holy is your name. May your kingdom come, may your will be done on earth just as in heaven. Give us today our daily bread, and forgive our debts, as we also forgive our debtors. And do not lead us into temptation, but rescue us from the evil one. For yours is the power and the glory forever and ever.

Three times in the day pray you so.

9. Now concerning the Eucharistic thanksgiving, give thanks as follows. First, as regards the cup:

> We give you thanks, our Father, for the holy vine of your son David, which you revealed to us through your son Jesus. Yours is the glory forever and ever.

Then as regards the broken bread:

> We give you thanks, our Father, for the life and knowledge which you revealed to us through your son Jesus. Yours is the glory forever and ever. Just as this broken bread was scattered on the mountains and being gathered together became one, so may your Church be gathered together in your kingdom from the ends of the earth. For yours is the glory and the power through Jesus Christ forever and ever.

But do not let anyone eat or drink of this Eucharistic thanksgiving, except those that have been baptized into the name of the Lord. For concerning this also the Lord has said: do not give that which is holy to the dogs.

10. And after this is completed, give thanks as follows:

> We give you thanks, holy Father, for your holy name which you made to dwell in our hearts, and for the knowledge and faith and

immortality which you revealed to us through your son Jesus. Yours is the glory forever and ever. You, almighty master, created everything for your name's sake, and gave food and drink to men to enjoy, so that we might give thanks to you. And you have given us spiritual food and drink and eternal life through your Son. Above everything, we give you thanks that you are powerful. Yours is the glory forever and ever. Remember, Lord, to deliver your Church from all evil and to perfect it in your love. And gather it together from the four winds (even the Church which as been sanctified) into your kingdom which you have prepared for it. For yours is the power and the glory forever and ever. May grace come and may this world pass away. Hosanna to the God of David. If anyone is holy, let him come to the Eucharist. If anyone is not, let him repent. Maranatha. Amen.

But permit the prophets to offer thanksgiving as much as they wish.

[*Didache*, 6–10]

INFANCY GOSPEL OF JAMES

Early Christians were interested in accounts of Jesus' childhood, which filled the gaps in the four Gospel narratives. Many childhood gospels circulated, but most of the information in these derive from two texts written about 150 C.E.: the Infancy Gospel of James, *and the* Infancy Gospel of Thomas. *The* Infancy Gospel of James, *also called the* Protoevangelium, *or first gospel, is pseudonomously ascribed to James, the brother of Jesus, and scholars believe that its author was a non-Jewish Christian from outside of Palestine. The text presents the oldest account of the early life of Mary, including her espousal to Joseph, and describes the virgin birth of Jesus. The tradition of Mary's life-long virginity runs counter to statements in the gospels referring to Jesus' brothers. The* Infancy Gospel of James *reconciles these two traditions by presenting Joseph as a widower with children from his previous marriage. The feast of Mary's presentation in the temple (November 21) in Catholic and Orthodox traditions is based on events in the selection below.*[8]

7. Many months passed, but when the child reached two years of age, Joachim said, "Let's take her up to the temple of the Lord, so that we can keep the promise we made, or else the Lord will be angry with us and our gift will be unacceptable."

    And Anna said, "Let's wait until she is three, so she won't miss her father or mother."

    And Joachim agreed: "Let's wait."

    When the child turned three years of age, Joachim said, "Let's send for the undefiled Hebrew daughters. Let them each take a lamp and light it, so the child won't turn back and have her heart captivated by things outside the Lord's temple." And this is what they did until the time they ascended to the Lord's temple.

The priest welcomed her, kissed her, and blessed her: "The Lord God has exalted your name among all generations. In you the Lord will disclose his redemption to the people of Israel during the last days."

And he sat her down on the third step of the altar, and the Lord showered favor on her. And she danced, and the whole house of Israel loved her.

8. Her parents left for home marveling and praising and glorifying the Lord God because the child did not look back at them. And Mary lived in the temple of the Lord. She was fed there like a dove, receiving her food from the hand of a heavenly messenger.

When she turned twelve, however, there was a meeting of the priests. "Look," they said, "Mary has turned twelve in the temple of the Lord. What should we do with her so she won't pollute the sanctuary of the Lord our God?" And they said to the high priest, "You stand at the altar of the Lord. Enter and pray about her, and we'll do whatever the Lord God discloses to you."

And so the high priest took the vestment with the twelve bells, entered the Holy of Holies, and began to pray about her. And suddenly a messenger of the Lord appeared: "Zechariah, Zechariah, go out and assemble the widowers of the people and have them each bring a staff. She will become the wife of the one to whom the Lord God shows a sign." And so heralds covered the surrounding territory of Judea. The trumpet of the Lord sounded and all the widowers came running.

9. And Joseph, too, threw down his carpenter's axe and left for the meeting. When they had all gathered, they went to the high priest with their staffs. After the high priest had collected everyone's staff, he entered the temple and began to pray. When he had finished his prayer, he took the staffs and went out and began to give them back to each man. But there was no sign of any of them. Joseph got the last staff. Suddenly a dove came out of this staff and perched on Joseph's head. "Joseph, Joseph," the high priest said, "you've been chosen by lot to take the virgin of the Lord into your care and protection."

But Joseph objected: "I already have sons and I'm an old man; she's only a young woman. I'm afraid that I'll become the butt of jokes among the people of Israel."

13. She was in her sixth month when one day Joseph came home from his building projects, entered the house, and found her pregnant. He struck himself in the face, threw himself to the ground on sackcloth, and began to cry bitterly: "What sort of face should I present to the Lord God? What prayer can I say on her behalf since I received her as a virgin from the temple of the Lord God and didn't protect her? Who has set this trap for me? Who has done this evil deed in my house? Who has lured this virgin away from me and violated her? The story of Adam has been repeated in my case, hasn't it? For just as Adam was praying when the serpent came and found Eve alone, deceived her, and corrupted her, so the same thing has happened to me."

So Joseph got up from the sackcloth and summoned Mary and said to her, "God has taken a special interest in you—how could you have done this? Have you forgotten the Lord your God? Why have you brought shame on yourself, you who were raised in the Holy of Holies and fed by a heavenly messenger?"

But she began to cry bitter tears: "I'm innocent. I haven't had sex with any man."

And Joseph said to her, "Then where did the child you're carrying come from?"

And she replied, "As the Lord my God lives, I don't know where it came from."

14. And Joseph became very frightened and no longer spoke with her as he pondered what he was going to do with her. And Joseph said to himself, "If I try to cover up her sin, I'll end up going against the law of the Lord. And if I disclose her condition to the people of Israel, I'm afraid that the child inside her might be heaven-sent and I'll end up handing innocent blood over to a death sentence. So what should I do with her? [I know,] I'll divorce her quietly."

But when night came a messenger of the Lord suddenly appeared to him in a dream and said: "Don't be afraid of this girl, because the child in her is the holy spirit's doing. She will have a son and you will name him Jesus—the name means 'he will save his people from their sins.'" And Joseph got up from his sleep and praised the God of Israel, who had given him this favor. And so he began to protect the girl.

15. Then Annas the scholar came to him and said to him, "Joseph, why haven't you attended our assembly?"

And he replied to him, "Because I was worn out from the trip and rested my first day home."

Then Annas turned and saw that Mary was pregnant.

He left in a hurry for the high priest and said to him, "You remember Joseph, don't you—the man you yourself vouched for? Well, he has committed a serious offense."

And the high priest asked, "In what way?"

"Joseph has violated the virgin he received from the temple of the Lord," he replied. "He had his way with her and hasn't disclosed his action to the people of Israel."

And the high priest asked him, "Has Joseph really done this?"

And he replied, "Send temple assistants and you'll find the virgin pregnant."

And so the temple assistants went and found her just as Annas had reported, and then they brought her, along with Joseph, to the court.

"Mary, why have you done this?" the high priest asked her. "Why have you humiliated yourself? Have you forgotten the Lord your God, you who were raised in the Holy of the Holies and were fed by heavenly messengers? You of all people, who heard their hymns and danced for them—why have you done this?"

And she wept bitterly: "As the Lord God lives, I stand innocent before him. Believe me, I've not had sex with any man."

And the high priest said, "Joseph, why have you done this?"

And Joseph said, "As the Lord lives, I am innocent where she is concerned."

And the high priest said, "Don't perjure yourself, but tell the truth. You've had your way with her and haven't disclosed this action to the people of Israel. And you haven't humbled yourself under God's mighty hand, so that your offspring might be blessed."

But Joseph was silent.

16. Then the high priest said, "Return the virgin you received from the temple of the Lord."

And Joseph, bursting into tears . . . [said nothing]

And the high priest said, "I'm going to give you the Lord's drink test, and it will disclose your sin clearly to both of you."

And the high priest took the water and made Joseph drink it and sent him into the wilderness, but he returned unharmed. And he made the girl drink it, too, and sent her into the wilderness. She also came back unharmed. And everybody was surprised because their sin had not been revealed. And so the high priest said, "If the Lord God has not exposed your sin, then neither do I condemn you." And he dismissed them. Joseph took Mary and returned home celebrating and praising the God of Israel.

[*Infancy Gospel of James*, 7–9, 13–16]

INFANCY GOSPEL OF THOMAS

Written about 150 c.e., the Infancy Gospel of Thomas *was among the most popular apocryphal writings in the early church. The text deals with Jesus' childhood up to his 12th year. The youthful Jesus is presented as having deadly divine powers, which he angrily uses to get his way. As he grows, though, his sense of moral responsibility progressively develops, and he uses his powers to heal rather than harm. The story provides an interesting commentary on the divine and human natures of Jesus: his power and knowledge are fully divine, but his conscience and emotions are human and require maturing. The text is reconstructed from several surviving manuscripts which vary greatly; some scholars believe that the original included sayings, although only the story lines are preserved.*[9]

1. I, Thomas the Israelite, am reporting to you, all my non-Jewish brothers and sisters, to make known the extraordinary childhood deeds of our Lord Jesus Christ—what he did after his birth in my region. This is how it all started:

2. When this boy, Jesus, was five years old, he was playing at the ford of a rushing stream. He was collecting the flowing water into ponds and made the water instantly pure. He did this with a single command. He

then made soft clay and shaped it into twelve sparrows. He did this on the sabbath day, and many other boys were playing with him.

But when a Jew saw what Jesus was doing while playing on the sabbath day, he immediately went off and told Joseph, Jesus' father: See here, your boy is at the ford and has taken mud and fashioned twelve birds with it, and so has violated the sabbath."

So Joseph went there, and as soon as he spotted him he shouted, "Why are you doing what's not permitted on the sabbath?"

But Jesus simply clapped his hands and shouted to the sparrows: "Be off, fly away, and remember me, you who are now alive!" And the sparrows took off and flew away noisily.

The Jews watched with amazement, then left the scene to report to their leaders what they had seen Jesus doing.

3. The son of Annas the scholar, standing there with Jesus, took a willow branch and drained the water Jesus had collected. Jesus, however, saw what had happened and became angry, saying to him, "Damn you, you irreverent fool! What harm did the ponds of water do to you? From this moment you, too, will dry up like a tree, and you'll never produce leaves or root to bear fruit."

In an instant the boy had completely withered away. Then Jesus departed and left for the house of Joseph. The parents of the boy who had withered away picked him up and were carrying him out, sad because he was so young. And they came to Joseph and accused him: "It's your fault—your boy did all this."

4. Later he was going through the village again when a boy ran by and bumped him on the shoulder. Jesus got angry and said to him, "You won't continue your journey." And all of a sudden he fell down and died.

Some people saw what had happened and said, "Where has this boy come from? Everything he says happens instantly!"

The parents of the dead boy came to Joseph and blamed him, saying, "Because you have such a boy, you can't live with us in the village, or else teach him to bless and not curse. He's killing our children!"

14. When Joseph saw the child's aptitude, and his great intelligence for his age, he again resolved that Jesus should not remain illiterate. So he took him and handed him over to another teacher. The teacher said to Joseph, "First I'll teach him Greek, then Hebrew." This teacher, of course, knew of the child's previous experience [with a teacher] and was afraid of him. Still, he wrote out the alphabet and instructed him for quite a while, though Jesus was unresponsive.

Then Jesus spoke: "If you're really a teacher, and if you know the letters well, tell me the meaning of the letter alpha, and I'll tell you the meaning of beta."

The teacher became exasperated and hit him on the head. Jesus got angry and cursed him, and the teacher immediately lost consciousness and fell face down on the ground.

The child returned to Joseph's house. But Joseph was upset and gave this instruction to his mother: "Don't let him go outside, because those who annoy him end up dead."

15. After some time another teacher, a close friend of Joseph, said to him, "Send the child to my schoolroom. Perhaps with some flattery I can teach him his letters."

Joseph replied, "If you can muster the courage, brother, take him with you." And so he took him along with much fear and trepidation, but the child was happy to go.

Jesus strode boldly into the schoolroom and found a book lying on the desk. He took the book but did not read the letters in it. Rather, he opened his mouth and spoke by [the power of] the holy spirit and taught the law to those standing there.

A large crowd gathered and stood listening to him, and they marveled at the maturity of this teaching and his readiness of speech—a mere child able to say such things.

When Joseph heard about this he feared the worst and ran to the schoolroom, imagining that his teacher was having trouble with Jesus.

But the teacher said to Joseph, "Brother, please know that I accepted this child as a student, but already he's full of grace and wisdom. So I'm asking you, brother, to take him back home."

When the child heard this, he immediately smiled at him and said, "Because you have spoken and testified rightly, that other teacher who was struck down will be healed." And right away he was. Joseph took his child and went home.

16. Joseph sent his son James to tie up some wood and carry it back to the house, and the child Jesus followed. While James was gathering the firewood, a viper bit his hand. And as he lay sprawled out on the ground, dying, Jesus came and blew on the bite. Immediately the pain stopped, the animal burst apart, and James got better on the spot.

17. After this incident an infant in Joseph's neighborhood became sick and died, and his mother grieved terribly. Jesus heard the loud wailing and the uproar that was going on and quickly ran there.

When he found the child dead, he touched its chest and said, "I say to you, infant, don't die but live, and be with your mother."

And immediately the infant looked up and laughed. Jesus then said to the woman, "Take it, give it your breast, and remember me."

The crowd of onlookers marveled at this: "Truly this child was a god or a heavenly messenger of God—whatever he says instantly happens." But Jesus left and went on playing with the other children.

18. A year later, while a building was under construction, a man fell from the top of it and died. There was quite a commotion, so Jesus got up and went there. When he saw the man lying dead, he took his hand and said, "I say to you, sir, get up and go back to work." And he immediately got up and worshipped him.

The crowd saw this and marveled: "This child's from heaven—he must be, because he has saved many souls from death, and he can go on saving all his life."

[*Infancy Gospel of Thomas*, 1–4, 14–18]

GOSPEL OF THOMAS

The 1945 discovery of several dozen Gnostic texts has redefined the study of early Christianity. The jewel in the crown of these texts is the Gospel of Thomas, *which broadens our understanding of the historical Jesus. The text is a sayings gospel insofar as it contains no story line, and little dialogue. The 114 sayings are organized around particular catchwords, but do not systematically develop themes. Although the text was ultimately compiled in the second century, it may be based on an original core of short sayings as early as those in any other Gospel. These, in turn, come from orally transmitted accounts of Jesus' teachings. The challenge for scholars is to identify that core from embellishments penned by later writers. A Gnostic component of the text suggests that these are secret teachings of Jesus, knowledge of which will free one's spirit from the material world. Many of the sayings parallel those found in the four canonical Gospels. Some of the parables in Thomas are more concise and thus, perhaps, earlier than their canonical counterparts (8, 9, 57, 63, 64, 65). A large group of sayings is unique to this text, although it probably did not originate with Jesus (15, 17, 18, 19). Most interesting, however, are two sayings that scholars believe originated with Jesus, but which are absent from the canonical Gospels, (97, 98).*[10]

Prologue. These are the secret sayings that the living Jesus spoke and Didymos Judas Thomas recorded

1. And he said, "Whoever discovers the interpretation of these sayings will not taste death."
2. Jesus said, "Those who seek should not stop seeking until they find. When they find, they will be disturbed. When they are disturbed, they will marvel, and will rule over all."
3. Jesus said, "If your leaders say to you, 'Look, the [Father's] imperial rule is in the sky,' then the birds of the sky will precede you. If they say to you, 'It is in the sea,' then the fish will precede you. Rather, the [father's] imperial rule is inside you and outside you. When you know yourselves, then you will be known, and you will understand that you are children of the living Father. But if you do not know yourselves, then you live in poverty, and you are the poverty."
4. Jesus said, "The person old in days won't hesitate to ask a little child seven days old about the place of life, and that person will live. For many of the first will be last, and will become a single one."
5. Jesus said, "Know what is in front of your face, and what is hidden from you will be disclosed to you. For there is nothing hidden that won't be revealed."

6. His disciples asked him and said to him, "Do you want us to fast? How should we pray? Should we give to charity? What diet should we observe?"

   Jesus said, "Don't lie, and don't do what you hate, because all things are disclosed before heaven. After all, there is nothing hidden that won't be revealed, and there is nothing covered up that will remain undisclosed."

7. Jesus said, "Lucky is the lion that the human will eat, so that the lion becomes human. And foul is the human that the lion will eat, and the lion still will become human."

8. And he said, "The human one is like a wise fisherman who cast his net into the sea and drew it up from the sea full of little fish. Among them the wise fisherman discovered a fine large fish. He threw all the little fish back into the sea, and easily chose the large fish. Anyone here with two good ears had better listen!"

9. Jesus said,

   > Look, the sower went out, took a handful (of seeds), and scattered (them). Some fell on the road, and the birds came and gathered them. Others fell on rock, and they didn't take root in the soil and didn't produce heads of grain. Others fell on thorns, and they choked the seeds and worms ate them. And others fell on good soil, and it produced a good crop: it yielded sixty per measure and one hundred twenty per measure.

10. Jesus said, "I have cast fire upon the world, and look, I'm, guarding it until it blazes."

11. Jesus said, "This heaven will pass away, and the one above it will pass away. The dead are not alive, and the living will not die. During the days when you ate what is dead, you made it come alive. When you are in the light, what will you do? On the day when you were one, you became two. But when you become two, what will you do?"

12. The disciples said to Jesus, "We know that you are going to leave us. Who will be our leader?"

    Jesus said to them, "No matter where you are, you are to go to James the Just, for whose sake heaven and earth came into being."

13. Jesus said to his disciples, "Compare me to something and tell me what I am like."

    Simon Peter said to him, "You are like a just angel."

    Matthew said to him, "You are like a wise philosopher."

    Thomas said to him, "Teacher, my mouth is utterly unable to say what you are like."

    Jesus said, "I am not your teacher. Because you have drunk, you have become intoxicated from the bubbling spring that I have tended."

    And he took him, and withdrew, and spoke three sayings to him.

    When Thomas came back to his friends, they asked him, "What did Jesus say to you?"

Thomas said to them, "If I tell you one of the sayings he spoke to me, you will pick up rocks and stone me, and fire will come from the rocks and devour you."

14. Jesus said to them, "If you fast, you will bring sin upon yourselves, and if you pray, you will be condemned, and if you give to charity, you will harm your spirits. When you go into any region and walk about in the countryside, when people take you in, eat what they serve you and heal the sick among them. After all, what goes into your mouth won't defile you; what comes out of your mouth will."

15. Jesus said, "When you see one who was not born of woman, fall on your faces and worship. That one is your Father."

16. Jesus said, "Perhaps people think that I have come to cast peace upon the world. They do not know that I have come to cast conflicts upon the earth: fire, sword, war. For there will be five in a house: there'll be three against two and two against three, father against son and son against father, and they will stand alone."

17. Jesus said, "I will give you what no eye has seen, what no ear has heard, what no hand has touched, what has not arisen in the human heart."

18. The disciples said to Jesus, "Tell us, how will our end come?"

Jesus said, "Have you found the beginning, then, that you are looking for the end? You see, the end will be where the beginning is. Congratulations to the one who stands at the beginning: that one will know the end and will not taste death."

19. Jesus said, "Congratulations to the one who came into being before coming into being. If you become my disciples and pay attention to my sayings, these stones will serve you. For there are five trees in Paradise for you; they do not change, summer or winter, and their leaves do not fall. Whoever knows them will not taste death."

20. The disciples said to Jesus, "Tell us what Heaven's imperial rule is like."
He said to them,

It's like a mustard seed. [It's] the smallest of all seeds, but when it falls on prepared soil, it produces a large branch and becomes a shelter for birds of the sky.

57. Jesus said,

The Father's imperial rule is like a person who had [good] seed. His enemy came during the night and sowed weeds among the good seed. The person did not let the workers pull up the weeds, but said to them, "No, otherwise you might go to pull up the weeds and pull up the wheat along with them." For on the day of the harvest the weeds will be conspicuous, and will be pulled up and burned.

63. Jesus said,

There was a rich man who had a great deal of money. He said, "I shall invest my money so that I may sow, reap, plant, and fill my storehouses with produce, that I may lack nothing." These were the things he was thinking in his heart, but that very night he died. Anyone here with two ears had better listen!

64. Jesus said,

Someone was receiving guests. When he had prepared the dinner, he sent his slave to invite the guests. The slave went to the first and said, "My master invites you." The first replied, "Some merchants owe me money; they are coming to me tonight. I have to go and give them instructions. Please excuse me for dinner." The slave went to another and said, 'My master has invited you." The second said to the slave, "I have bought a house, and I have been called away for a day. I shall have no time." The slave went to another and said, "My master invites you." The third said to the slave, "My friend is to be married, and I am to arrange the banquet. I shall not be able to come. Please excuse me from dinner." The slave went to another and said, "My master invites you." The fourth said to the slave, "I have bought an estate, and I am going to collect the rent. I shall not be able to come. Please excuse me." The slave returned and said to his master, "Those whom you invited to dinner have asked to be excused." The master said to his slave, " Go out on the streets and bring back whomever you find to have dinner."
Buyers and merchants [will] not enter the places of my Father.

65. He said,

A person owned a vineyard and rented it to some farmers, so they could work it and he could collect its crops from them. He sent his slave so the farmers would give him the vineyard's crop. They grabbed him, beat him, and almost killed him, and the slave returned and told his master. His master said, "Perhaps he didn't know them." He sent another slave, and the farmers beat that one as well. Then the master sent his son and said, "Perhaps they'll show my son some respect." Because the farmers know that he was the heir to the vineyard, they grabbed him and killed him. Anyone here with two ears had better listen!

97. Jesus said,

The [Father's] imperial rule is like a woman who was carrying a [jar] full of meal. While she was walking along [a] distant road, the handle of the jar broke and the meal spilled behind her [along] the road. She didn't know it; she hadn't noticed a problem. When she reached her house, she put the jar down and discovered that it was empty.

98. Jesus said,

The Father's imperial rule is like a person who wanted to kill someone powerful. While still at home he drew his sword and thrust it into the wall to find out whether his hand would go in. Then he killed the powerful one.

[*Gospel of Thomas*, 1–20, 57, 63, 64, 65, 97, 98]

GOSPEL OF MARY

Gnostic writings contained feminine imagery typical of ancient mythology, which was ultimately removed from mainstream Christianity. Much of this imagery is cosmological, and it involves various layers of God's being and creative activity. Some Gnostic texts portray God as having both a male and female quality: God is the primal father and the mother of all things. Others describe God as radiating divine beings or personalities, one of which is the female spirit of wisdom, the womb of everything. Finally, and most interestingly, several texts depict the divine Trinity as the father, mother, and son. In addition to their feminine theological themes, Gnostic texts defend the role of women as teachers of divine knowledge. This is most evident in the Gospel of Mary *(named after Mary Magdalene) where, after Mary presents some private teachings of Jesus, her authority is first challenged by Peter, and then defended by Levi. Much of the* Gospel of Mary *is lost; the surviving sections are presented below.*[11]

1. [Six manuscript pages are missing.]
2. [Jesus said] " . . . Will matter then be utterly destroyed or not?"

    The Savior replied, "Every nature, every modeled form, every creature, exists in and with each other. They will dissolve again into their own proper root. For the nature of matter is dissolved into what belongs to its nature. Anyone with two ears capable of hearing should listen!"
3. Then Peter said to him, "You have been expounding every topic to us; tell us one further thing. What is the sin of the world?"

    The Savior replied, "There is no such thing as sin; rather, you yourselves are what produces sin when you act according to the nature of adultery, which is called 'sin.' For this reason, the Good came among you approaching what belongs to every nature. It will set it within its root."

    Then he continued. He said, "This is why you get sick and die, for [you love] what de[c]ei[ve]s you. Anyone with a mind should use it to think!

    [Ma]tter gav[e bi]rth to a passion which has no [true] image because it derives from what is contrary to nature. Then a disturbing confusion occurred in the whole body. This is why I told you. 'Be content of heart.' And do not conform [to the body], but form yourselves in the presence of that other image of nature. Anyone with two ears capable of hearing should listen!"
4. When the Blessed One had said this, he greeted them all. "Peace be with you!" he said. Acquire my peace within yourselves!

    Be on your guard so that no one deceives you by saying, 'Look over here!' or 'Look over there!' For the seed of true humanity exists within you. Follow it! Those who search for it will find it.

    Go then, preach the good news of the domain. Do not lay down any rule beyond what I ordained for you, nor promulgate law like the lawgiver, or else it will dominate you."

    After he said these things, he left them.

5. But they were distressed and wept greatly. How are we going to go out to the rest of the world to preach the good news, about the domain of the seed of true humanity?" they said. "If they didn't spare him, how will they spare us?"

Then Mary stood up. She greeted them all and addressed her brothers: "Do not weep and be distressed nor let your hearts be irresolute. For his grace will be with you all and will shelter you. Rather we should praise his greatness, for he has joined us together and made us true human beings."

When Mary said these things, she turned their minds [to]ward the Good, and they began to [as]k about the wor[d]s of the Savi[or].

6. Peter said to Mary, "Sister, we know that the Savior loved you more than any other woman. Tell us the words of the Savior that you know, but which we haven't heard."

Mary responded, "I will rep[ort to you as much as] I remember that you don't know." And she began to speak these words to them.

7. She said, "I saw the Lord in a vision and I said to him, 'Lord, I saw you today in a vision.'

"He said to me, 'Congratulations to you for not wavering at seeing me. For where the mind is, there is the treasure.'

"I said to him, 'Lord, how does a person who sees a vision see it— [with] the soul [or] with the spirit?'

"The Savior answered, 'The [visionary] does not see with the soul or with the spirit, but with the mind which exists between these two— that is [what] sees the vision and that is w[hat . . .]'

8. [Four manuscript pages are missing.]

9. . . . "And Desire said, 'I did not see you go down, yet now I see you go up. So why do you lie since you belong to me?'

"The soul answered, 'I saw you. You did not see me nor did you know me. You [mis]took the garment [I wore] for my [true] self. And you did not recognize me.'

"After it had said these things, [the soul] left rejoicing greatly.

Again, it came to the third Power, which is called 'Ignorance.' [It] examined the soul closely, saying, 'Where are you going? You are bound by fornication. Indeed you are bound! Do not pass judgment!'

"And the soul said, 'Why do you judge me, since I have not passed judgment? I am bound, but I have not bound. They did not recognize me, but I have recognized that the universe is to be dissolved, both the things of earth and those of heaven.'

"When the soul had overcome the third Power, it went upward and it saw the fourth Power. It had seven forms. The first form is Darkness; the second, Desire; the third, Ignorance; the fourth Zeal of Death; the fifth, the Domain of the Flesh; the sixth, the Foolish Wisdom of the Flesh, and seventh is the Wisdom of the Wrathful Person. These are seven Powers of Wrath.

"They interrogated the soul, 'Where are you coming from human-killer, and where are you going, space-conqueror?'

"The soul replied, 'What binds me has been slain, and what surrounds me has been destroyed, and my desire has been brought to an end, and my ignorance has died. In a world, I was set loose from a world and in a type, from a type which is above, and [from] the chain of forgetfulness that exists in time. For now on, for the rest of the course of the [due] measure of the time of the age, I will rest i[n] silence.'"

When Mary said these things, she fell silent, since it was up to this point that the Savior had spoken to her.

10. Andrew sai[d, "B]rothers, what is your opinion of what was just said? I for one don't believe that the S[a]vior said these things, be[cause] these opinions seem to be so different from h[is th]ought."

After reflecting on these ma[tt]ers, [Peter said], "Has the Sa[vior] spoken secretly to a wo[m]an and [not] openly so that [we] would all hear? [Surely] he did [not wish to indicate] that [she] is more worthy than we are?"

Then Mary wept and said to Peter, "Peter, my brother, what are you imagining about this? Do you think that I've made all this up secretly by myself or that I am telling lies about the Savior?"

Levi said to Peter, "Peter, you have a constant inclination to anger and you are always ready to give way to it. And even now you are doing exactly that by questioning the woman as if you're her adversary. If the Savior considered her to be worthy, who are you to disregard her? For he knew her completely [and] loved her devotedly.

"Instead, we should be ashamed and, once we clothe ourselves with perfect humanity, we should do what we were commanded. We should announce the good news as the Savior ordered, and not be laying down any rules or making laws."

After he said these things, Levi left [and] began to announce the good news.

[*Gospel of Mary*]

NICENE CREED

The Nicene Creed was initially composed during the early church period and adopted in revised form at the Council at Nicea in 325 c.e. It was further modified at the Council of Constantinople in 381 c.e., although some scholars believe it took its penultimate form at the Council at Chalcedon in 451 c.e. At the local Council of Toledo in 589 c.e., the sentence "I believe in the Holy Ghost . . . who proceeds from the father" was expanded to read "who proceeds from the father and the son (filioque)." The issue involves whether the Holy Ghost originated from the father alone, or both the father and the son. Known as the filioque *clause, its inclusion provoked discord with the Eastern Orthodox churches, and became their rallying cry in the Great Schism of 1054. The* filioque *clause was definitively added to the creed by the Catholics at the Second Council of Lyons in 1274. Today, the Nicene Creed remains the most popular confession of faith in Catholic, Orthodox, and most Protestant liturgies, although Orthodox churches omit the* filioque *clause.*[12]

> I believe in one God the father almighty, maker of heaven and earth, and of all things visible and invisible. And in one lord Jesus Christ, the only begotten son of God, begotten of his father before all worlds, God of God, light of light, true God of true God, begotten, not made, being of one substance with the father, by whom all things were made. Who for us men, and for our salvation came down from heaven, and was incarnate by the Holy Ghost of the Virgin Mary, and was made man, and was crucified also for us under Pontius Pilate. He suffered and was buried, and the third day he rose again according to the scriptures, and ascended into heaven, and sits on the right hand of the father. And he shall come again with glory to judge both the quick and the dead: whose kingdom shall have no end. And I believe in the Holy Ghost, the lord and giver of life, who proceeds from the father and the son, who with the father and the son together is worshipped and glorified, who spoke by the prophets. And I believe in one catholic and apostolic church. I acknowledge one baptism for the remission of sins, and I look for the resurrection of the dead, and the life of the world to come. Amen.

SELECTIONS FROM MYSTICAL WRITINGS

MYSTICAL THEOLOGY OF PSEUDO-DIONYSIUS

Acts 17:34 mentions an Athenian convert of Paul's named Dionysius, a member of Athens's high court, the Areopagus. Eusibius, a fourth-century church historian, reports that Dionysius became bishop of Athens, and was later martyred. An unknown author of four mystical essays pseudonymously ascribed them to Dionysius, thereby guaranteeing their notice by his contemporaries. The pious fraud was more than successful, and the essays were consulted by mystics and scholars for the next millennium. One of these, the brief Mystical Theology, *was perhaps the single most influential text in medieval Christian mysticism. Pseudo-Dionysius argues that to know God directly one must progress through a series of assertions about what God is, and then denials about what God is not. There are three progressively detailed groups of assertions. The first are assertions that God is Father, Son, and Holy Spirit. Though profound, these assertions do not lend themselves to much detail. The second group, which is less profound but more detailed, describes God philosophically as powerful, wise, good. The third and final group, even less profound and more detailed yet, are metaphors describing God as sleeping, angry, grieved, or enraged. Once one's affirmative knowledge of God peaks in detail, one then extends knowledge of him negatively, in three reverse stages. One first denies metaphors about God: he has no emotions as humans understand them. Next one denies philosophical attributes of God: he is not power, knowledge, or goodness as humans understand the terms. Finally, one denies the most profound attributes: he is not father, son, or spirit as humans understand the terms. Dionysius concludes that the more one denies such features of God, the closer one comes to approaching God directly.*[13]

Chapter 3. What are the affirmative theologies and what are the negative? In my *Theological Representations*, I have praised the notions which are most appropriate to affirmative theology. I have shown the sense in which the divine and good nature is said to be one and then tri-une, how Fatherhood and Sonship are predicated of it, the meaning of the theology of the Spirit, how these core lights of goodness grew from the incorporeal and indivisible good, and how in this sprouting they have remained inseparable from their co-eternal foundation in it, in them-selves, and in each other. I have spoken of how Jesus, who is above indi-vidual being, became a being with a true human nature. Other revela-tions of scripture were also praised in *The Theological Representations*.

In *The Divine Names* I have shown the sense in which God is described as good, existent, life, wisdom, power, and whatever other things pertain to the conceptual names for God. In my *Symbolic Theology* I have discussed analogies of God drawn from what we perceive. I have spoken of the im-ages we have of him, of the forms, figures, and instruments proper to him, of the places in which he lives and of the ornaments he wears. I have spo-ken of his anger, grief, and rage, of how he is said to be drunk and hung-over, of his oaths and curses, of his sleeping and waking, and indeed of all those images we have of him, images shaped by the workings of the sym-bolic representations of God. And I feel sure that you have noticed how these latter come much more abundantly than what went before, since *The Theological Representations* and a discussion of the names appropriate to God are inevitably briefer than what can be said in *The Symbolic Theology*. The fact is that the more we take flight upward, the more our words are confined to the ideas we are capable of forming; so that now as we plunge into that darkness which is beyond intellect, we shall find ourselves not simply running short of words but actually speechless and unknowing. In the earlier books my argument traveled downward from the most exalted to the humblest categories, taking in on this downward path an ever-increasing number of ideas which multiplied with every stage of the de-scent. But my argument now rises from what is below up to the transcen-dent, and the more it climbs, the more language falters, and when it has passed up and beyond the ascent, it will turn silent completely, since it will finally be at one with him who is indescribable.

Now you may wonder why it is that, after starting out from the high-est category when it involves a denial. The reason is this. When we assert what is beyond every assertion, we must then proceed from what is most akin to it, and as we do so we make the affirmation on which everything else depends. But when we deny that which is beyond every denial, we have to start by denying those qualities which differ most from the goal we hope to attain. Is it not closer to reality to say that God is life and good-ness rather than that he is air or stone? Is it not more accurate to deny that drunkness and rage can be attributed to him than to deny that we can apply to him the terms of speech and thought?

Chapter 4. That the supreme Cause of every perceptible thing is not itself perceptible. So this is what we say. The Cause of all is above all and is not inexistent, lifeless, speechless, mindless. It is not a material body, and hence has neither shape nor form, quality, quantity, or weight. It is not in any place and can neither be seen nor be touched. It is neither perceived nor is it perceptible. It suffers neither disorder nor disturbance and is overwhelmed by no earthly passion. It is not powerless and subject to the disturbances caused by sense perception. It endures no deprivation of light. It passes through no change, decay, division, loss, no ebb and flow, nothing of which the senses may be aware. None of all this can either be identified with it nor attributed to it.

Chapter 5. That the supreme Cause of every conceptual thing is not itself conceptual. Again, as we climb higher we say this. It is not soul or mind, nor does it possess imagination, conviction, speech, or understanding. Nor is it speech per se, understanding per se. It cannot be spoken of and it cannot be grasped by understanding. It is not number or order, greatness or smallness, equality or inequality, similarity or dissimilarity. It is not immovable, moving, or at rest. It has no power, it is not power, nor is it light. It does not live nor is it life. It is not a substance, nor is it eternity or time. It cannot be grasped by the understanding since it is neither knowledge nor truth. It is not kingship. It is not wisdom. It is neither one nor oneness, divinity nor goodness. Nor is it a spirit, in the sense in which we understand that term. It is not sonship or fatherhood and it is nothing known to us or to any other being. It falls neither within the predicate of nonbeing nor of being. Existing beings do not know it as it actually is and it does not know them as they are. There is no speaking of it, nor name nor knowledge of it. Darkness and light, error and truth—it is none of these. It is beyond assertion and denial. We make assertions and denials of what is next to it, but never of it, for it is both beyond every assertion, being the perfect and unique cause of all things, and, by virtue of its pre-eminently simple and absolute nature, free of every limitation, beyond every limitation; it is also beyond every denial.

[*Mystical Theology*, Pseudo-Dionysius the Areopagite, 3–5]

HESYCHIUS OF SINAI ON THE JESUS PRAYER

From as early as the sixth century, the dominant form of mystical contemplation in Eastern Orthodoxy involved continuously repeating the Jesus prayer: "Lord Jesus Christ, Son of God, have mercy on me." By the 13th century, recitation of the Jesus prayer was supplemented with techniques of regular breathing, and taking postures with one's chin placed on the chest, eyes fixed on the heart. The purpose of this technique, known as hesychasm *(literally* stillness*), was to clear one's mind from all distraction and directly encounter God within one's heart. The heart was the focal point of the Jesus prayer since Hesychists believed it to be one's spiritual center. Hesychasm was violently* *attacked in the 14th century by those who maintained that direct encounter with God was impossible. Nevertheless, Hesychasm was too firmly grounded in monastic practice, and thus was confirmed by Orthodox councils in 1341 and 1351. The following selection, one of the earliest sustained discussions of the Jesus prayer, is from* On Watchfulness and Holiness *by Hesychius of Sinai, an eighth-century Abbot.*[14]

102. Forgetfulness can extinguish our guard over our intellect as water extinguishes fire; but the continuous repetition of the Jesus Prayer combined with strict watchfulness uproots it from our heart. The Jesus Prayer requires watchfulness as a lantern requires a candle.

103. We should strive to preserve the precious gifts which preserve us from all evil, whether on the plane of the senses or on that of the intellect. These gifts are the guarding of the intellect with the invocation of Jesus Christ, continuous insight into the heart's depths, stillness of mind unbroken even by thoughts which appear to be good, and the capacity to be empty of all thought. In this way the demons will not steal in undetected; and if we suffer pain through remaining centered in the heart, consolation is at hand.

104. The heart which is constantly guarded, and is not allowed to receive the forms, images and fantasies of the dark and evil spirits, is conditioned by nature to give birth from within itself to thoughts filled with light. For just as coal engenders a flame, or a flame lights a candle, so will God, who from our baptism dwells in our heart, kindle our mind to contemplation when He finds it free from the winds of evil and protected by the guarding of the intellect.

105. The name of Jesus should be repeated over and over in the heart as flashes of lightning are repeated over and over in the sky before rain. Those who have experience of the intellect and of inner warfare know this very well. We should wage this spiritual warfare with a precise sequence: first, with attentiveness; then, when we perceive the hostile thought attacking, we should strike at it angrily in the heart, cursing it as we do so; thirdly, we should direct our prayer against it, concentrating the heart through the invocation of Jesus Christ, so that the demonic fantasy may be dispersed at once, the intellect no longer pursuing it like a child deceived by some conjurer.

106. Let us exert ourselves like David, crying out 'Lord Jesus Christ' until our throats are sore; and let our spiritual eyes never cease to give us hope in the Lord our God (cf. Ps. 69:3).

107. If we constantly bear in mind the parable of the unjust judge, which the Lord related in order to show us that we ought always to pray and not to lose heart, we shall both profit and be vindicated (cf. Luke 18:1–8).

108. Just as he who looks at the sun cannot but fill his eyes with light, so he who always gazes intently into his heart cannot fail to be illumined.

174. The single-phrased Jesus Prayer destroys and consumes the deceits of the demons. For when we invoke Jesus, God and Son of God, constantly and tirelessly, He does not allow them to project in the mind's mirror even the first hint of their infiltration—that is to say, their

provocation—or any form, nor does He allow them to have any converse with the heart. If no demonic form enters the heart, it will be
empty of evil thoughts, as we have said; for it is the demons' habit to
converse with the soul by means of evil thoughts and so deceitfully
to pervert it.

175. It is through unceasing prayer that the mind is cleansed of the dark
clouds, the tempests of the demons. And when it is cleansed, the divine light of Jesus cannot but shine in it, unless we are puffed up with
self-esteem and delusion and a love of ostentation, and elevate ourselves towards the unattainable, and so are deprived of Jesus' help.
For Christ, the paradigm of humility, loathes all such self-inflation.

176. Let us hold fast, therefore, to prayer and humility, for together with
watchfulness they act like a burning sword against the demons. If we
do this, we shall daily and hourly be able to celebrate a secret festival
of joy within our hearts.

188. Noxious foods give trouble when taken into the body; but as soon as
he feels the pain, the person who has eaten them can quickly take
some emetic and so be unharmed. Similarly, once the intellect that
has imbibed evil thoughts senses their bitterness, it can easily expel
them and get rid of them completely by means of the Jesus Prayer uttered from the depths of the heart. This lesson, and the experience
corresponding to it, have by God's grace conveyed understanding to
those who practice watchfulness.

189. With your breathing combine watchfulness and the name of Jesus, or
humility and the unremitting study of death. Both may confer great
blessing.

[Hesychius of Sinai, *On Watchfulness and Holiness*, 102–108, 174–176,
188–189]

ST. TERESA ON PRAYER OF UNION

*Teresa of Avila (1515–1582), 16th-century Spanish mystic, entered a Carmelite con-
vent at age 19. With St. John of the Cross she established the Discalced (barefoot)
order, which was more strict and wore only sandals. She had visions and raptures and,
in her most memorable vision, an angel pierced her heart with a flaming arrow, which
when removed left her with a love for God. Teresa's most systematic work, the* Interior Castle *(1577), uses the metaphor of seven series of mansions to represent various
stages of spiritual development. The mystic enters the castle door through prayer, and
then roams the mansions' millions of rooms at will. She describes the fifth series of
mansions as the Prayer of Union by which the mystic's soul is possessed by God. In
the selection below, she explains the effects of this union using the analogy of a silkworm. The silkworm starts from a tiny egg that feeds on mulberry leaves, spins a cocoon, and emerges as a butterfly. The silkworm represents the soul, its nourishment is
the Church, the silk house is Christ, and the spinning of the cocoon is the prayer of
union. Thus, the union experience, which does not last even a half hour, transforms
the mystic, and the new "butterfly" feels like a stranger in its new world.*[15]

You will have heard of the wonderful way in which silk is made—a way which no one could invent but God—and how it comes from a kind of seed which looks like tiny peppercorns. (I have never seen this, but only heard of it, so if it is incorrect in any way the fault is not mine). When the warm weather comes, and the mulberry-trees begin to show leaf this seed starts to take life, until it has this sustenance, on which it feeds, it is as dead. The silkworms feed on the mulberry-leaves until they are full-grown, when people put down twigs, upon which, with their tiny mouths, they start spinning silk, making themselves very tight little cocoons, in which they bury themselves. Then, finally, the worm, which was large and ugly, comes right out of the cocoon a beautiful white butterfly.

. . . The silkworm is like the soul which takes life when, through the heat which comes from the Holy Spirit, it begins to utilize the general help which God gives to us all, and to make use of the remedies which He left in His Church—such as frequent confessions, good books and sermons, for these are the remedies for a soul dead in negligences and sins and frequently plunged into temptation. The soul begins to live and nourishes itself on this food, and on good meditations, until it is full grown—and this is what concerns me now: the rest is of little importance.

When it is full-grown, then, as I wrote at the beginning, it starts to spin its silk and to build the house in which it is to die. This house may be understood here to mean Christ. I think I read or heard somewhere that our life is hid in Christ, or in God (for that is the same thing), or that our life is Christ. (The exact form of this is little to my purpose.)

Here, then, daughters, you see what we can do, with God's favor. May His Majesty Himself be our Mansion as He is in this Prayer of Union which, as it were, we ourselves spin. When I say He will be our Mansion, and we can construct it for ourselves and hide ourselves in it, I am to be suggesting that we can subtract from God, or add to Him. But of course we cannot possibly do that! We can neither subtract from, nor add to God, but we can subtract from, and add to, ourselves, just as these little silkworms do. And, before we have finished doing all that we can in that respect, God will take this tiny achievement of ours, which is nothing at all, unite it with His greatness and give it such worth that its reward will be the Lord Himself. And as it is He Whom it has cost the most, so His Majesty will unite our small trials with the great trials which He suffered, and make both of them into one.

On, then, my daughters. Let us hasten to perform this task and spin this cocoon. Let us renounce our self-love and self-will, and our attachment to earthly things. Let us practice penance, prayer, mortification, obedience, and all the other good works that you know of. Let us do what we have been taught; and we have been instructed about what our duty is. Let the silkworm die—let it die, as in fact it does when it has completed the work which it was created to do. Then we shall see God and shall ourselves be as completely hidden in His greatness as is this little worm in its cocoon. Note that, when I speak of seeing God, I am referring to the way in which, as I have said, He allows Himself to be apprehended in this kind of union.

And now let us see what becomes of this silkworm, for all that I have been saying about it is leading up to this. When it is in this state of prayer, and quite dead to the world, it comes out a little white butterfly. Oh, greatness of God, that a soul should come out like this after being hidden in the greatness of God, and closely united with Him, for so short a time—never, I think, for as long as half an hour! I tell you truly, the very soul does not know itself. For think of the difference between an ugly worm and a white butterfly, it is just the same here. The soul cannot think how it can have merited such a blessing—whence such a blessing could have come to it, I meant to say, for it knows quite well that it has not merited it at all. It finds itself so anxious to praise the Lord that it would gladly be consumed and die a thousand deaths for His sake. Then it finds itself longing to suffer great trials and unable to do otherwise. It has the most vehement desires for penance, for solitude, and for all to know God. And hence, when it sees God being offended, it becomes greatly distressed. In the following Mansion we shall treat of these things further and in detail, for, although the experiences of this Mansion and of the next are almost identical, their effects come to have much greater power, for, as I have said, if after God comes to a soul here on earth it strives to progress still more, it will experience great things.

[*Interior Castle*, Fifth Mansions, Chapter 2.]

SELECTIONS FROM RECENT SECTARIAN WRITINGS

BOOK OF MORMON

The Book of Mormon, *published in 1830, chronicles the history and religious practices of a band of Israelites who migrated to America in 600 B.C.E. Under two leaders, two distinct conflicting cultures emerged: the civilized Nephites, and the nomadic and warring Lamanites. Ostensibly the forefathers of the Native Americans, the Lamanites exterminated the Nephites. Anticipating their demise, Moroni, a Nephite Chronicler, buried a golden copy of the Book of Mormon to preserve their story. A 20-page section of the Book of Mormon describes how Jesus visited the Nephites and gave them Christian Doctrine, much of which is paraphrased from the Gospels. Selections from this are below.*

11. . . . And it came to pass, as they understood they cast their eyes up again towards heaven; and behold, they saw a Man descending out of heaven; and he was clothed in a white robe; and he came down and stood in the midst of them; and the eyes of the whole multitude were turned upon him, and they durst not open their mouths, even one to another and wist not what it meant, for they thought it was an angel that had appeared unto them. And it came to pass that he stretched forth his hand and spake unto the people, saying:

Behold, I am Jesus Christ, whom the prophets testified shall come into the world. . . .

Behold, verily, verily, I say unto you, I will declare unto you my doctrine. And this is my doctrine, and it is the doctrine which the Father hath given unto me; and I bear record of the Father, and the Father beareth record of me, and the Holy Ghost beareth record of the Father and me; and I bear record that the Father commandeth all men, everywhere, to repent and believe in me. And whoso believeth in me, and is baptized, the same shall be saved; and they are they who shall inherit the kingdom of God. And whoso believeth not in me, and is not baptized, shall be damned.

Verily, verily, I say unto you, that this is my doctrine, and I bear record of it from the Father; and whoso believeth in me believeth in the Father also; and unto him will the Father bear record of me, for he will visit him with fire and with the Holy Ghost. And thus will the Father bear record of me, and the Holy Ghost will bear record unto him of the Father and me; for the Father, and I, and the Holy Ghost are one.

And again I say unto you, ye must repent, and become as a little child, and be baptized in my name, or ye can in nowise receive these things. And again I say unto you, ye must repent, and be baptized in my name, and become as a little child, or ye can in nowise inherit the kingdom of God. Verily, verily, I say unto you, that this is my doctrine, and whoso buildeth upon this buildeth upon my rock, and the gates of hell shall not prevail against them. And whoso shall declare more or less than this, and establish it for my doctrine, the same cometh of evil, and is not built upon my rock; but he buildeth upon a sandy foundation, and the gates of hell stand open to receive such when the floods come and the winds beat upon them. Therefore, go forth unto this people, and declare the words which I have spoken, unto the ends of the earth.

17. Behold, now it came to pass that when Jesus had spoken these words he looked round about again on the multitude, and he said unto them: Behold, my time is at hand. I perceive that ye are weak, that ye cannot understand all my words which I am commanded of the Father to speak unto you at this time. Therefore, go ye unto your homes, and ponder upon the things which I have said, and ask of the Father, in my name, that ye may understand, and prepare your minds for the morrow, and I come unto you again. But now I go unto the Father, and also to show myself unto the lost tribes of Israel, for they are not lost unto the Father, for he knoweth wither he hath taken them.

And it came to pass that when Jesus had thus spoken, he cast his eyes round about again on the multitude, and beheld they were in tears, and did look steadfastly upon him as if they would ask him to tarry a little longer with them. And he said unto them: Behold my bowels are filled with compassion towards you. Have ye any that are sick among you? Bring them hither. Have ye any that are lame, or blind, or halt, or maimed, or leprous, or that are withered, or that are dear, or that are afflicted in any manner? Bring them hither and I will heal them, for I have compassion upon you; my bowels are filled with mercy. . . .

18. . . . Therefore, keep these sayings which I have commanded you that ye come not under condemnation; for wo unto him whom the Father condemneth. And I give you these commandments because of the disputations which have been among you. And blessed are ye if ye have no disputations among you. And now I go unto the Father, because it is expedient that I should go unto the Father for your sakes.

And it came to pass that when Jesus had made an end of these sayings, he touched with his hand the disciples whom he had chosen, one by one, even until he had touched them all, and spake unto them as he touched them. And the multitude heard not the words which he spake, therefore they did not bear record; but the disciples bear record that he gave them power to give the Holy Ghost. And I will show unto you hereafter that this record is true. And it came to pass that when Jesus had touched them all, there came a cloud and overshadowed the multitude that they could not see Jesus. And while they were overshadowed he departed from them, and ascended into heaven. And the disciples saw and did bear record that he ascended again into heaven.

[*Book of Mormon*, Third Nephi, 11:8–10, 31–41; 17:1–7; 18:33–39]

GLOSSARY

Apostles   early followers of Jesus commissioned to lead the church after his death.

Catholic   the largest Christian denomination which follows a church hierarchy led by the bishop of Rome (i.e., the Pope).

Disciples   Jesus' followers.

Eastern Orthodox   the church diocese originally of the eastern Roman Empire, which rejects the supreme authority of the bishop of Rome.

Gnosticism   the Near Eastern religious movement from 100–400 C.E., which aims to free one's spirit from the evil material world by acquiring special knowledge (gnosis).

Hesychasm   literally "stillness"; method of Orthodox mysticism involving controlled breathing and body postures while repeating the Jesus prayer: "Lord Jesus Christ, Son of God, have mercy on me."

Holy Spirit   divine presence and agent of guidance for Christians. One person of the Trinity, along with the father and son.

Judaizers   first-century Jewish Christians who maintained that Christians were still bound by traditional Jewish laws.

Messiah   Hebrew term for "anointed one," or "king," indicating that someone is set aside for a divinely appointed office either in a religious apocalyptic sense, or political revolutionary sense.

Protestant   Christian denominations whose lineages derive from the 16th-century Protestant Reformation.

Quelle (or Q)   a no longer extant written sayings list that Matthew and Luke used as a source for Jesus' teachings.

Son of Man   literally *son of Adam*, an Old Testament term sometimes meaning human being, other times referring to a messianic figure.

Synoptic Gospels   Gospels of Mark, Matthew and Luke, which are similar in content, in contrast to John which vastly differs.

Trinity   doctrine that God is a unity of three persons: the Father, Son, and Holy Spirit.

SUGGESTIONS FOR FURTHER READING

BORG, MARCUS J. *Jesus in Contemporary Scholarship*. Valley Forge: Trinity, 1994.

BAINTON, R. H. *The Reformation of the Sixteenth Century*. Boston: Beacon Press, 1962.

CHADWICK, OWEN, ed., *The Pelican History of the Church*, 5 vols. London: Penguin, 1960–70.

CROSSAN, JOHN DOMINIC. *Jesus: A Revolutionary Biography*. San Francisco: HarperCollins, 1994.

DAVIES, STEVAN L. *The Gospel of Thomas and Christian Wisdom*. New York: Seabury, 1983.

JACOBSON, ARLAND, *The First Gospel: An Introduction to Q*. Sonoma: Polebridge, 1992.

HACKEL, S. *The Orthodox Church*. London: Ward Lock Educational, 1971.

HUGHES, P. *A Short History of the Catholic Church*. London: Burns and Oates, 1978.

LATOURETTE, KENNETH S. *A History of Christianity*. 2 vols., rev. ed. San Francisco: HarperCollins, 1975.

PELIKAN, JAROSLAV. *The Christian Tradition*. 4 vols. 1971–83.

RAHNER, K. *Foundations of Christian Faith*. New York: Seabury Press, 1978.

SCHWEITZER, ALBERT. *The Quest of the Historical Jesus*. New York: MacMillan, 1961.

Islam

Islam's basic tenets are expressed in its most holy creed: "There is no God but Allah, and Muhammad is his messenger." *Islam* means surrender, and adherents to the religion are called *Muslims,* meaning those who surrender. Staunchly monotheistic, Islam sees Allah as the omnipotent creator God who, through a series of prophets, has called people to obedience. At the end of time, Allah will resurrect the dead, condemn the wicked to hell, and entrust believers to eternal peace in his garden. Following prophets such as Moses and Jesus, Muhammad is the final and greatest prophet, who delivered the definitive expression of Allah's voice in the Qur'an, Islam's most holy book. Drawing on Jewish narratives, Muslims trace their religious heritage from Adam, to Noah, to Abraham, and finally, to Ishmael, Abraham's first son. Muslim faith is embodied not only in religious practice but in a social order governed by Islamic law.

HISTORY OF ISLAM

Time of Ingratitude

The cradle of Islam was the Arabian Peninsula, during a period which Muslims contemptuously refer to as the *time of ingratitude (al-jahiliyyah),* that is, ingratitude toward God. Economically, desert conditions of the peninsula disallowed for widespread agriculture, so inhabitants depended on trade with the surrounding empires. When the Arabs later lost their spice monopoly, trading cities such as Petra died. As a convenient stopping place on well-traveled trade routes, though, Mecca survived as the prosperous center of trading in the Arab world. Politically, Mecca was plagued by warring factions involving their two main tribes, the Quraysh and the Khuza'a, each with divisive clans.

Religiously, inhabitants believed in a range of spiritual forces and deities. Belief in polydemonism prevailed, involving supernatural *jinn,* sprites, and demons, some good and others evil, which inhabited special objects or locations. Tapping into their ancient Semitic heritage, they set up shrines to various nature gods and goddesses. Hubal, god of the moon, was the principal deity of the Meccans, and before his idol people would cast lots and divining arrows. Three chief goddesses of Mecca, Al-Lat, Al-Manat, and Al-Uzza, were worshiped. There was widespread belief in a creator deity, named Allah, who was high god of the regional pantheon. Sacred shrines with carved and uncarved stones were thought to be the dwelling places of these spirits and deities, and they became the focus of offerings and prayers. There was also a significant Jewish and Christian monotheistic presence. Large numbers of Diaspora Jews, fleeing enemies for over a thousand years, settled in Arabia's desert. The Jews interacted well with their new neighbors, and many Arabs converted to Judaism. Hermit Christian monks settled in the desert regions, along with heretical Christian sects escaping the authority of the Roman church. Muslim tradition also notes the presence of pre-Islamic monotheists, known as *Hanif,* who carried the torch of Abraham's religion through the time of ingratitude.

Festivals and pilgrimages dominated the religious activities of the Meccans. Annual festivals lasting weeks drew inhabitants from throughout the peninsula to the two cities of Mina and Ukaz. With its 365 shrines, one for each day of the year, Mecca was a constant attraction to pilgrims. Meccan religious activity centered on the Ka'bah, an austere cubical structure housing idols, murals of the gods, and the Black Stone. The stone, believed to have fallen from heaven, was the object of a special ritual in which naked pilgrims would circle it seven times and then kiss it. Muslim tradition maintains that the Ka'bah was originally built by Abraham.

Early Years of Muhammad

Even a brief survey of world religions indicates that the lives of the religious founders are shrouded in legend, often to the point that their historical lives can no longer be recovered. Although many accounts of Muhammad are also legendary, Islam has the advantage of early written sources, not just by early Muslims, but by Muhammad himself.

Born about 570 C.E., Muhammad was from the Hashimite family clan of Mecca, part of the Quraysh tribe. The clan's founder, from whom Muhammad descended, traced his lineage back to Ishmael, Abraham's first son according to Jewish legend. Muhammad's birth name is unknown, although his honorific title, *Muhammad,* means "highly praised." Tragedy marked his infant and childhood years. His father died before he was born, and as a minor under pre-Islamic law he was unable to acquire inheritance. He was entrusted to his grandfather who, according to one tradition, had him raised by a Bedouin foster mother. His natural mother died when he was six, and his grandfather two years later. Under the care of his uncle, he became involved with caravans. A story relates that the 12-year-old Muhammad accompanied his uncle to Syria on a caravan, where he met a Christian monk who recognized him as the future great prophet. Because of his reputation for honesty, Muhammad was soon entrusted with the leadership of caravans. A pivotal moment in his life arrived when, at 25, he led a caravan for a wealthy widow named Khadija. Although she was 15 years his senior, the two married, and for years she became an important source of encouragement for Muhammad. She bore him four daughters and three sons who died in infancy. Fatima, the most well known daughter, later married his cousin Ali.

According to his tribal custom, during one month of every year Muhammad retreated for religious reflection. He reflected on the good fortune given him by Allah, in view of his family and successful caravan career. He also thought about Jews and Christians who had a *book,* the Bible, by virtue of which they were prospering more than his own people. This moved him toward monotheism. Islam was born on the *Night of Power* (Laylat al-Qadr) when, on retreat in a cave outside of Mecca, the 40-year-old Muhammad had a life-changing vision. In a voice like reverberating bells, the angel Gabriel approached him, commanding him to recite a phrase: "And the Lord is most Generous, who by the pen has taught mankind things they knew not." He went through a period of doubt for a few months, even contemplating suicide, fearing he was an ecstatic visionary, an occupation not held in high esteem in his society. He also considered that he might be mad, or that he had heard the voice of a *jinn.* Eventually his doubts dispersed and his wife became his first convert, believing that he was a prophet.

Visions and revelations of this kind continued throughout his life. They were recorded or memorized by others as they occurred, and then compiled into the text of the Qur'an. The moments of revelation began with Muhammad becoming entranced while shaking and sweating. Then, in rhymed prose, rhapsodies in Arabic flowed from his mouth. During his early prophetic career, the main points of his message were that Allah is the only God, that the dead will resurrect, and that Allah will judge all. After his wife, his next converts included his cousin Ali and a merchant named Abu Bakr, both of whom assumed leadership positions after Muhammad's death. As his following grew, the first Muslims experienced verbal attacks, threats, and later physical violence. The opposition was in part economically motivated by those whose livelihoods depended on religious pilgrimages to the Ka'bah; Muhammad's message of a single God, they assumed, threatened this. Many Meccan merchants assumed that a single god would draw fewer pilgrims than the many idols housed in their city.

For protection, Muhammad first sent a band of his followers to Ethiopia, where they were warmly received by local Christians. He and about 50 followers were then placed under siege in their Meccan neighborhood in an attempt to starve them into submission. Under pressure, Muhammad strangely reported a new revelation: Along with Allah, the three key Meccan goddesses were acknowledged. The siege was then lifted, and the exiles returned from Ethiopia. Later Muhammad announced that the new revelation was inspired by the devil, and the relevant passages were removed from his record of revelations. Hostility increased when his wife and uncle died. He tried to establish himself in an oasis town named Taif, about 60 miles southeast of Mecca, but failed.

Later Years of Muhammad

The turning point in Muhammad's mission occurred during a pilgrimage festival. He met residents of the northern city Yathrib who suggested that their people would be more receptive to him, in part because the city had many Jews who were awaiting the arrival of a prophet. The city was in political turmoil, and the residents believed that they could benefit from Muhammad's administrative skills. A period of negotiations followed. It was agreed that Muhammad would be the final arbiter of all disputes and that the various religious groups, including the Jews and Muslims, would be autonomous. The migration to Yathrib, called the *hijrah* (flight) began with around 100 of his follower's families. In 622 C.E., at age 52, Muhammad joined them, fleeing Meccan authorities as he made the journey. This migration is so momentous for Islam that it marks the starting point of the Muslim calendar.

Muhammad quickly became a successful administrator and statesman, an accomplishment with which even his enemies agreed. He renamed the city *Medina,* city of the prophet. Living unpretentiously in a clay house and milking goats, he was ever available for consultation. He punished the guilty, but was merciful toward his personal enemies. Of his several diplomatic marriages, his primary wife, A'isha, daughter of Abu Bakr, had particular influence over him, and is the source of many of the traditions later ascribed to him.

Although successful in Medina, hostilities with Mecca continued. Believing that he had a responsibility to provide for the Meccan emigrant followers living in Medina, Muhammad intercepted a caravan to Mecca for its booty. Attempting this a second time, his band of 300 encountered an army of 1,000 Meccans at a site called Badr. The ensuing battle was a victory for Muhammad. Not dissuaded, a few years later the Meccans launched a military offensive against Muhammad's army. Known as the Battle of Uhud, the Muslims were badly outnumbered, forced to retreat, and Muhammad himself was slightly wounded. Even so, the battle was a moral victory since the Meccans failed to eradicate Muhammad. Two years later the Meccans attacked Medina directly with a confederate army of surrounding cities and nomads. By recommendation of a Persian soldier in his camp, Muhammad ordered a trench dug around the entire city, a strategy that resulted in victory.

With each military victory (and moral victories like Uhud), his converts increased, and his control over Medina became more firm. The Jewish population, which attracted him to the city, ironically failed to accept him as God's prophet. Some even aided the Meccans in their attack. Now with increased authority, Muhammad drove them out. His disappointment with the Jews had theological consequences as well. The Jewish and Christian elements of his religion were suppressed, and the traditional Arab elements were emphasized. No longer would Muslims pray facing Jerusalem, but towards Mecca. Qur'anic passages of this period enjoined Muslims to make pilgrimages to Mecca, which included circumambulation of the Ka'bah and kissing its Black Stone. Friday became the official day of rest, not Saturday or Sunday. During his rule in Medina, other central Muslim doctrines were established, such as fasting, alms giving, and ritual prayer. Social laws involving marriage, divorce, inheritance, and treatment of slaves and prisoners were also formalized.

In the fifth year of the migration, Muhammad and his followers approached Mecca with the intention of making a pilgrimage, but were met with resistance from the city leaders. The two sides reached a face-saving compromise, in which Muhammad and his followers withdrew, with the understanding that the next year they would return and the city would be open to them for a pilgrimage. However, in the intervening year a Meccan broke the truce, and Muhammad responded by marching on the city. Realizing that they were unable to resist his force, the leaders of the city surrendered and bloodshed was avoided. Riding into the Ka'bah on his camel, with his own hands he smashed its 360 idols, declaring, "Truth has come and falsehood has vanished." Thus, he reclaimed the shrine for God. All of Mecca converted, giving no resistance. The territory around the Ka'bah was declared sacred (*haram*), and non-Muslims were prohibited from entering the area. Muhammad then returned to Medina.

In the tenth year after his migration, he made a final announcement at the Ka'bah: "Today I have completed my religion for you and I have fulfilled the extent of my favor towards you. It is my will that Islam be your religion. I have completed my mission. I have left you the Book of Allah and clear commandments. If you keep them you will never go wrong." Shortly thereafter, reporting severe headaches, he died while in A'isha's house and was buried on that spot.

The Caliphate

Muhammad founded both a new religion and a new social order. Although he believed that his mission as a religious prophet was complete at the time of his death, plans for a larger Muslim social community (*umma*) were not as yet realized. He had planned to conquer Syria and Iraq, but died too soon. Upon his death, key political decisions were made by Muhammad's early companions (*Sahaba*), many of whom were his first converts. Their first task was to appoint a successor, or Caliph, who would fill Muhammad's political leadership role, but not his prophetic role. From the start, however, there was political dissent. To the consternation of Ali, Muhammad's cousin who expected to step into the leadership role, the early companions selected Abu Bakr as the first Caliph. For the sake of unity, Ali deferred to his rival. Plans were drawn for military expansion, but the aged Caliph died only two years into his rule.

For the next ten years, the newly appointed Caliph Umar expanded Muslim territory far into the Persian and Byzantine empires. Non-Arab converts were denied equal political rights, and it would be almost a hundred years until a unified Muslim political order would emerge. Umar was stabbed to death by a Persian slave, and Uthman became the third Caliph. According to legend, trouble started for Uthman when he lost Muhammad's seal ring in a well. He prompted further negative reaction by favoring his family clan, the Umayyads, which originally opposed Muhammad in Mecca. A small rebellion erupted in Medina, in which a disaffected faction (which later became the Kharajites) laid siege to his house. Civil war broke later and, 12 years into his rule, Uthman was assassinated by rebel Muslim troops from Egypt. The early companions finally elected Ali as the fourth Caliph, but he was immediately opposed by Syrian governor Mu'awiyah, who sought to avenge the death of Uthman, his cousin. War broke out between Ali and Mu'awiyah and, on the eve of the decisive battle, Ali was killed by a soldier from a rebel group that had split with him as a result of disagreement with his policies. The Caliphate fell to Ali's son, Husan, but he quickly ceded it to Mu'awiyah.

Under the first wave of Muslim expansion by the first four Caliphs, all of Arabia, Persia, and North Africa were conquered. For the next 90 years the Caliphate was held by the secular Umayyad Dynasty (661–750), established by Mu'awiyah. After Mu'awiyah's death, the Caliphate was passed to his unpopular son Yazid. In 680 an insurrection against Yazid was launched by Ali's son, Husayn. Husayn and his followers were massacred in what is now the Iraqi city of Kerbala (a tragedy which became the rallying cry of the Shi'i Muslims). Centered in Damascus, the Umayyads continued to push Muslim boundaries. Moving across north Africa and into Spain, expansion into Europe halted at the French borders in the Battle of Tours in 732. The Caliphate was next held by the Abbasid Dynasty (750–1285), centered in Baghdad, and then by the Ottoman Empire (1300–1922), centered in Istanbul. In 1924 the Caliphate was abolished by the Turkish National Assembly, inheritors of the Ottoman Empire. To justify this controversial decision the Assembly maintained that "The idea of a single caliph, exercising supreme religious authority over all the peoples of Islam, is an idea taken from fiction, not from reality."

Sunni and Shi'a

Just as political factions divided early Islam, so did theological differences, the key issue being whether Ali and his successors had a special spiritual status. Islam today is divided into two main groups over this issue. The Sunni, or Sunnite, attribute no special function to Ali, whereas the Shi'a, or Shi'ite, do. Sunnis make up approximately 90 percent of Muslims worldwide. Their full name is *Ahl al-Sunnah wa 'l-Hadith,* that is, followers of the path laid out by the prophet in his sayings. In addition to rejecting the special spiritual status of Ali, Sunnis recognize the first four Caliphs as political successors to Muhammad and acknowledge the political authority of the Caliphate in general. Sunnis must also follow one of the four schools of Islamic law (*madhahib*), developed in the eighth and ninth centuries.

Prior to the emergence of the four Sunni schools of law, Muslims used several guides to determine proper conduct. After the Qur'an was consulted for guidance, appeals were made to practices of Muhammad (*sunna*) as compiled by scholars into texts called *Hadith.* When these avenues failed, decisions were made in one of three ways: analogical deductions from existing laws (*qiyas*), consensus of the Muslim community or its leading scholars (*ijma*), and independent decisions of a single jurist (*ijtihad*).

The four schools of Islamic law not only systematized the above appeal routes, but developed their own codes of behavior from these. The methodological differences between the four schools are subtle, although their geographical domains are more distinct. The *Hanafite* school, which provides the greatest scope of reasoning, predominates in former Turkish empire areas (Turkey, Palestine, Egypt), and India. The *Malikite* school, which focuses more on the traditions of Muhammad's companions rather than Muhammad, is dominant in west Africa. The *Shafi'ite* school, which developed the standard hierarchy of appeals, is most prominent in Indonesia. Finally, the *Hanbalite* school, the most literalist in adhering to the letter of the Qur'an, is found in Saudi Arabia and Qatar.

Shi'a Muslims, consisting of 10 percent of the Muslim population, are located primarily in Iran. Shi'a origins are difficult to trace because of negative Sunni chronologies and biased reports by later Shi'as. However, with the assassination of Ali and the creation of the Umayyad Caliphate in 661, a faction loyal to the memory of Ali emerged. Devotion to Ali and his selected descendants became the test for true faith. Early Shi'as were in continual opposition to the ruling Caliph, some groups advocating armed resistance.

About 40 factions of Shi'as have emerged over the years. The most numerous are the Twelvers (*Ithna 'Asha-Riyyah*), who comprise about 80 percent of their number. The central Twelver doctrine is that of the Imam, or leader. Twelvers believe that Muhammad's spiritual abilities (*wilaya*) were passed on to a series of Imams, beginning with Ali. Twelver theology holds that human beings require inspired leadership in order to adhere faithfully to the dictates of Islam and that successive Imams are clearly designated by predecessors (*nass*). Imams are also thought to be guided by Allah and to be infallible (*isma*). Eleven Imams have appeared so far, and they await the appearance of the 12th and final, named Mahdi, who is alive but hidden from view. More precisely, the Mahdi is in a state called *occultation,* in which he can see others, but others cannot see him; at age four, Allah placed him in that state for protection after the death of his father, the 11th Imam, 873 C.E. It is believed that the Mahdi made four representations (*wakils*) between 873–940, a period called the *lesser occultation.* He will return at the end of time, take vengeance on unbelievers, and initiate an era of peace. Until then, leaders called the *Mujtahid* make decisions of canon law on behalf of the hidden Imam. In this century, the Ayatollahs have this function.

Two other Shi'a factions deserve mentioning. The Fivers (*Zaydis*) split from Twelver tradition by recognizing Zaydis as the fifth Imam (as opposed to Muhammad al-Baqir). Concentrated in Yemen, they do not assert the necessity of Imams and accept some of the early Caliphs. The Seveners (*Isma'ili*) split from Twelver tradition by recognizing Isma'il as the seventh Imam (rather than Musa-l-Kazim). They see Isma'il as the final Imam, Mahdi, who will return for the day of judgment.

MUSLIM SCRIPTURES

The sacred literature of Islam falls into three categories. First and foremost is the Qur'an, its most holy scripture. Next, at a deuterocanonical level, are the *Hadith* canons. Finally, there are sectarian texts that are revered by Sunni, Shi'i, and Sufi practitioners.

The Qur'an

The Qur'an is the collected revelations of Muhammad written during the last 23 years of his life. It is the primary sacred text for all sects of Islam. The text is divided into 114 sections called *surahs,* in lengths varying from three verses to almost 300 verses. The term "Qur'an" means "to recite," in the sense that Muhammad is verbally delivering Allah's message to the people. The traditional arrangement of the *surahs* is neither chronological nor topical, but according to length, beginning with the longest and ending with the shortest. *Surah* titles are derived from a prominent or recurring word, such as Cow, Abraham, Mary, Angels, Muhammad, Divorce, Infidels. Every *surah* (save one[1]) begins with the phrase, "In the name of God, the Merciful, the Compassionate," which was probably the original indicator of the *surah* divisions.

The exact chronology of the *surahs* was forgotten even during Muhammad's life, and many short revelations from different periods were joined together to form longer *surahs.* Modern scholars have offered several chronological schemes for organizing the *surahs,* although traditional Muslims believe that such attempts compromise the inherent beauty of the nonhistorical arrangement. Nevertheless, each *surah* is associated with either the Meccan or Medinan periods of Muhammad's life. The Meccan *surahs* are the earliest and reflect Muhammad's struggle to persuade his skeptical Meccan listeners to abandon polytheism and idolatry. They are shorter and more poetic than the Medinan sections, and they are characterized by vivid imagery. Meccan *surahs* describe the world's cataclysmic end and emphasize Allah's omnipotence and active role in history.

Within the Meccan period itself the style and content of the *surahs* developed. The earliest use short sentences, particularly powerful imagery and are the most lyrical. The later ones, by contrast, are longer, more direct and sermonizing, and less heated. Stories of the early prophets become more developed. When Muhammad and his followers migrated to Medina, political circumstances were considerably more favorable, and the *surahs* reflect the confident voice of a lawgiver concerned with social and political issues. These are the longest *surahs* in the Qur'an, and deal with the giving of the law.

Stylistically, most of the Qur'an is written in first, second, and third person, with Allah addressing believers, unbelievers, or Muhammad. The first person is used when God describes his divine attributes, and the second when describing actions in which humans participate. Passages not in the voice of Allah are prefaced by the word "say," indicating that they are to be recited by believers. Most of the Qur'an is written in rhymed prose, as opposed to poetry with meter. The latter approach was typical of poets who were thought to be guided by *jinn,* an association which Muhammad strongly resisted. Phrases are repetitive and well-suited for reciting; indeed, several traditional Qur'anic division schemes break the text into sections for daily reading. Muslims believe that the literary quality of the Qur'an itself validates Muhammad's claims of prophethood. For, although illiterate, he produced a literary work of great merit.

The initial compilation of the Qur'an is a remarkable story. After each of Muhammad's revelations, efforts were made to record their content, either through writing or memorization by specially assigned reciters. Although Muhammad may have done some editing of the earlier *surahs* when in Medina, no definitive "book" existed at the time of his death. A year after Muhammad's death, many of the original reciters were killed in battle. Fearing that the Qur'an's contents would be lost through time, the first Caliph, Abu Bakr, ordered the compilation of the first complete text of the Qur'an. The task was assigned to Zayd ibn Thabit, an aide of Muhammad, who pieced the text together from oral and written sources in Medina. Variant Qur'an fragments continued to circulate for 24 more years, until the third Caliph, Uthman, ordered the creation of a definitive text. Again Zayd supervised the compilation. He gathered all existing manuscript fragments and met with the original reciters accompanying Muhammad who had the complete contents memorized. When the compilation was complete, all previous written versions were destroyed, assuring that only one version of the Qur'an would remain. Although variant editions appeared later, the definitive text of the Qur'an we have today is the work of Zayd. Diacritical marks were later introduced to fix proper vocalization for recitation.

The content of the Qur'an covers a variety of subjects. Many stories parallel accounts in the Old Testament, and some from the New Testament, especially those of Adam, Noah, Abraham, Joseph, and Jesus. It is unlikely that Muhammad had access to Arabic translations of Jewish or Christian texts, but instead relied on oral traditions of the local Jewish and Christian populace. Other narratives are of Arabian origin.[2] Large sections of the Qur'an provide legislation for the newly formed Muslim community in Medina.

For Muslims, the Qur'an records more than the words of Muhammad; it is Allah's eternal speech; the Torah and Bible are earlier and incomplete revelations of Allah. Most Muslims believe that the Qur'an is uncreated, existing from eternity, with an original engraved tablet of the Qur'an in heaven. This eternal Qur'an is written in the Arabic language, and so authentic copies of the Qur'an will also only be in Arabic. The first unofficial translation appeared in 1141 in Latin, which was loathed by Muslims for its disparaging renderings. The physical book itself is sacred, and copies of the Qur'an are touched only after ceremonial cleansing of the handler.

Hadith *Canons*

After the Qur'an, the second most authoritative group of texts in Islam are the *Hadith* canons. The term *Hadith* means talk or speech, and it refers to collected narratives reporting actions and sayings of Muhammad recounted by his companions. These monumental collections are the principal basis for interpreting the Qur'an and were used to develop early Islamic legal systems.

While Muhammad was alive, his companions took note of his life events and his sayings. Within the first hundred years after Muhammad's death, individual sayings were transmitted both orally and in written form from teachers of *Hadith* to their students. Within the second hundred years, booklets of *Hadith* appeared on single topics, and later on several topics. The number of *Hadith* grew to about three quarters of a million, most being duplicates with only slight variations as generated by the continually growing number of teachers and students of *Hadith*. Finally, they were systematically compiled in the 9th and 10th centuries into no less than 12 multivolume collections.

The Sunnis have nine collections, six of which are particularly revered. The most widely accepted of these are referred to as the *Two Sahih* (authentic): *Sahih al-Bukhari* and *Sahih Muslim*. The first of these, compiled by al-Bukhari (d. 875), is the most important. A prominent teacher of *Hadith,* al-Bukhari examined 600,000 sayings, the majority being duplicate versions, and sifted them down to 7,275 authentic ones. Of these, about 2,700 are nonrepititious. Limited by space constraints, he remarks that he left out other sayings that he believed were authentic. The sayings are topically categorized in 97 books, with some longer sayings split and categorized into two distinct topical divisions. The second most revered collection is that by Muslim ibn al-Hajjaj (d. 875), who examined 300,000 traditions and reduced them to 4,000. A student of al-Bukhari, al-Hajjaj is thought to have been more critical in deeming a saying "authentic" and, unlike his teacher, presents the longer sayings in their integrated form. The remaining four collections (or *Sunan*) were compiled by Abu Dawud (d. 886), at-Tirmidhi (d. 892), an-Nasa'i (d. 915), and Ibn Majah (d. 886).[3] Of the six *Hadith* collections, those by al-Bukhari, Muslim al-Hajjaj and Dawud have been made available in English translation. Three Shi'a collections, called *akhbar* (as opposed to *Hadith*) are traditionally thought to originate with Ali and the Imams (Ja'far al-Sadiq in particular). Larger than the Sunni collections, they were compiled by al-Kafi of al-Kulini (d. 939) (whose collection is the most widely respected), al-Qummi (d. 991), and al-Tusi (d. 1067).

Hadith sayings are in two parts. First is the story itself (*matn*), and second is a list of names constituting the chain of sources which establish the story's authenticity (*isnad*). The stories themselves are of two types. The first, called sacred *Hadith* (*Hadith qudsi*), contain divine revelations similar to those in the Qur'an. The second, called noble *Hadith* (*Hadith sharif*), relate to Muhammad's personal life and nonprophetic utterances. For *Hadith* compilers, a story's authenticity rested on the integrity of each person mentioned in the chain of sources. A discipline emerged that critically scrutinized the lives of the transmitters. According to the norms of this field of study, even an otherwise authentic statement that bears a faulty chain of transmitters should be regarded as inauthentic. Muslims agree that many of the *Hadith* were invented in the early days of Islam to answer questions of law, support religious factions, or serve political needs in struggles for power. Thousands were rejected early on for this very reason. An early *Hadith* scholar was even executed for confessing he fabricated 4,000 sayings for financial gain. Critical *Hadith* scholarship is still in its infancy, however, and judgment regarding the extent of their authenticity must be postponed.

Sectarian Writings

Muslim sectarian writings are voluminous, and the lines distinguishing sacred texts from works of mere theology are often blurred. Writings from the various schools of Islamic law are particularly respected. Foundational works in the *Hanafite* school are *The Book of Roots* by Muhammad ibn al-Hasan al-Shaybani (d. 805) and the *Hidaya* by Burhan al-Din al-Marghinani (d. 1197). From the Malikite school there is the *Muwatta* by Malik ibn Anas (712–795), the school's founder. From the Shafi'ite tradition there is the *Rasala* by al-Shafi'i (767–820), founder of the school. Finally, from the Hanbalite school there is the *Musnad* by founder ibn Hanbal (780–855), and the *Kitab -al-'Umada* by Ibn Qudama (1146–1223).

There are also a number of important writings by Sufis, that is, Islamic mystics whose writings emphasize mystical union with Allah. Key writers among the Sufis include: Rabi'a al-'Adawiya (717–801), a freed slave girl whose writings stress the intense love of Allah; al-Ghazali (1058–1111), a scholar of Islamic Law; and ibn-al-Arabi (1165–1240), a Spanish-born metaphysician. The most widely influential Sufi writer is Jalal ad-Din ar-Rumi (1207-1273). Rumi's six book *Masnawi*, sometimes refereed to as the "Qur'an in Persian," is a compendium of lyric poetry and stories allegorizing Sufi doctrine.

SELECTIONS FROM THE QUR'AN[4]

THE NIGHT OF POWER

Muhammad's first revelation occurred on the Night of Power *when on retreat in a cave near Mecca. It is recorded in the Clot (surah 96). An early sequel to this surah, called the Power (surah 97), celebrates Muhammad's call to prophethood on the Night of Power. Both are reprinted in the following.*

96: Clots of Blood

Recite in the name of your Lord who created—created man from clots of blood

Recite! Your Lord is the Most Bountiful One, who by the pen taught man what he did not know.

Indeed, man transgresses in thinking himself his own master: for to your Lord all things return.

Observe the man who rebukes Our servant when he prays.

Think: does he follow the right guidance or enjoin true piety?

Think: if he denies the Truth and gives no heed, does he not know that God observes all things?

No. Let him desist, or We will drag him by the forelock, his lying, sinful forelock.

Then let him call his helpmates. We, in Our turn, will call the guards of Hell.

No, never obey him! Prostrate yourself and come nearer.

97: Qadr (Glory)

We revealed this on the Night of Qadr. Would that you knew what the Night of Qadr is like!

Better is the Night of Qadr than a thousand months.

On that night the angels and the Spirit by their Lord's leave come down with each decree.

That night is peace, till break of dawn.

[*surah* 96, 97]

DIVINE JUDGMENT

After his call to prophethood, Muhammad lived in Mecca for about 12 years, trying to convince his fellow citizens to worship only Allah. As illustrated in the following four early Meccan surahs, *Muhammad's earliest revelations were short, poetic declamations about punishment in hell for unbelievers. Since the context of most of the Meccan revelations was quickly lost, it is not known who the specific offenders were who incited these harsh condemnations.*

101: The Disaster

The disaster! What is the Disaster?

Would that you knew what the Disaster is!

On that day men shall become like scattered moths and the mountains like tufts of carded wool.

Then he whose scales are heavy shall dwell in bliss; but he whose scales are light, the Abyss shall be his home

Would that you knew what this is like!

It is a scorching fire.

102: Worldly Gain

Your hearts are taken up with worldly gain from the cradle to the grave.

But you shall know. You shall before long come to know.

Indeed, if you knew the truth with certainty, you would see the fire of Hell: you would see it with your very eyes.

Then, on that day, you shall be questioned about your joys.

103: The Declining Day

I swear by the declining day that perdition shall be the lot of man, except for those who have faith and do good works; who exhort each other to justice and to fortitude.

104: The Slanderer

Woe to every back-biting slanderer who amasses riches and sedulously hoards them, thinking his wealth will render him immortal!

By no means! He shall be flung to the Destroying Flame.

Would that you knew what the Destroying Flame is like!

It is God's own kindled fire, which will rise up to the hearts of men. It will close upon them from every side, in towering columns.

[*surahs* 101–104]

THE OPENING

The opening surah *of the Qur'an is the most commonly repeated prayer in Islam and an integral part of worship. Scholars give it an early date from about the fourth year of Muhammad's Meccan mission.*

> Praise be to God, Lord of the Universe,
> The compassionate, the Merciful,
> Sovereign of the Day of Judgment!
> You alone we worship, and to You alone we turn for help.
> Guide us to the straight path,
> The path of those whom You have favoured,
> Not of those who have incurred Your wrath,
> Nor of those who have gone astray.

[*surah* 1]

EVILS OF IDOLATRY

The overriding theme of Muhammad's message while in Mecca was the rejection of idolatry and commitment to Allah. The following selection from Jonah (surah 10), *a late Meccan* surah, *describes how idolaters forfeit paradise and are blind to the powers of the creator.*

God invites you to the Home of Peace. He guides whom He will to a straight path. Those that do good works shall have a good reward, and more besides. Neither blackness nor misery shall overcast their faces. They are the heirs of Paradise: in it they shall abide for ever.

As for those that have doe evil, evil shall be rewarded with like evil. Misery will oppress them (they shall have none to protect them from God), as though patches of the night's own darkness veiled their faces. They are the heirs of Hell: in it they shall abide for ever.

On the day We assemble them all together, We shall say to the idolaters: 'Keep to your places, you had your idols!' We will separate them one from another, and then their idols will say to them: 'It was not us that you worshipped. God is our all-sufficient witness. Nor were we aware of your worship.'

Thereupon each soul will know what it has done. They shall be sent back to God, their true Lord, and the idols they invented will forsake them.

Say: 'Who provides for you from heaven and earth? Who has endowed you with sight and hearing? Who brings forth the living from the dead, and the dead from the living? Who ordains all things?'

They will reply: 'God'

Say: 'Will you not take heed, then? Such is God, your true Lord. That which is not true must needs be false. How then can you turn away from Him?'

Thus is the Word of your Lord made good. The evil-doers have no faith.

Say: 'Can any of your idols conceive Creation, then renew it?' Say: 'God conceives Creation, then renews it. How is it that you are so misled?'

Say: 'Can any of your idols guide you to the truth?' Say: 'God can guide you to the truth. Who is more worthy to be followed: He that can guide to the truth, or he that cannot and is himself in need of guidance? What has come over you that you so judge?'

Most of them follow nothing but mere conjecture. But conjecture is in no way a substitute for truth. God is cognizant of all their actions.

[*surah* 10:26–37]

EARLY PROPHETS

The Qur'an states that every nation has its prophet (surah 13:7). About 30 prophets who preceded Muhammad are mentioned. Most of these are also mentioned in the Bible. The prophets typically spoke to unreceptive idolatrous people, and Allah subsequently destroyed the idolaters for their continued disbelief. The hillsides are scattered with the ruins of the idolater's cities as monuments to their recalcitrance. As Muhammad's own prophetic message was met with disbelief and hostility, he warned the Meccans of the consequences. During Muhammad's late Meccan period of revelation, detailed accounts of early prophets are prominent. Surah 11, titled Hud, recounts the stories of Noah, Hud, Salih, Abraham, Lot, Shu'aib, and Moses. Noah, Abraham, Lot, and Moses are from Jewish tradition. The Qur'an's account of these prophets differs from biblical accounts, explaining in surah 6:91 that the Jews suppressed much of Moses' revelation and that Muhammad is revealing new information. Unique to Qur'anic tradition, Hud, Salih, and Shu'aib, are prophets sent by Allah to the Arabs.

[*HUD.*] To Ad We sent their compatriot Hud. He said: 'Server God, my people; you have no god but Him. False are your inventions. I demand of you no recompense, my people, for none can reward me except my Creator. Will you not understand?

'My people, seek forgiveness of your Lord and turn to Him in repentance. He will send from the sky abundant rain upon you; He will add strength to your strength. Do not turn away from Him with wrongdoing.'

They replied: 'Hud, you have given us no clear proof. We will not forsake our gods at your behest, nor will we believe in you. We can only suppose that our gods have afflicted you with evil.'

He said: 'God is my witness, and you are my witnesses too: I am done with your idols. Scheme against me if you will, and give me no respite. I have put my trust in God, my Lord and your Lord. There is not a living creature on the earth whose destiny He does not control. Straight is the path of my Lord.

'If you give no heed, I have made known to you my message, and my Lord will replace you by other men. You will in no way harm Him. My Lord is watching over all things.'

And when our judgment came to pass, We delivered Hud through Our mercy, together with those who shared his faith. We delivered them from a horrifying scourge.

Such were Ad. They denied the revelations of their Lord, disobeyed His apostles, and did the bidding of every headstrong reprobate. Cursed were they in this world, and cursed they shall be on the Day of Resurrection.

Ad denied their Lord. Gone are Ad, the people of Hud.

[*SALIH.*] And to Thamud We sent compatriot Salih. He said: 'Serve God, my people; you have no god but Him. It was He who brought you into being from the earth and gave you means to dwell upon it. Seek forgiveness of him, and turn to Him in repentance. My Lord is near at hand and answers all.'

'Salih,' they replied, 'great were the hopes we placed in you. Would you now forbid us to serve the gods our fathers worshipped? Truly, we strongly doubt the faith to which you call us.'

He said: 'Do but consider, my people! If my Lord has revealed to me His will and bestowed on me His grace, who would protect me from God if I rebelled against Him? You would surely aggravate my ruin.

'My people, here is God's she-camel, a sign for you. Leave her to graze at will in God's own land, and do not molest her lest an instant scourge should fall upon you.'

Yet they slew her. He said: 'You have but three days to live in your dwellings. This prophecy shall not prove false.'

And when Our judgment came to pass, We delivered Salih through Our mercy from the ignominy of that day, together with those who shared his faith. Mighty is your Lord and all-powerful. A dreadful cry rang above the evil-doers, and when morning came they were prostrate in their dwellings, as though they had never prospered there.

[*Abraham and Lot.*] Our messengers came to Abraham with good news. They said 'Peace!' 'Peace!' he answered, and hastened to bring them a roasted calf. But when he saw their hands being withheld from it, he mistrusted them and was afraid of them. They said: 'Have no fear. We are sent forth to the people of Lot.'

His wife, who was standing by, laughed. We bade her rejoice in Isaac, and in Jacob after him.

'Alas!' she replied. 'How shall I bear a child when I am old and my husband is well-advanced in years? This is indeed a strange thing.'

They replied: 'Do you marvel at the ways of God? May God's mercy and blessings be upon you, dear hosts! Worthy of praise is He and glorious.'

And when fear left him as he pondered the good news, Abraham pleaded with Us for the people of Lot. Abraham was gracious, tenderhearted, and devout.

We said; 'Abraham, plead no more. Your Lord's will must needs be done. Irrevocable is the scourge which shall smite them.'

And when Our messengers came to Lot, he grew anxious about them, for he was powerless to offer them protection. 'This is indeed a day of woe,' he said.

His people, long addicted to evil practices, came running towards him. 'My people,' he said, 'here are my daughters: surely they are more wholesome to you. Fear God, and do not humiliate me by insulting my guests. Is there not one good man among you?'

They replied: "You know we have no need of your daughters. You know full well what we are seeking.'

He cried: 'Would that I had strength enough to overcome you, or could find refuge in some mighty man!'

They said: 'Lot, we are the messengers of your Lord: They shall not touch you. Depart with your kinsfolk in the dead of night and let none of you turn back, except your wife. She shall suffer the fate of the others. In the morning their hour will come. Is not the morning near?'

And when Our judgment came to pass, We turned their city upside down and let loose upon it a shower of clay-stones bearing the tokens of your Lord. The punishment of the unjust was not far off.

[*Shu'aib.*] And to the people of Midian We sent their compatriot Shu'aib. He said: 'Serve God, my people; you have no god but Him. Do not give short weight or measure. Prosperous though you are, beware the torment of a fateful day!

'My people, give just weight and measure in all fairness. Do not defraud your fellow men of their possessions, nor shall you corrupt the land with evil. Better for you is God's reward, if you are true believers. I am not your keeper.'

'Shu'aib,' they replied, 'did your prayers teach you that we should renounce the gods of our fathers and not conduct our affairs in the manner we pleased? Truly, you are a wise and gracious man!'

He said: 'Do but consider, my people! If my Lord has revealed to me His will and bestowed on me a gracious gift, should I not guide you? I do not wish to argue with you, only to practice what I forbid you. I seek only to reform you: as far as I am able. Nor can I succeed without God's help. In Him I have put my trust and to Him I turn in repentance.

'Let your dispute with me not bring upon you the doom which overtook the peoples of Noah, Hud, and Salih; nor is it long since the tribe of Lot was punished. Seek forgiveness of your lord and turn to Him in repentance. Merciful and loving is my Lord.'

They replied: 'Shu'aib, much of what you say we cannot comprehend. We know how weak you are in our midst. But for our tribe, we should have stoned you. You shall on no account prevail against us.'

He said: 'My people, have you more regard for my tribe than for God? Dare you turn you backs upon Him? My Lord has knowledge of all your actions. Do what you will, my people, and so will I. You shall know who will be punished and held up to shame, and who is lying. Wait if you will; I too am waiting.'

And when our judgment was carried out We delivered Shu'aib through Our mercy, together with those who shared his faith. A dreadful cry overtook the evil-doers, and when morning came they were prostrate in their dwellings, as though they had never prospered there. Like Thamud, gone are the people of Midian.

[*Moses.*] We sent forth Moses with Our signs and with clear authority to Pharaoh and his nobles. But they followed the behests of their master; misguided were Pharaoh's behests. He shall stand at the head of his people on the Day of Resurrection, and shall lead them into the Fire. Dismal is the place they shall be led to.

A curse followed them in this world, and a curse shall follow them on the Day of Resurrection. Evil is the gift they shall receive.

We have recounted to you the annals of these nations: some have survived, while others have ceased to exist. We did not wrong them, but they wronged themselves. The gods they called on besides God availed them nothing: and when your Lord's will was done, they only added to their ruin.

Such was the scourge you Lord visited upon the nations while they sinned. Harrowing and relentless is His scourge.

Surely in this there is a sign for him that dreads the torment of the hereafter. On that day all men shall be assembled. That shall be a fateful day.

We shall defer it only to its appointed hour. And when that day arrives, no man shall speak but by His leave. Some shall be damned, and others shall be blessed. The damned shall abide as long as the heavens and the earth endure, unless our Lord ordain otherwise: your Lord shall accomplish what he will. As for the blessed, they shall abide in Paradise as long as the heavens and the earth endure, unless your Lord ordain otherwise. Theirs shall be an endless recompense.

Have no doubt as to what they worship. They serve the idols which their fathers served before them. We shall requite them in full measure.

We gave the Book to Moses, but differences arose about it. And but for a Word from your Lord, already decreed, their fate would have been long sealed. Yet they strongly doubt this.

[*surah* 11:50–110]

RESURRECTION OF THE DEAD

Muhammad met with resistance concerning the concept of the bodily resurrection of the dead. In the following, from two late Meccan surahs, he makes this doctrine more palpable by offering analogies to bodily resurrection, and also by illustrating Allah's power, which implies Allah's ability to resurrect even dead bodies.

22:5–10. Men, if you doubt the Resurrection remember that We first created you from dust, then from a living germ, then from a clot of blood, and them from a half-formed lump of flesh, so that We might manifest to you Our power.

We cause to remain in the womb whatever We please for an appointed term, and then We bring you forth as infants, that you may grow up and reach your prime. Some die young, and some live on to abject old age when all that they once know they know no more.

You sometimes see the earth dry and barren: but no sooner do We send down rain upon it than it begins to stir and swell, putting forth every kind of radiant bloom. That is because God is Truth: He resurrects the dead and has power over all things.

The Hour of Doom is sure to come—in this there is no doubt. Those who are in the grave God will raise to life.

Some wrangle about God, though they have neither knowledge nor guidance nor divine revelation. They turn away in scorn and lead others astray from God's path. Such men shall incur disgrace in this life and taste the torment of Hell on the Day of Resurrection. 'This,' We shall say, 'is the reward of your misdeeds. God is not unjust to His servants.'

23:12–22. We first created man from an essence of clay: then placed him, a living germ, in a safe enclosure [i.e., the womb]. The germ We made a clot of blood, and the clot a lump of flesh. This We fashioned into bones, then clothed the bones with flesh, thus bringing forth another creation. Blessed be God the noblest of creators.

You shall surely die hereafter, and be restored to life on the Day of Resurrection. We have created seven heavens above you; of Our creation We are never heedless.

We sent down water from the sky in due measure, and lodged it into the earth. But if We please, We can take it all away.

With it We caused vineyards and palm-groves to spring up, yielding abundant fruit for your sustenance. The tree which on Mount Sinai grows gives oil and a condiment for men.

In the cattle, too, you have an example of Our power. You drink of that which is in their bellies, you eat their flesh, and gain other benefits from them besides. By them, as by the ships that sail the sea, you are carried.

[*surahs* 22:5–10; 23:12–22]

THE REVEALED QUR'AN

As Muhammad's revelations grew to a sizable collection within a few years, the Qur'an itself frequently became a subject of further revelation. A middle Meccan surah recounts, "We have divided the Qur'an into sections so that you may recite it to the people with deliberation. We have imparted it by gradual revelation" (surah 17:106). Another states, "We have revealed the Qur'an in the Arabic tongue that you may understand its meaning. It is a transcript of the eternal book in our keeping, sublime, and full of wisdom" (surah 43:3–4). In a late Meccan surah, Muhammad's illiteracy is offered as proof that the Qur'an was divinely revealed (surah 29:48). The following from Jonah (surah 10), of the late Meccan period, discusses the fate of those who deny the divine authority of the Qur'an.

. . . These are the verses of the Wise Book: Does it seem strange to mankind that We revealed Our will to a mortal from among themselves, saying: 'Give warning to mankind, and proclaim good tidings to the faithful: their endeavors shall be rewarded by their Lord?'

The unbelievers say: 'This man [i.e., Muhammad] is a skilled enchanter.' Yet your Lord is God, who in six days created the heavens and the earth and then ascended His throne, ordaining all things. None has power to intercede for you, except him who has received His sanctions. Such is God, your Lord: therefore serve Him. Will you not take heed?

To Him you shall all return: God's promise shall be fulfilled. He gives being to all His creatures, and in the end he will bring them back to life, so that he may justly reward those who have believed in Him and done good works. As for the unbelievers, they shall drink scalding water and be sternly punished for their unbelief. . . .

When Our clear revelations are recited to them, those who entertain no hope of meeting Us say to you: 'Give us a different Koran, or make some changes in it.'

Say: 'Had God pleased, I would never have recited it to you, nor would he have made you aware of it. A whole lifetime I dwelt among you before it was revealed. Will you not understand?'

Who is more wicked than the man who invents a falsehood about God or denies His revelations? Truly, the evil-doer shall not triumph. . . .

This Koran could not have been devised by any but God. It confirms what was revealed before it and fully explains the Scriptures. It is beyond doubt from the Lord of the Universe.

If they say: 'He invented it himself,' say: 'Bring me one chapter like it. Call on whom you may besides God to help you, if what you say be true!'

Indeed, they disbelieve what they cannot grasp, for they have not yet seen its prophecy fulfilled. Likewise did those who passed before them disbelieve. But see what was the end of the wrongdoers.

Some believe in it, while others do not. But your Lord best knows the evil-doers.

[*surah* 10:2–4, 16–18, 38–41]

LAWS

In 622 Muhammad and his early followers migrated to Medina, where he became the city administrator. The focus of his revelations soon shifted from being a lone defender of monotheism to his being a lawgiver. The following selections from the Cow (surah 2) present laws concerning drinking, gambling, orphans, divorce, weaning, widows, and dowries.

They ask you about drinking and gambling. Say: 'There is great harm in both, although they have some benefits for men; but their harm is far greater than their benefits.'

They ask you what they should give in alms. Say: 'What you can spare.' Thus God makes plain to you His revelations so that you may reflect upon this world and the hereafter.

They question you concerning orphans. Say: 'To deal justly with them is best. If you mix their affairs with yours, remember they are your brothers. God knows the just from the unjust. If God pleased, he could afflict you. He is mighty and wise.'

You shall not wed pagan women, unless they embrace the Faith. A believing slave-girl is better than an idolatress, although she may please you. Nor shall you wed idolaters, unless they embrace the Faith. A believing slave is better than an idolater, although she may please you. These call you to hell-fire; but God calls you, by his will, to Paradise and forgiveness. He makes plain His revelations to Mankind, so that they may take heed.

They ask you about menstruation. Say: 'It is an indisposition. Keep aloof from women during their menstrual periods and do not touch them until they are clean again. Then have intercourse with them in the way God enjoined you. God loves those that turn to Him in repentance and strive to keep themselves clean.'

Women are your fields: go, then, into your fields whence you please. Do good works and fear God. Bear in mind that you shall meet Him. Give good tidings to the believers.

Do not make God, when you swear by Him, a means to prevent you from dealing justly, from guarding yourselves against evil, and from making peace among men. God knows all and hears all. God will not call you to account from that which is inadvertent in your oaths. But He will take you to task for that which is intended in your hearts. God is forgiving and lenient.

Those that renounce their wives on oath must wait four months. If they change their minds, God is forgiving and merciful; but if they decide to divorce them, know that God hears all and knows all.

Divorced women must wait, keeping themselves from men, three menstrual courses. It is unlawful for them, if they believe in God and the Last Day, to hide what God has created in their wombs; in which case their husbands would do well to take them back, should they desire reconciliation.

Women shall with justice have rights similar to those exercised against them, although men have a status above women. God is mighty and wise.

Divorce[5] may be pronounced twice, and then a woman must be retained in honor or allowed to go with kindness. It is unlawful for husbands to take from them anything they have given them, unless both fear that they may not be able to keep within the bounds set by God; in which case it shall be no offense for either of them if the wife ransom herself.

These are the bounds set by God; do not transgress them. Those that transgress the bounds of God are wrongdoers.

If a man divorces his wife,[6] he cannot remarry her until she has wedded another man and been divorced by him; in which case it shall be no offense for either of them to return to the other, if they think that they can keep within the bounds set by God.

Such are the bounds of God. He makes them plain to men of understanding.

When you have renounced your wives and they have reached the end of their waiting period, either retain them in honor or let them go with kindness. But you shall not retain them in order to harm them or to wrong them. Whoever does this wrongs his own soul.

Do not make game of God's revelations. Remember the favors God has bestowed upon you, and the book and the wisdom He has revealed for your instruction. Fear God and know God has knowledge of all things.

If a man has renounced his wife and she has reached the end of her waiting period, do not prevent her from remarrying her husband if they have come to an honorable agreement. This is enjoined on every one of you who believes in God and the Last Day; it is more honorable for you and more chaste. God knows, but you do not.

Mothers shall give such to their children for two whole years if the father wishes the sucking to be completed. They must be maintained and clothed in a reasonable manner by the child's father. None should be charged with more than one can bear. A mother should not be allowed to suffer on account of her child, nor should a father on account of his child. The same duties devolve upon the father's heir. But if, after consultation, they choose by mutual consent to wean the child, they shall incur no guilt. Nor shall it be any offense for you if you prefer to have a nurse for your children, provided that you pay her what you promise, according to usage. Have fear of God and know that God is cognizant of all your actions.

Widows shall wait, keeping themselves apart from men, for four months and ten days after their husband's death. When they have reached the end of their waiting period, it shall be no offense for you to let them do whatever they choose for themselves, provided that it is decent. God is cognizant of all your actions.

It shall be no offense for you openly to propose marriage to such women or to cherish them in your hearts. God knows that you will remember them. Do not arrange to meet them in secret, and if you do, speak to them honorably. But you shall not consummate the marriage before the end of the waiting period. Know that God has knowledge of all your thoughts. Therefore take heed and bear in mind that God is forgiving and lenient.

It shall be no offense for you to divorce your wives before the marriage is consummated or the dowry settled. Provide for them with fairness; the rich man according to his means and the poor man according to his. This is binding on the righteous men. If you divorce them before the marriage is consummated, but after their dowry has been settled, give them the half of their dowry, unless they or the husband agree to waive it. But it is more proper that the husband should waive it. Do not forget to show kindness to each other. God observes your actions.

Attend regularly to your prayers, including the middle prayer, and stand up with all devotion before God. When you are exposed to danger pray on foot or while riding; and when you are restored to safety remember God, as He has taught you what you did not know.

You shall bequeath your widows a year's maintenance without causing them to leave their homes; but if they leave of their own accord, no blame shall be attached to you for any course they may deem fit to pursue. God is mighty and wise. Reasonable provisions shall also be made for divorced women. That is incumbent on righteous men.

[*surah* 2:219–241]

TREATMENT OF WOMEN

In spite of contemporary criticism of the treatment of women in Muslim societies, Islam introduced women's rights where virtually none existed previously. Before Muhammad, women were essentially property, with no inheritance rights, and often buried alive in infancy. Marriage contracts were loose, and often temporary. Muhammad condemned infanticide and required that daughters be given a share of inheritance. In matters of marriage, adultery was denounced, women were allowed the right of consent for marriage, and divorce became more difficult. Written about 626, the following selections from Women (surah 4) are laws pertaining to women and include some of these reforms.

. . . God has thus enjoined you concerning your children:

A male shall inherit twice as much as a female. If there be more than two girls, they shall have two-thirds of the inheritance; but if there be one only, she shall inherit the half. Parents shall inherit a sixth each, if the deceased have a child; but if he leave no child and his parents be his heirs, his mother shall have a third. If he have brothers, his mother shall have a sixth after payment of any legacy he may have bequeathed or any debt he may have owed.

You may wonder whether your parents or your children are more beneficial to you. But this is the law of God; God is all-knowing and wise.

You shall inherit the half of your wives' estate if they die childless. If they leave children, a quarter of their estate shall be yours after payment of any legacy they may have bequeathed or any debt they may have owed.

Your wives shall inherit one quarter of your estate if you die childless. If you leave children, they shall inherit one eighth, after payment of any legacy you may have bequeathed or any debt you may have owed.

If a man or a woman leave neither children nor parents and have a brother or a sister, they shall each inherit one-sixth. If there be more, they shall equally share the third of the estate, after payment of any legacy he may have bequeathed or any debt he may have owed, without prejudice to the rights of the heirs. That is a commandment from God. God is all-knowing, and gracious.

Such are the bounds set by God. He that obeys God and His apostle shall dwell for ever in gardens watered by running streams. That is the supreme triumph. But he that defies God and His apostle and transgresses His bounds, shall be cast into a Fire wherein he will abide for ever. A shameful punishment awaits him.

If any of your women commit fornication, call in four witnesses from among yourselves against them; if they testify to their guilt confine them to their houses till death overtakes them or till God finds another way for them.

If two men among you commit indecency, punish them both. If they repent and mend their ways, let them be. God is forgiving and merciful.

God forgives those who commit evil in ignorance and then quickly turns to Him in repentance. God will pardon them. God is all-knowing and wise. But He will not forgive those who do evil and, when death comes to them, say: 'Now we repent!' Nor those who die unbelievers: for them We have prepared a woeful scourge.

Believers, it is unlawful for you to inherit the women of your deceased kinsmen against their will, or to bar them from re-marrying, in order that you may force them to give up a part of what you have given them, unless they be guilty of a proven crime. Treat them with kindness; for even if you dislike them, it may well be that you dislike a thing which God has meant for your own abundant good.

If you wish to replace a wife with another, do not take from her the dowry you have given her even if it be a talent of gold. That would be improper and grossly unjust; for how can you take it back when you have lain with each other and entered into a firm contract?

You shall not marry the women whom your fathers married: all previous such marriages excepted. That was an evil practice, indecent and abominable.

Forbidden to you are your mothers, your daughters, your sisters, your paternal and maternal aunts, the daughters of your brothers and sisters, your foster-mothers, your foster sisters, the mothers of your wives, your step-daughters who are in your charge, born of the wives with whom you have lain (it is no offense for you to marry your step-daughters if you have not consummated your marriage with their mothers), and the wives of your own begotten sons. You are also forbidden to take in marriage two sisters at one and the same time: all previous such marriages excepted. God is forgiving and merciful. Also married women, except those whom you own as slaves. Such is the decree of God. All women other than these are lawful to you, provided you seek them with your wealth in modest conduct, not in fornication. Give them their dowry for the enjoyment you have had of them as a duty; but it shall be no offense for you to make any other agreement among yourselves after you have fulfilled your duty. God is all-knowing and wise.

If any one of you cannot afford to marry a free believing woman, let him marry a slave-girl who is a believer (God best knows your faith: you are born one of another). Marry them with the permission of their masters and give them their dowry in all justice, provided they are honorable and chaste and have not entertained other men. If after marriage they commit adultery, they shall suffer half the penalty inflicted upon free adulteresses. Such is the law for those of you who fear to commit sin: but if you abstain, it will be better for you. God is forgiving and merciful. . . .

Men have authority over women because God has made the one superior to the other, and because they spend their wealth to maintain them. Good women are obedient. They guard their unseen parts because God has guarded them. As for those from whom you fear disobedience, admonish them and send them to beds apart and beat them. Then if they obey you, take no further action against them. God is high, supreme.

If you fear a breach between a man and his wife, appoint an arbiter from his people and another from hers. If they wish to be reconciled God will bring them together again. God is all-knowing and wise. . . .

They consult you concerning women. Say: 'God has instructed you about them, and so have the verses proclaimed to you in the Book, concerning the orphan girls whom you deny their lawful rights and refuse to marry; also regarding helpless children. He has instructed you to deal justly with orphans. God has knowledge of all the good you do.'

If a woman fear ill-treatment or desertion on the part of her husband, it shall be no offense for them to seek a mutual agreement, for agreement is best. Man is prone to avarice. But if you do what is right and guard yourselves against evil, know then that God is cognizant of all your actions.

Try as you may, you cannot treat all your wives impartially. Do not set yourself altogether against any of them, leaving her, as it were, in suspense. If you do what is right and guard yourselves against evil, you will find God forgiving and merciful. If they separate, God will compensate both out of His own abundance: God is munificent and wise. . . .

[*surah* 4:11–25, 34–35, 127–130]

JESUS THE PROPHET

According to the Qur'an, Jesus is a highly exalted prophet who was born of a virgin, performed miracles, delivered God's message, and will return at the end of time. However, the Qur'an denies the reality of the crucifixion, implying that it was either an illusion or someone else was substituted. More significantly, it denies the Trinity and the divine nature of Jesus, as seen in the following selection from the Table (surah 5), written about 629.

. . . One day God will gather all the apostles and ask them: 'How were you received?' They will reply: "We have no knowledge. You alone know what is hidden.' God will say: 'Jesus, son of Mary, remember the favor I have bestowed on you and on your mother: how I strengthened you with the Holy Spirit, so that you preached to men in your cradle and in the prime of manhood; how I instructed you in the Book and in wisdom, in the Torah and in the Gospel; how by My leave you fashioned from clay the likeness of a bird and breathed into it so that, by My leave, it became a living bird; how, by My leave, you healed the blind man and the leper, and by my leave restored the dead to life; how I protected you from the Israelites when you had come to them with clear signs: when those of them who disbelieved declared: "This is but plain sorcery"; how when I enjoined the disciples to believe in Me and in My apostle they replied: "We believe; bear witness that we submit."'

'Jesus, son of Mary,' said the disciples, 'can your Lord send down to us from heaven a table spread with food?'

He replied: 'Have fear of God, if you are true believers.'

'We wish to eat of it,' they said, 'so that we may reassure our hearts and know that what you said to us is true, and that we may be witnesses of it.'

'Lord,' said Jesus, the son of Mary, 'send down to us from heaven a table spread with food, that it may mark a feast for us and for those that will come after us: a sign from You. Give us our sustenance; You are the best provider.'

God replied: 'I am sending one to you. But whoever of you disbelieves hereafter shall be punished as no man will ever be punished.'

Then God will say: 'Jesus, son of Mary, did you ever say to mankind; "Worship me and my mother as gods besides God?"'

'Glory to You,' he will answer, 'how could I ever say that to which I have no right? If I had ever said so, You would have surely known it. You know what is in my mind, but I know not what is in Yours. You alone know what is hidden. I told them only what You bade me. I said: "Serve God, my Lord and your Lord." I watched over them while living in their midst, and ever since You took me to Yourself, You have been watching over them. You are the witness of all things. If You punish them, they surely are Your servants; and if You forgive them, surely You are mighty and wise.'

God will say: 'This is the day when their truthfulness will benefit the truthful. They shall for ever dwell in gardens watered by running streams. God is pleased with them, and they are pleased with Him. That is the supreme triumph.'

God has sovereignty over the heavens and the earth and all that they contain. He has power over all things.

[*surah* 5:109–120]

UNBELIEVING PEOPLE OF THE BOOK

According to the Qur'an, certain groups of people had received revealed scriptures prior to Muhammad. These "people of the book" include the Jews, Christians, Zoroastrians, and Sabians. The Qur'an acknowledges the legitimacy of these religions, maintaining a place for such believers in the afterlife. However, many people of the book have abandoned their revealed teachings by adopting false gods and denying God's true prophets. The following selection from the Table (surah 5) admonishes the unbelieving people of the book.

. . . We have revealed the Torah, in which there is guidance and light. By it the prophets who surrendered themselves judged the Jews, and so did the rabbis and the divines, according to God's Book which had been committed to their keeping and to which they themselves were witnesses.

Have no fear of man; fear Me, and do not sell My revelations for a paltry end. Unbelievers are those who do not judge according to God's revelations.

We decreed for them a life for a life, an eye for an eye, a nose for a nose, an ear for an ear, a tooth for a tooth, and a wound for a wound. But if a man charitably forbears from retaliation, his remission shall atone for him. Transgressors are those that do not judge according to God's revelations.

After them We sent forth Jesus, the son of Mary, confirming the Torah already revealed, and gave him the Gospel in which there is guidance and light, corroborating what was revealed before it in the Torah, a guide and an admonition to the righteous. Therefore let those who follow the Gospel judge according to what God has revealed therein. Evil-doers are those that do not base their judgments on God's revelations. . . .

Believers, take neither Jews nor Christians for your friends. They are friends with one another. Whoever of you seeks their friendship shall become one of their number. . . .

If the People of the Book accept the true faith and keep from evil, We will pardon them their sins and admit them to the gardens of delight. If they observe the Torah and the Gospel and what is revealed to them from their Lord, they shall enjoy abundance from above and from beneath.

There are some among them who are righteous men; but there are many among them who do nothing but evil.

Apostle, proclaim what is revealed to you from your Lord; if you do not, you will surely fail to convey His message. God will protect you from all men. God does not guide the unbelievers.

Say: 'People of the Book, you will attain nothing until you observe the Torah and the Gospel and that which is revealed to you from your Lord.'

That which is revealed to you from your Lord will surely increase the wickedness and unbelief of many of them. But do not grieve for the unbelievers.

Believers, Jews, Sabaeans and Christians—whoever believes in God and the Last Day and does what is right shall have nothing to fear or to regret.

We made a covenant with the Israelites and sent forth apostles among them. But whenever an apostle came to them with a message that did not suit their fancies, some they accused of lying and others they put to death. They thought no harm would follow: they were blind and deaf. God turned to them in mercy, but many again were blind and deaf. God is ever watching their actions.

Unbelievers are those that say: 'God is the messiah, the son of Mary.' For the Messiah himself said: 'Children of Israel, serve God, my Lord and your Lord.' He that worships other gods besides God, God will deny him Paradise, and Hell shall be his home. None shall help the evil-doers.

Unbelievers are those that say: 'God is one of three.' There is but one God. If they do not desist from so saying, those of them that disbelieve shall be sternly punished.

Will they not turn to God in repentance and seek forgiveness of Him? God is forgiving and merciful.

The Messiah, the son of Mary, was no more than an apostle: other apostles passed away before him. His mother was a saintly woman. They both ate earthly food.

See how We make plain to them Our revelations. See how they ignore the truth.

Say: 'Will you serve instead of God that which can neither harm nor help you? God is He who hears all and knows all.'

Say: 'People of the Book! Do not transgress the bounds of truth in your religion. Do not yield to the desires of those who have erred before; who have led many astray and have themselves strayed from the even path.'

Those of the Israelites who disbelieved were cursed by David and Jesus, the son of Mary, because they rebelled and committed evil. Nor did they censure themselves for any wrong they did. Evil were their deeds.

[*surah* 5:44–48, 51, 65–78]

FIVE PILLARS OF ISLAM

The primary ritual requirements of Islam are known as the Five Pillars of Islam (arkan ad-din). *They are (1) sincerely uttering the creed, "there is no God but Allah, and Muhammad is his messenger"* (shahada), *(2) praying five times a day facing Mecca* (salat), *(3) paying an alms tax for the needy* (zakat), *(4) fasting during the month of Ramadan* (sawm), *and (5) making a pilgrimage to Mecca once in one's life, if possible* (hajj). *Each of these has its foundation in the Qur'an. Elements of the first pillar, the creed, are found in* surahs 37:35, 47:19, and 48:29. *The remaining four pillars are discussed in the following selections from the Cow* (surah 2) *from the late Medinan period.*

[**Prayer.**] Many a time have We seen you turn your face towards heaven. We will make you turn towards a *qiblah* that will please you. Turn your face towards the Holy Mosque; wherever you be, turn your faces towards it.

Those to whom the Scriptures were given know this to be the truth from their Lord. God is never heedless of what they do. But even if you gave them every proof they would not accept your *qiblah,* nor would you accept theirs; nor would any of them accept the *qiblah* of the other. If, after all the knowledge you have been given, you yield to their desires, then you will surely become an evil-doer.

Those to whom We gave the Scriptures know Our apostle as they know their own sons. But some of them deliberately conceal the truth. This is the truth from your Lord: therefore never doubt it.

Each one has a goal towards which he turns. But wherever you be, emulate one another in good works. God will bring you all before Him. God has power over all things.

Whichever way you depart, face towards the Holy Mosque. This is surely the truth from your Lord. God is never heedless of what you do.

Whichever way you depart, face towards the Holy Mosque: and wherever you are, face towards it, so that men will have no cause to reproach you, except the evil-doers among them. Have no fear of them; fear Me, so that I may perfect My favor to you and that you may be rightly guided. . . .

[*Fasting.*] Believers, fasting is decreed for you as it was decreed for those before you; perchance you will guard yourselves against evil. Fast a certain number of days, but if any one among you is ill or on a journey, let him fast a similar number of days later; and for those that cannot endure it there is a ransom: the feeding of a poor man. He that does good of his own accord shall be well rewarded; but to fast is better for you, if you but knew it.

In the month of Ramadan the Qur'an was revealed, a book of guidance with proofs of guidance distinguishing right from wrong. Therefore whoever of you is present in that month let him fast. But he who is ill or on a journey shall fast a similar number of days later on.

God desires your well-being, not your discomfort. He desires you to fast the whole month so that you may magnify Him and render thanks to Him for giving you His guidance.

When My servants question you about Me, tell them that I am near. I answer the prayer of the suppliant when he calls to Me; therefore let them answer My call and put their trust in Me, that they may be rightly guided.

It is now lawful for you to lie with your wives on the night of the fast; they are a comfort to you as you are to them. God know that you were deceiving yourselves. He has relented towards you and pardoned you. Therefore you may now lie with them and seek what God has ordained for you. Eat and drink until you can tell a white thread from a black one in the light of the coming dawn. Then resume the fast till nightfall and do not approach them, but stay at your prayers in the mosques.

These are the bounds set by God: do not come near them. Thus he makes known His revelations to mankind that they may guard themselves against evil. . . .

[*Alms.*] Give generously for the cause of God and do not with your own hands cast yourselves into destruction. Be charitable; God loves the charitable. . . .

[*Pilgrimage.*] Make the pilgrimage and visit the Sacred House for His sake. If you cannot, send such offerings as you can afford and do not shave your heads until the offerings have reached their destination. But if any of you is ill or suffers from an ailment of the head, he must pay a ransom either by fasting or by almsgiving or by offering a sacrifice.

If in peacetime anyone among you combines the visit with the pilgrimage, he must offer such gifts as he can afford; but if he lacks the means let him fast three days during the pilgrimage and seven when he has returned; that is, ten days in all. That is incumbent on him whose family are not present at the Holy Mosque. Have fear of God: know that he is stern in retribution.

Make a pilgrimage in the appointed months. He that intends to perform it in those months must abstain from sexual intercourse, obscene language, and acrimonious disputes while on the pilgrimage. God is aware of whatever good you do. Provide well for yourselves: the best provision is piety. Fear Me, then, you that are endowed with understanding.

It shall be no offense for you to seek the bounty of our Lord. When you come running from Arafat [near Mecca] remember God as you approach the sacred monument. Remember Him that gave you guidance when you were in error. Then go out from the place whence the pilgrims will go out and implore the forgiveness of God. He is forgiving and merciful. And when you have fulfilled your sacred duties, remember God as you remember your forefathers or with deeper reverence.

[*surah* 2:144–150, 183–187, 195–200]

JIHAD

Often called the sixth pillar of Muslim obligation, Jihad, or holy war, is struggling for Allah's cause. Islam divides the world into two abodes: the abode of submission, encompassing Muslim territories (Dar al-Islam), and the abode of struggle, encompassing non-Islamic territories (Dar al-Harb). The obligation of jihad is to extend the abode of submission through missionary activities or, when necessary, through armed force. Jihad aims at political control over societies, to govern them by the principles of Islam. In theory, forced conversion of individuals is not intended. Originally the responsibility of the Caliphs, Jihad should only be undertaken when success is likely. Although the explicit obligation of jihad first appears in the Hadith, *its foundations are laid in the Qur'an. The following selection from the Women (surah 4), written just after the unsuccessful battle of Uhud, advises Muslims who fight for Allah.*

Believers, show discernment when you go to fight for the cause of God, and do not say to those that offer you peace; 'You are not believers,'— seeking the chance of booty of this world; for with God there are abundant gains. Such was your custom in days gone by, but now God has bestowed on you His grace. Therefore show discernment; God is cognizant of all your actions.

The believers who stay at home—apart from those that suffer from a grave impediment—are not equal to those who fight for the cause of God with their goods and their persons. God has given those that fight with their goods and their persons a higher rank than those who stay at home. God has promised all a good reward; but far richer is the recompense of those who fight for Him: ranks of His own bestowal, forgiveness, and mercy. God is forgiving and merciful.

The angels will ask those whom they carry off whole steeped in sin; 'What were you doing?' 'We were oppressed in our land,' they will reply. They will say: 'Was not the earth of God spacious enough for you to fly for refuge?' Hell shall be their home: an evil fate.

As for the helpless men, women, and children who have neither the strength nor the means to escape, God may pardon them: God pardons and forgives.

He that flies his homeland for the cause of God shall find numerous places of refuge in the land and great abundance. He that leaves his dwelling to fight for God and His apostle and is then overtaken by death, shall be rewarded by God. God is forgiving and merciful.

It is no offense for you to shorten your prayers when traveling the road if you fear that the unbelievers may attack you. The unbelievers are your inveterate enemies.

When you (Prophet) are with the faithful, conducting their prayers, let one party of them rise up to pray with you, armed with their weapons. After making their prostrations, let them withdraw to the rear and then let another party who have not prayed come forward and pray with you; and let these also be on their guard, armed with their weapons. It would much please the unbelievers if you neglected your arms and your baggage, so that they could swoop upon you with one assault. But it is no offense for you to lay aside your arms when overtaken by heavy rain or stricken with an illness, although you must be always on your guard. God has prepared a shameful punishment for the unbelievers.

When your prayers are ended, remember God standing, sitting, and lying down. Attend regularly to your prayers so long as you are safe: for prayer is a duty incumbent on the faithful, to be conducted at appointed hours.

Seek out your enemies relentlessly. If you have suffered, they too have suffered: but you at least hope to receive from God what they cannot hope for. God is all-knowing, and wise.

[*surah* 4:94–105]

MUHAMMAD'S WIVES

The selection below from the Clans (surah 33), revealed about 629, presents the domestic side of Muhammad in his final years. At the time he had nine wives, several previously widowed, and additional slave girls. This surah advises his wives on proper conduct and discusses his relations with them. Recommendations are also made on etiquette when visiting Muhammad.

. . . Wives of the Prophet! Those of you who commit a proven sin shall be doubly punished. That is easy enough for God. But those of you who obey God and His apostle and do good works shall be doubly rewarded; for them We have made a generous provision.

Wives of the Prophet, you are not like other women. If you fear God, do not be too complaisant in your speech, lest the lecherous-hearted should lust after you. Show discretion in what you say. Stay in your homes and do not display your finery as women used to do in the days of ignorance [i.e., the *time of ingratitude*]. Attend to your prayers, give alms and obey God and His apostle.

Women of the household, God seeks only to remove uncleanness from you and to purify you. Commit to memory the revelations of God and the wise sayings that are recited in your dwellings. Benignant is God and all-knowing.

Those who surrender themselves to God and accept the true Faith; who are devout, sincere, patient, humble, charitable, and chaste; who fast and are ever mindful of God—on these, both men and women, God will bestow forgiveness and a rich reward.

It is not for true believers—men or women—to take their choice in their affairs if God and His apostle strays far indeed.

You [Muhammad] said to the man [Zayd, Muhammad's adopted son] whom God and yourself have favoured: 'Keep your wife and have fear of God.' You sought to hide in your heart what God was to reveal [Muhammad's intention to marry Zayd's wife]. You were afraid of man, although it would have been more proper to fear God. And when Zayd divorced his wife, We gave her to you in marriage, so that it should become legitimate for true believers to wed the wives of their adopted sons if they divorced them. God's will must needs be done.

No blame shall be attached to the Prophet for doing what is sanctioned for him by God. Such was the way of God with the prophets who passed away before him (God's decrees are pre-ordained); who fulfilled the mission with which God had charged them, fearing God and fearing none besides Him. Sufficient is God's reckoning.

Muhammad is the father of no man among you [i.e., he left no male heirs]. He is the Apostle of God and the Seal of the Prophets. God has knowledge of all things. . . .

Prophet, We have made lawful to you the wives to whom you have granted dowries and the slave-girls whom God has given you as booty; the daughters of your paternal and maternal uncles and of your paternal and maternal aunts who fled with you; and any believing woman who gives herself to the Prophet and whom the Prophet wished to take in marriage.[7] This privilege is yours alone, being granted to no other believer.

We well know the duties We have imposed on the faithful concerning their wives and slave-girls. We grant you this privilege so that none may blame you. God is forgiving and merciful.

You may put off any of your wives you please and take to your bed any of them you please. Nor is it unlawful for you to receive any of those whom you have temporarily set aside. That is more proper, so that they may be contented and not vexed, and may all be pleased with what you give them.

God knows what is in your [i.e., the believer's] hearts. He is all-knowing and gracious.

It shall be unlawful for you [i.e., Muhammad] to take more wives or to change your present wives for other women, though their beauty please you, except where slave-girls are concerned. God takes cognizance of all things.

Believers, do not enter the houses of the Prophet for a meal without waiting for the proper time, unless you are given leave. But if you are invited, enter; and when you have eaten, disperse. Do not engage in familiar talk, for this would annoy the Prophet and he would be ashamed to bid you go; but of the truth God is not ashamed. If you ask his wives for anything, speak to them from behind a curtain. This is more chaste for your hearts and their hearts.

You must not speak ill of God's apostle, nor shall you ever wed his wives after him; this would be a grave offense in the sight of God. Whether you hide or reveal them, God has knowledge of all things.

It shall be no offense for the Prophet's wives to be seen unveiled by their fathers, their sons, their brothers, their brother's sons, their sisters' sons, their women, or their slave-girls. Women, have fear of God, for he observes all things.

[*surah* 33:30–40, 50–55]

IDOLATRY ABOLISHED

By 630, the tables had clearly turned against idolatry in Mecca in favor of Islam. Muhammad rode into the Ka'bah and destroyed its idols. In the following selection from the Repentance (surah 9), a declaration of immunity is announced: Muslims would no longer be bound by obligations to idolatrous tribes which repeatedly broke agreements with Muslims. Idolaters would also be barred from the Ka'bah.

A declaration of immunity from God and His apostle to the idolaters with whom you have made agreements:

For four months you shall go unmolested in the land. But know that you shall not escape God's judgment, and that God will humble the unbelievers.

A proclamation to the people from God and His apostle on the day of the greater pilgrimage:

God and His apostle are under no obligation to the idolaters. If you repent, it shall be well with you; but if you give no heed, know that you shall not be immune from God's judgment.

Proclaim a woeful punishment to the unbelievers, except to those idolaters who have honored their treaties with you in every detail and aided none against you. With these keep faith, until their treaties have run their term. God loves the righteous.

When the sacred months are over slay the idolaters wherever you find them. Arrest them, besiege them, and lie in ambush everywhere for them. If they repent and take to prayer and render the alms levy, allow them to go their way. God is forgiving and merciful.

If an idolater seeks asylum with you, give him protection so that he may hear the Word of God, and then convey him to safety. For the idolaters are ignorant men.

God and His apostle repose no trust in idolaters, save those with whom you have made treaties at the Sacred Mosque. So long as they keep faith with you, keep faith with them. God loves the righteous.

How can you trust them? If they prevail against you they will respect neither agreements nor ties of kindred. They flatter you with their tongues, but their hearts reject you. Most of them are evil-doers.

They sell God's revelations for trifling gain and debar others from His path. Evil is what they do. They break faith with the believers and set at nought all ties of kindred. Such are the transgressors.

If they repent and take to prayer and render the alms levy, they shall become your brothers in the Faith. Thus do We make plain Our revelations for men of understanding.

But if, after coming to terms with you, they break their oaths, and revile your faith, make war on the leaders of unbelief—for no oaths are binding with them—so that they may desist.

Will you not fight against those who have broken their oaths and conspired to banish the Apostle? Surely God is more deserving of your fear, if you are true believers.

Make war on them: God will chastise them at your hands and humble them. He will grant you victory over them and heal the spirit of the faithful. He will take away all rancor from their hearts: God shows mercy to whom he pleases. God is all-knowing and wise.

Did you imagine you would be forsaken before God has had time to know those of you who have fought valiantly and served none but God, His Apostle and the faithful? God is cognizant of all your actions.

It ill becomes idolaters to visit the mosques of God, for they are self-confessed unbelievers. Vain shall be their works, and in the fire they shall abide for ever.

None should visit the mosques of God except those who believe in God and the Last Day, attend to their prayers and render the alms levy and fear none but God. These shall be rightly guided. . . .

Believers, know that the idolaters are unclean. Let them not approach the Sacred Mosque after this year is ended. If you fear poverty, God, if he pleases, will enrich you through His own bounty. God is all-knowing and wise.

[*surah* 9:1–18, 28]

FINAL REVELATION

In 632, just months before his death, Muhammad delivered his final revelation while on pilgrimage to Mecca. Set within the context of dietary regulations, the completion of Islam is proclaimed.

Believers, be true to your obligations. It is lawful for you to eat the flesh of all beasts other than that which is hereby announced to you. Game is forbidden while you are on pilgrimage. God decrees what He will.

Believers, do not violate the rites of God, or the sacred month, or the offerings or their ornaments, or those that repair to the Sacred House seeking God's grace and pleasure. Once your pilgrimage is ended, you shall be free to go hunting.

Do not allow your hatred for those who would debar you from the Holy Mosque lead you into sin. Help one another in what is good and pious, not in what is wicked and sinful. Have fear of God; God is stern in retribution.

You are forbidden carrion, blood, and the flesh of swine; also any flesh dedicated to any other than God. You are forbidden the flesh of strangled animals and of those beaten or gored to death; of those killed by a fall or mangled by beasts of prey (unless you make it clean by giving the death-stroke yourselves); also of animals sacrificed to idols.

You are forbidden to settle disputes by consulting the Arrows. That is a pernicious practice.

The unbelievers had this day abandoned all hope of vanquishing your religion. Have no fear of them: fear Me.

This day I have perfected your religion for you and completed My favor to you. I have chosen Islam to be your faith.

He that is constrained by hunger to eat of what is forbidden, not intending to commit sin, will find God forgiving and merciful.

They ask you what is lawful to them. Say: 'All good things are lawful to you, as well as that which you have taught the birds and beasts of prey to catch, training them as God has taught you. Eat of what they catch for you, pronouncing upon it the name of God. And have fear of God: swift is God's reckoning.'

All good things have this day been made lawful to you. The food of those to whom the Book was given is lawful to you, and yours to them. . . .

[*surah* 5:1–5]

SELECTIONS FROM THE HADITH[8]

THE CALL TO PROPHETHOOD

The story of Muhammad's call to prophethood on the night of power is recorded in the Hadith.

Narrated A'isha the mother of the faithful believers: The commence-
ment of the Divine Inspiration to Allah's Apostle was in the form of good
dreams which came true like bright day light, and then the love of seclusion was bestowed upon him. He used to go in seclusion in the cave of
Hira' where he used to worship (Allah alone) continuously for many days
before his desire to see his family. He used to take with him the journey
food for the stay and then come back to (his wife) Khadija to take his food
like-wise again till suddenly the Truth descended upon him while he was
in the cave of Hira'. The angel came to him and asked him to read. The
Prophet replied, "I do not know how to read."

The Prophet added, "The angel caught me (forcefully) and pressed
me so hard that I could not bear it any more. He then released me and
again asked me to read and I replied, 'I do not know how to read.'
Thereupon he caught me again and pressed me a second time till I
could not bear it any more. He then released me and again asked me to
read but again I replied, 'I do not know how to read (or what shall I
read)?' Thereupon he caught me for the third time and pressed me, and
then released me and said, 'Read in the name of your lord, who has created (all that exists) has created man from a clot. Read! And your Lord
is the Most Generous.'" (96: 1, 2, 3) Then Allah's Apostle returned with
the Inspiration and with his heart beating severely. Then he went to
Khadija bint Khuwailid and said, "Cover me! Cover me!" They covered
him till his fear was over and after that he told her everything that had
happened and said, "I fear that something may happen to me." Khadija
replied, "Never! By Allah, Allah will never disgrace you. You keep
good relations with your Kith and kin, help the poor and the destitute,
serve your guests generously and assist the deserving calamity-
afflicted."

Khadija then accompanied him to her cousin Waraqa ibn Naufal ibn
Asad ibn 'abdul 'Uzza, who, during the Pre-Islamic Period became a
Christian and used to write the writing with Hebrew letters. He would
write from the Gospel in Hebrew as much as Allah wished him to write.
He was an old man and had lost his eyesight. Khadija said to Waraqa,
"Listen to the story of your nephew, O my cousin!" Waraqa asked, "O my
Nephew! What have you seen?" Allah's Apostle described whatever he
had seen. Waraqa said, "This is the same one who keeps the secrets (angel
Gabriel) whom Allah had sent to Moses. I wish I were young and could
live up to the time when your people would turn you out." Allah's Apostle asked, "Will they drive me out?" Waraqa replied in the affirmative and
said, "Anyone (man) who came with something similar to what you have
brought was treated with hostility; and if I should remain alive till the day
when you will be turned out then I would support you strongly." But
after a few days Waraqa died and the Divine Inspiration was also paused
for a while.

[*Sahih al-Bukhari*, 1:3]

THE NIGHT JOURNEY

Surah 17:1 of the Qur'an, written in the middle Meccan period, reads, "Glory be to him who made his servant go by night from the sacred temple [of Mecca] to the farther temple [of Jerusalem] whose surroundings we have blessed, that we might show him some of our signs." Referred to as the Night Journey, Muhammad was carried by Gabriel to the temple of Jerusalem (isra), and brought through the seven heavens to God (mi'raj). Although some Muslims interpret this as a vision, most see it as a literal journey. In commemoration of this event, a Muslim shrine called the Dome of the Rock stands on the place of Muhammad's ascent, the former site of the Jewish temple of Jerusalem. It is Islam's third most holy place, after Mecca and Medina. The story of the Night Journey from the Hadith *is recounted here.*

Narrated Anas ibn Malik from Malik ibn Sa'sa'a that Allah's Apostle described to them his Night Journey saying, While I was lying in Al-Hatim or Al-Hijr, suddenly someone came to me and cut my body open from here to here [across the chest]. He then took out my heart. Then a gold tray full of Belief was brought to me and my heart was washed and was filled (with Belief) and then returned to its original place. Then a white animal which was smaller than a mule and bigger than a donkey was brought to me. . . . The animal's step (was so wide that it) reached the nearest heaven. When he asked for the gate to be opened it was asked, "Who is it?" Gabriel answered, "Gabriel." It was asked, "Who was accompanying you?" Gabriel replied, "Muhammad." It was asked, "Has Muhammad been called?" Gabriel replied in the affirmative. Then it was said, "He is welcomed. What an excellent visit his is!" The gate was opened, and when I went over the first heaven, I saw Adam there. Gabriel said (to me), "This is your father, Adam; pay him your greetings." So I greeted him and he returned the greeting to me and said, "You are welcomed, o pious son and pious Prophet." The Gabriel ascended with me till we reached the second heaven. . . . There I saw Yahya (i.e., John) and 'Isa (i.e., Jesus) who were cousins of each other. . . . Then Gabriel ascended with me to the third heaven and . . . there I saw Joseph. . . . Then Gabriel ascended with me to the fourth heaven and . . . there I saw Idris. . . .

Then Gabriel ascended with me to the fifth heaven and . . . there I saw Harun (i.e., Aaron). Then Gabriel ascended with me to the sixth heaven and . . . there I saw Moses. . . . When I left him (i.e., Moses) he wept. Someone asked him, "What makes you weep?" Moses said, "I weep because after me there has been sent (as Prophet) a young man whose followers will enter Paradise in greater numbers than my followers." Then Gabriel ascended with me to the seventh heaven and . . . there I saw Abraham. . . . Then I was made to ascend to Sidrat-ul-Muntaha (i.e., the Lote Tree of the farthest limit). Behold! Its fruits were like the jars of Hajr (i.e., a place near Medina) and its leaves were as big as the ears of elephants. Gabriel said, "This is the Lote Tree of the farthest limit." Behold! There ran four rivers, two were hidden and two were visible. I asked, "What are these two kinds of rivers, O Gabriel?" He replied, "As for the hidden rivers, they are two rivers in Paradise and the visible rivers are the Nile and the Euphrates." Then Al-Bait-ul-Ma'mur (i.e., the Sacred House) was shown to me and a container full of wine and another full of milk and a third full of honey were brought to me. I took the milk. Gabriel remarked, "This is the Islamic religion which you and your followers are following." Then the prayers were enjoined on me: They were fifty prayers a day.

When I returned, I passed by Moses who asked (me), "What have you been ordered to do?" I replied, "I have been ordered to offer fifty prayers a day." Moses said, "Your followers cannot bear fifty prayers a day, and by Allah, I have tested people before you, and I have tried my level best with Bani Israil (in vain). Go back to your Lord and ask for reducing your followers' burden." So I went back, and Allah reduced ten prayers for me. Then again I went back to Allah and he reduced ten more prayers. When I came back to Moses he said the same, I went back to Allah and he ordered me to observe ten prayers a day. When I came back to Moses, he repeated the same advice, so I went back to Allah and was ordered to observe five prayers a day. When I came back to Moses, he said . . . go back to your Lord and ask for reducing your followers' burden." I said, "I have requested so much of my Lord that I feel ashamed, but I am satisfied now and surrender to Allah's Order." When I left, I heard a voice saying, "I have passed My Order and have reduced the burden of My Worshippers."

[*Sahih al-Bukhari*, 5:227]

RECITING THE QUR'AN

Many Hadith *passages indicate that the memorization and recitation of Qur'anic verses was an expected form of piety for Muslims during Muhammad's life. Muhammad himself ritually recited its passages. Special reciters memorized the Qur'an's entirety and recited it daily. At least one function of recitation was to preserve its content, as illustrated in the following* Hadith *passage: "The Prophet heard a reciter reciting the Qur'an in the mosque at night. The Prophet said, May Allah bestow his mercy on him, as he has reminded me of such-and-such verses of such-and-such surahs, which I missed!" (Sahih al-Bukhari, 6:562). Recitation was also a daily ritual for lay people: "The Prophet said, 'if one recites the last two verses of surah-al-Baqara at night, it is sufficient for him (for that night)'" (Sahih al-Bukhari, 6:560). In Qur'anic recitation, not only were the words memorized, but the tonal songlike vocalizations as well. The following describes the variety of vocalizations that were permitted.*

Narrated Umar ibn Al-Khattab: I heard Hisham ibn Hakim reciting *surah* Al-Furqan during the lifetime of Allah's Apostle and I listened to his recitation and noticed that he recited in several different ways which Allah's Apostle had not taught me. I was about to jump over him during his prayer, but I controlled my temper, and when he had completed his prayer, I put his upper garment around his neck and seized him by it and said, "Who taught you this Surah which I heard you reciting?" He replied, "Allah's Apostle taught it to me." I said, "You have told a lie, for Allah's Apostle has taught it to me in a different way from yours." So I dragged him to Allah's Apostle and said (to Allah's Apostle), "I heard this person reciting Surah Al-Furqan in a way which you haven't taught me!" On that Allah's Apostle said, "Release him (O 'Umar)! Recite, O Hisham!" Then he recited in the same way as I heard him reciting. Then Allah's Apostle said,, "It was revealed in this way," and added "Recite, O "Umar!" I recited it as he had taught me. Allah's Apostle then said, "It was revealed in this way. This Koran has been revealed to be recited in seven different ways, so recite of it whichever is easier for you.

[*Sahih al-Bukhari*, 6: 514]

STONING OF ADULTEROUS JEWS

The Hadith *provides a narrative context for many Qur'anic passages, the meanings of which would otherwise be lost. For example, surah 17:81 states, "Truth has come and falsehood vanished. Falsehood is ever bound to vanish." Although the surrounding verses provide no context, the* Hadith *does: "Allah's Apostle entered Mecca (in the year of the conquest) and there were three-hundred and sixty idols around the Ka'bah. He then started hitting them with a stick in his hand and said, Truth has come and falsehood vanished. Falsehood is ever bound to vanish" (Sahih al-Bukhari 6:244). The following Hadith narrative sets the context for another equally obscure Qur'anic passage: "Bring the Torah and read it, if what you say be true" (surah 3:93). The* Hadith *story, from about the fourth year of the migration to Medina, highlights the interaction between the Jews and early Muslims, Muhammad's administrative function in settling legal questions, and the prohibition against adultery.*

Narrated Abdullah ibn Umar: The Jews brought to the Prophet a man and a woman from among them who had committed illegal sexual intercourse. The Prophet said to them, "How do you usually punish the one amongst you who has committed illegal sexual intercourse?" They replied, "We blacken their faces with coal and beat them." He said, "Don't you find the order of Ar-Rajm (i.e., stoning to death) in the Torah?" They replied, "We do not find anything in it." 'Abdullah ibn Salam (after hearing this conversation) said to them, "You have told a lie!" Bring here the Torah and recite it if you are truthful." (So the Jews brought the Torah). And the religious teacher who was teaching it to them put his hand over the Verse of Ar-Rajm and started reading what was written above and below the place hidden with his hand, but he did not read the Verse of Ar-Rajm. 'Abdullah ibn Salam removed his (i.e., the teacher's) hand from the Verse of Ar-Rajm and said, "What is this?" So when the Jews saw that Verse, they said, "This is the Verse of ar-Rajm." So the Prophet ordered the two adulterers to be stoned to death, and they were stoned to death near the place where biers are placed near the Mosque. I saw her companion (i.e., the adulterer) bow-ing over her so as to protect her from the stones.

[*Sahih al-Bukhari,* 6:79]

THE DEATH OF MUHAMMAD

After complaining of severe headaches, Muhammad died in the house of his favorite wife, A'isha. The Hadith *narratives surrounding his death describe his companions' concern about a possible successor to Muhammad and their fear that Muhammad might become an object of worship. The following account of Muhammad's death, at-tributed to A'isha, maintains that Muhammad appointed no successor.*

A'isha, the wife of the Prophet said, When the ailment of Allah's Apos-tle became aggravated, he requested his wives to permit him to be treated in my house, and they gave him permission. He came out (to my house), walking between two men with his feet dragging on the ground. . . . When Allah's Apostle entered my house and his disease became aggra-vated, he said, "Pour on me the water of seven waterskins, the mouths of which have not been untied, so that I may give advice to the people." So we let him sit in a big basin . . . and then started to pour water on him from these waterskins till he started pointing to us with his hands intend-ing to say "You have done your job". . . . Then he went out to the people and led them in prayer and preached to them. . . .

When Allah's Apostle became ill seriously, he started covering his face with his woolen sheet, and when he felt short of breath, he removed it from his face and said, "That is so! Allah's curse be on the Jews and the Christians, as they took the graves of their prophets as (places of wor-ship)," intending to warn (the Muslims) of what they had done. . . . I ar-gued with Allah's Apostle repeatedly about the matter (i.e., his order that Abu Bakr should lead the people in prayer in his place when he was ill), and what made me argue so much was that it never occurred to my mind that after the Prophet, the people would ever love a man who had taken his place, and I felt that anybody standing in his place would be a bad omen to the people, so I wanted Allah's Apostle to give up the idea of choosing Abu Bakr (to lead his people in prayer).

[*Sahih al-Bukhari,* 5:727]

Narrated A'isha: It was one of favors towards me that Allah's Apostle expired in my house on the day of my turn while leaning against my chest and Allah made my saliva mix with his saliva at his death. 'Abdur-Rahman entered upon me with a Siwak in his hand and I was supporting (the back of) Allah's Apostle (against my chest). I saw the Prophet looking at the Siwak and I knew that he loved the Siwak, so I said (to him), "Shall I take it for you?" He nodded in agreement. So I took it and it was too stiff for him to use, so I said, "Shall I soften it for you?" He nodded his approval. So I softened it and he cleaned his teeth with it. In front to him there was a jug or a tin containing water. He started dipping his hand in the water and rubbing his face with it. He said, "None has the right to be worshipped except Allah. Death has its agonies." He then lifted his hands (towards the sky) and started saying, "With the highest companion," till he expired and his hand dropped down.

[*Sahih al-Bukhari*, 5:730]

Narrated Al-Aswad: It was mentioned in the presence of A'isha that the Prophet had appointed Ali as successor by will. Thereupon she said, "Who said so? I saw the Prophet while I was supporting him against my chest. He asked for a tray, and then fell on one side and expired, and I did not feel it. So how (do the people say) he appointed Ali as his successor?

[*Sahih al-Bukhari*, 5:736]

THE FIRST COMPILATION OF THE QUR'AN

During Muhammad's life, isolated Qur'anic verses were preserved in writing, but the only complete copies existed in the memories of the reciters. The following describes the circumstances surrounding the first written compilation of the Qur'an, initiated by the first Caliph, Abu Bakr, a year after Muhammad's death.

Narrated Zayd ibn Thabit: Abu Bakr As-Siddiq sent for me when the people of Yama-ma had been killed (i.e., a number of the Prophet's Companions who fought against Musailama). (I went to him) and found Umar ibn Al-Khattab sitting with him. Abu Bakr then said (to me), "Umar has come to me and said, 'Casualties were heavy among the Qurra of the Koran (i.e., those who knew the Koran by heart) on the day of the Battle of Yamama, and I am afraid that more heavy casualties may take place among the Qurra on other battlefields, whereby a large part of the Koran may be lost. Therefore I suggest you (Abu Bakr) order that the Koran be collected.' I said to Umar, 'How can you do something which Allah's Apostle did not do?' Umar said, 'By Allah, that is a good project.' Umar kept on urging me to accept his proposal till Allah opened my chest for it and I began to realize the good in the idea which Umar had realized." Then Abu Bakr said (to me), "You are a wise young man and we do not have any suspicion about you, and you used to write the Divine Inspiration for Allah's Apostle. So you should search for (the fragmentary scripts of) the Koran and collect it (in one book)." By Allah! If they had ordered me to sift one of the mountains, it would not have been heavier for me than this ordering me to collect the Koran. . . . So I started looking for the Koran and collecting it from (what was written on) palm-leaf stalks, thin white stones and also from the men who know it by heart, till I found the last verse of Surah At-Tauba (Repentance) Abi Khuzaima Al-Ansari. . . . Then the complete manuscripts (copy) of the

Koran remained with Abu Bakr till he died, then with Umar till the end of his life, and then with Hasfa, the daughter of Umar.

[*Sahih al-Bukhari*, 6:509]

THE DEFINITIVE COMPILATION OF THE QUR'AN

In spite of the existence of Abu Bakr's single written compilation of the Qur'an, the Qur'an was still principally transmitted through memorized accounts and scattered written verses. As conflicting versions arose, the third Caliph, Uthman, authorized a definitive written edition 24 years after Muhammad's death. The following recounts the story of Uthman's edition.

Narrated Anas ibn Malik: Hudhaifa ibn Al-Yaman came to 'Uthman at the time when the people of Sha'm and the people of Iraq were waging war to conquer Arminya and Adharbijan. Hudhaifa was afraid of their (the people of Sha'm and Iraq) differences in the recitation of the Koran, so he said to 'Uthman, "O the chief of the Believers! Save this nation before they differ about the Book (Koran) as Jews and the Christians did before." So 'Uthman sent a message to Hafsa saying, "Send us the manuscripts of the Koran so that we may compile the Koranic materials in perfect copies and return the manuscripts to you." Hafsa sent it to 'Uthman. 'Uthman then ordered Zayd ibn Thabit, 'Abdullah ibn Az-Zubair, Sa'id ibn Al-As and 'Abdur-Rahman ibn Harith ibn Hisham to rewrite the manuscripts in perfect copies. 'Uthman said to the three Quaishi men, "In case you disagree with Zayd ibn Thabit on any point in the Koran, then write it in the dialect of Quraish as the Koran was revealed in their tongue." They did so, and when they had written many copies, 'Uthman returned the original manuscripts to Hafsa. 'Uthman sent to every Muslim province one copy of what they had copied, and ordered that all the other Qur'anic materials, whether written in fragmentary manuscripts or whole copies, be burnt. Zayd ibn Thabit added, "A verse from Surah Ahzab was missed by me when we copied the Koran, and I used to hear Allah's Apostle reciting it. So we searched for it and found it with Khuzaima ibn Thabit Al-Ansari. (That verse was): "Among the believers are men who have been true in their covenant with Allah" (22:23).

[*Sahih al-Bukhari*, 6:510]

SELECTIONS FROM SUNNI AND SHI'I WRITINGS

SHAFI'I ON CONSENSUS, ANALOGY, AND PERSONAL REASONING

Ibn Idris al-Shafi'i (767–820) was the foremost scholar of early Islamic law. He is most well known for his analysis of the "four roots of jurisprudence." That is, legal questions

*are resolved by appealing firstly to the Qur'an, secondly to the Sunna, thirdly to con-
sensus, and lastly to analogical reasoning. After his death Shafi'i's disciples founded
the Shafi'ite school; his penetrating analysis of the four roots was also adopted by the
other schools of Islamic Law. The following from Shafi'i's* Risala *discusses the use of
consensus, analogy, and personal reasoning in legal questions.*[9]

Chapter 11, On Consensus *(ijma).*

480. Shafi'i said: Some asked me: I have understood your doctrine concerning God's commands and His Apostle's orders that he who obeys God
obeys His Apostle, [for] God has imposed [on men] the duty of obeying
His Apostle, and that the proof for what you held has been established
that it would be unlawful for a Muslim who has known the Book [of
God] and the sunna [i.e., Hadith tradition of the Prophet] to give an
opinion at variance with either one, for I know that this [i.e., acceptance
of the Book and the sunna] is a duty imposed by God. But what is your
proof for accepting the consensus of the public [on matters] concerning
which no explicit command of God nor any [sunna] related on the authority of the Prophet is to be found? Do you assert, with others, that
the consensus of the public should always be based on an established
sunna even if it were not related [on the authority of the Prophet]?

481. [Shafi'i] replied: That on which the public are agreed and which, as
they assert, was related from the Apostle, that is so. As to that which
the public do not relate [from the Prophet], which they may or may
not relate as a tradition from the Prophet, we cannot consider it as related on the authority of the Prophet—because one may relate only
what he has heard, for no one is permitted to relate [on the authority
of the Prophet] information which may or may not be true. So we accept the decision of the public because we have to obey their authority, and we know that wherever there are sunnas of the Prophet, the
public cannot be ignorant of them, although it is possible that some
are, and we know that the public can neither agree on anything contrary to the sunna of the Prophet nor on an error.

484. He asked: What is the meaning of the Prophet's order to follow the
community?

487. [Shafi'i] replied: When the community spread in the lands [of Islam],
nobody was able to follow its members who had been dispersed and
mixed with other believers and unbelievers, pious and impious. So it
was meaningless to follow the community [as a whole], because it was
impossible [to do so], except for what the [entire] community regarded
as lawful or unlawful [orders] and [the duty] to obey these [orders].

He who holds what the Muslim community holds shall be regarded as following the community, and he who holds differently
shall be regarded as opposing the community he was ordered to follow. So the error comes from separation: but in the community as a
whole there is no error concerning the meaning of the Qur'an, the
sunna, and analogy.

Chapter 12, On Analogy (*qiyas*).

488. He asked: On what ground do you hold that [on matters] concerning which no text is to be found in the Book, nor a sunna or consensus, recourse should be had to analogy? Is there any binding text for analogical deduction?

489. [Shafi'i] replied: If analogy were [stated] in the text of the Book or the sunna, such a text should be called either God's command or the Apostle's order rather than analogy.

490. He asked: What is analogy? Is it personal reasoning [ijtihad], or are the two different?

491. [Shafi'i] replied: They are two terms with the same meaning. . . .

493. On all matters touching the [life of a] Muslim there is either a bonding decision or an indication as to the right answer. If there is a decision, it should be followed; if there is no indication as to the right answer, it should be sought by personal reasoning, and personal reasoning is analogy [qiyas].

496. [He asked]: If [legal] knowledge is derived through analogy— provided it is rightly applied—should [the scholars] who apply analogy agree on most [of the decision], although we may find them disagreeing on some?

497. [Shafi'i replied]: Analogy is on two kinds: the first, if the case in question is similar to the original meaning [of the precedent], no disagreement on this kind [is permitted]. The second, if the case in question is similar to several precedents, analogy must be applied to the precedent nearest in resemblance and most appropriate. But those who apply analogy are likely to disagree [in their answers].

Chapter 13, On Personal Reasoning (*ijtihad*).

534. He asked: On what ground do you hold that [the exercise of] personal reasoning [ijtihad] is permitted in addition to what you have already explained?

535. [Shafi'i] replied: It is on the basis of God's saying: "from whatever place thou issuest, turn thy face in the direction of the Sacred Mosque; and wherever you may be, turn your faces in its direction" [Koran. II. 145]. Regarding him who [wishes to] face the Sacred Mosque [in prayer] and whose residence is at a distance from it, [legal] knowledge instructs [us] that he can seek the right direction through ijtihad on the basis of certain indications [guiding] toward it. For he who is under an obligation to face the Sacred House and does not know whether he is facing the right or wrong direction may be able to face the right one through certain indications known to him [which helps him] to face it as accurately as he can, just as another person may know other indications which help to orient him [in the right direction], although the direction sought by each person may be different from that sought by the other.

[*Risala*, 480, 481, 484, 487, 488–491, 493, 496, 497, 534, 535].

TWELVER SHI'I IMAMS

Eighty percent of Shi'i Muslims belong to the Twelver sect (Ithna 'Asha-Riyyah). *The most distinctive feature of Twelver theology is the belief in the twelve Imams (Ali and eleven of his descendants) who intermediate between God and humans. The Imams carried both a spiritual and civil authority derived from and virtually parallel- ing that of Muhammad. The following selections concerning the Imam are from one of the earliest Shi'i creeds, the* Risalatu'l-I'tiqadat, *compiled by Shi'i theologian ibn Babawayhi al-Qummi (918–991). Ibn Babawayhi was a collector of Hadith and assem- bled one of the Four Books of Shi'i Hadith.*[10]

> And the Prophet said: The Imams after me are twelve, the first of them is the Prince of Believers, 'Ali ibn Abi Talib, and the last of them is the Mahdi (rightly minded), the *Qa'im* (the upholder of the true religion); obedience to them is obedience to me and disobedience to them is disobe- dience to me; and he who denies one of them has verily denied me.

[*Risalatu'l-I'tiqadat* 147]

> [Concerning the first eleven Imam] the Prince of Believers [Ali ibn Abi Talib, the first Imam], on whom be peace, was murdered by 'Ab- du'r-Rahman ibn Muljam al-Muradi, may Allah curse him, and he was buried in Ghari. And Hasan ibn 'ali [the second Imam], on both of whom be peace,—he was poisoned by his wife Ja'da bint Ash'ath of Kinda, may Allah curse them both, and he died on account of that. And Husayn ibn 'Ali [the third Imam] was slain at Karbala. His murderer was Sinan ibn Anas an-Nakha'i, the curse of Allah on them both. And Ali ibn Husayn, the Sayyid Zaynu'l-Abidin [the fourth Imam], was poi- soned by al-Walid ibn 'Abdu'l-Malik, Allah cursed him. And Muham- mad al-Baqir ibn 'Ali [the fifth Imam] was poisoned by Ibrahim ibn al-Walid, may Allah curse him. And Ja'far as-Sadiq [the sixth Imam] was poisoned by Abu Ja'far al-Mansur ad-Dawaniqi, may Allah curse him. And Musa al-Kazim ibn Ja'far [the seventh Imam] was poisoned by Harunu'r-Rashid, may Allah curse him. And 'Ali ar-Rida ibn Musa [the eighth Imam] was poisoned by Ma'mun, may Allah curse him. And Abu Ja'far Muhammad at-Taqi ibn 'Ali [the ninth Imam] was poisoned by al-Mu'tasim, may Allah curse him. And 'Ali an-Naqi ibn Muhammad [the tenth Imam] was poisoned by al-Mutawakkil, may Allah curse him. And Hasan al-Askari ibn 'Ali [the eleventh Imam] was poisoned by al-Mu'tamid, may Allah curse him.
>
> And our belief is that these events actually occurred, and that there was no doubt in the minds of the people regarding the Imams' affairs, as some of those who exceed the bounds (of belief) allege.[11] . . . And verily the Prophets and Imams, on whom be peace, had informed (people) that they would all be murdered.

[*Risalatu'l-I'tiqadat* 142]

[Concerning the twelfth Imam, Mahdi] we believe that the Proof of Allah in His earth and His vicegerent (*khalifa*) among His slaves in this age of ours is the Upholder (*al-Qa'im*). . . . He it is concerning whose name and descent the Prophet was informed by Allah the Mighty and Glorious, and he it is *who will fill the earth with justice and equity, just as now it is full of oppression and wrong.* And he it is through whom Allah will make His faith manifest "in order to supersede all religion, though the polytheists may disliked (it)". He it is whom Allah will make victorious over the whole world until from every place the call to prayer will be heard, and all religion will belong entirely to Allah, Exalted is He above all. He it is who is the Rightly Guided (*mahdi*), about whom the Prophet gave information that when he appears, Jesus, son of Mary, will descend upon the earth and pray behind him, and he who prays behind him is like one who prays behind the Prophet of Allah, because he is his vicegerent (*khalifa*). And we believe that there can be no Qa'im other than him; he may live in the state of occultation (as long as he likes); and were he to live in the state of occultation for the space of the existence of this world, there would nevertheless be no Qa'im other than him. For, the Prophet and the Imams have indicated him by his name and descent; him they appointed as their successor, and of him they gave glad tidings—the Blessings of Allah on all of them.

[*Risalatu'l-I'tiqadat* 140]

SELECTIONS FROM SUFI WRITINGS

RABI'A ON LOVE

Almost as old as Islam itself, Sufism is the mystical tradition of Islam that emphasizes mystical union with God. Rabi'a al-'Adawiya (717–801) was one of the earliest and most admired Sufis and is sometimes referred to as the Muslim St. Teresa. She was kidnapped as a girl, sold into slavery, and was later freed because of her piety. Thereafter she lived as an ascetic with a small group of followers. Although she did not write systematic treatises on Sufism, her sayings were passed down to later generations of Sufis who recorded them and used them as sounding boards for their own mystical ideas. Her key theological contribution is the notion of unconditional love of God (mahabbah), *which parallels the Hindu notion of* bhakti *or Christian notion of* agape.[12]

Abd Allah b. Isa said: I entered Rabi'a's presence and I saw the light on her face, and she used to weep much, and a man related of her that at every mention of fire (representing the punishment of the unrepentant sinner), she swooned, and I heard the falling of her tears on the ground like the sound of water filling a vessel. . . . I came into Rabi'a's presence and she was worshipping, and when I reached my place, she raised her head, and lo, the place of her worship was like a marsh from her tears and I saluted her. Then she received me and said, "O my son, do you need anything?" and I said, "I came to you to greet you," and she wept and said, "May God censure thee!" Then she rose up for the ritual prayer and said, "I ask forgiveness of God for my lack of sincerity when I say those words "I ask forgiveness of God."

[*Siyar al-Salihat*, 26a]

It is related that at one time she saw someone who had a bandage bound about his head. She said, "Why is this bandage bound round your head?" He said, "My head is paining me." Rabi'a asked him how old he was. "Thirty years old," he replied. She asked him, "Were you in pain and trouble for the greater part of your life?" "No," he answered. Then she said, "For thirty years (God) has kept your body fit and you have never bound upon it the bandage of gratitude, but for one night of pain in your head you bind it with the bandage of complaint."

[Attar, *Tadhkirat al-Awliya*]

They told us that Rabi'a al-'Adawiyya once said: I praised God one night with the praises of dawn, then I slept and I saw a bright green tree, indescribable in its size and beauty, and lo, upon it were three kinds of fruit, unknown to me among the fruits of this world, like virgins' breasts, white, red and yellow, and they shone like spheres and suns in the green spaces of the tree, and I admired them and said, "Whose is this?" and one said to me, "This is yours, for your praises aforetime." Then I began to walk round it, and lo, under it were eighteen fruits on the ground, of the color of gold, and I said, "If only these fruits were with the fruits on the tree, it would surely be better." That personage said to me: "They would have been there, but that you, when you offered your praises, were thinking, 'Is the dough leavened or not?' and this fruit fell off."

[*Qut al-Qulub*, I, p. 103]

Some people were speaking in Rabi'a's presence of a devotee, who was known to be holy and in the favor of God, and who lived on what he collected from the refuse-heap of one of our kings, and a man said in her hearing, "What harm would there be in this, if he is in favor with God, and he should ask of him to provide him with food by some other means?" and Rabi'a said to him, "Be silent, O worthless one, have you not realized that the saints of God are satisfied with Him, that they accept his will even if he takes from them their means of livelihood, so long as it is he who chooses this for them?

[Abu Talib, *Qut al-Qulub*, p. 40]

I have loved you with two loves, a selfish love and a love that is worthy of you. As for the love which is selfish, I occupy myself therein with remembrance of you to the exclusion of all others. As for that which is worthy of you, therein you raise the veil that I may see you. Yet is there no praise to me in this or that, but the praise is to you, whether in that or this.

[*Rawd Al-Fa'iq*, p. 213]

AL-GHAZALI ON SUFISM

Abu Hamid al-Ghazali (1058–1111) was a scholar of Islamic law and philosopher who ultimately rejected academic approaches to truth in favor of immediate mystical experience. The following is from al-Ghazali's biography, Deliverer from Error *in which he describes his initial acquaintance with Sufism.*[13]

When God by His grace and abundant generosity cured me of this disease, I came to regard the various seekers (sc. after truth) as comprising four groups: (1) the *Theologians (mutakallimun),* who claim that they are the exponents of thought and intellectual speculation; (2) the *Batiniyah,* who consider that they, as the party of "authoritative instruction" *(ta'lim),* alone derive truth from the infallible *imam;* (3) the *Philosophers,* who regard themselves as the exponents of logic and demonstration; (4) the *Sufis or Mystics,* who claim that they alone enter into the "presence" [of God], and possess vision and intuitive understanding. . . .

When I had finished with these sciences [of the philosophers], I next turned with set purpose to the method of mysticism (or Sufism). I know that the complete mystic "way" includes both intellectual belief and practical activity; the latter consists in getting rid of the obstacles in the self and in stripping off its base characteristics and vicious morals, so that the heart may attain to freedom from what is not God and to constant recollection of Him.

The Intellectual belief was easier to me than the practical activity. I began to acquaint myself with their belief by reading their books. . . . I thus comprehended their fundamental teachings on the intellectual side, and progressed, as far as is possible by study and oral instruction, in the knowledge of mysticism. It became clear to me, however, that what is most distinctive of mysticism is something which cannot be apprehended by study, but only by immediate experience *(dhawq*—literally "tasting"), by ecstasy and by a moral change. What a difference there is between *knowing* the definition of health and satiety, together with their causes and presuppositions, and *being* healthy and satisfied! . . .

In general, then, how is a mystic "way" *(tariqah)* described? The purity which is the first condition of it [as bodily purity is the prior condition of formal Worship for Muslims] is the purification of the heart completely from what is other than God most high; the key to it, which corresponds to the opening act of adoration in prayer, is the sinking of the heart completely in the recollection of God; and the end of it is complete absorption *(fana')* in God. At least this is its end relatively to those first steps which almost come within the sphere of choice and personal responsibility; but in reality in the actual mystic "way" it is the first step, what comes before it being, as it were, the antechamber for those who are journeying towards it.

With this first stage of the "way" there begin the revelations and visions. The mystics in their waking state now behold angels and the spirits of the prophets; they hear these speaking to them and are instructed by them. Later, a higher state is reached; instead of beholding forms and figures, they come to stages in the "way" which it is hard to describe in language; if a man attempts to express these, his words inevitably contain what is clearly erroneous.

In general what they manage to achieve is nearness to God; some, however, would conceive of this as "inherence" (*hulul*), some as "union" (*itthad*), and some as "connection" (*wusul*). All that is erroneous. . . .

In general the man to whom He has granted no immediate experience at all, apprehends no more of what prophetic revelation really is than the name. The miraculous graces given to the saints are in truth the beginnings of the prophets; and that was the first "state" of the Messenger of God (peace be upon him) when he went out to Mount Hira, and was given up entirely to his Lord, and worshipped, so that the bedouin said, "Muhammad loves his Lord passionately."

Now this is the mystical "state" which is realized in immediate experience by those who walk in the way leading to it. Those to whom it is not granted to have immediate experience can become assured of it by trial [i.e., contact with mystics or observation of them] and by hearsay, if they have sufficiently numerous opportunities of associating with mystics to understand that [ecstasy] with certainty by means of what accompanies the "states". Whoever sits in their company derives from them this faith; and none who sits in their company is painted.

[*Deliverer from Error*, sections 78, 122–125, 132–135]

RUMI ON UNION AND SEPARATION

The most widely acclaimed Sufi writer is Jalal ad-Din ar-Rumi (1207–1273) whose poetic work entitled The Masnawi *is often referred to as the Qur'an in Persian. Central to Rumi's writings are the paired notions of union and separation. That is, moments of the mystic's life consist of blissful union with God, whereas, of necessity, other moments involve separation. Separation frequently manifests itself in human pain and suffering. Rumi argues that such suffering must be understood in a larger context: The spiritual happiness we achieve in the state of union is accentuated by the suffering we experience while in separation. The following selections are from Rumi's* Masnawi *and his other epic writing, the* Diwan.[14]

Only the imagination that has contemplated Unification, and then, after direct vision, has undergone separation;

Not a definitive separation, but one for a good purpose, since that station is secure from all separation;

In order to preserve the spiritualized body, the Sun pulls back from the snow for a moment.

[*Masnawi* 6:4012–15]

At the time of union, only God knows what that Moon is! For even during separation, what incredible joy and expansion of spirit!

[*Diwan* 30321]

Separation and parting from Thee is difficult, oh Beloved, especially after Thy embrace!

[*Diwan* 13901]

If man should see himself at all, if he should see that his wound is deadly and gangrenous,

Then from such looking within, pain would arise, and pain would bring him out from behind the veil.

Until mothers feel the pain of childbirth, the child finds no way to be born.

The trust is within the heart and the heart is pregnant; all the exhortations of the saints act as a midwife.

The midwife says, "The woman has no pain. Pain is necessary, for it will open a way for the child."

He that is without pain is a brigand, for to be without pain is to say "I am God."

To say "I" at the wrong time is a curse, but to say it at the right time is a mercy.

[*Masnawi* 2:2516–22]

The body is pregnant with the spirit, the body's suffering is the pain of childbirth—the coming of the embryo brings pain and torment for the woman.

Look not at the wine's bitterness, look at the joy of drunkards! Look not at the woman's affliction, look at the hope of the midwife!

[*Diwan* 5990]

How much the Beloved made me suffer before this work settled into the eye's water and the liver's blood!

A thousand fires and smokes and heartaches—and its name is Love! A thousand pains and regrets and afflictions—and its name is Beloved!

Let every enemy of his own spirit set out to work! Welcome to the spirit's sacrifice and a pitiful death!

My heart keeps saying, "I suffer because of Him," and I keep laughing at its weak hypocrisy.

[*Masnawi* 1:1773–82]

Union with this world is separation from that world. The health of this body is the sickness of the spirit.

It is hard to be separated from this caravanserai—so know that separation from that permanent abode is harder!

Since it is hard for you to be separated from the painting, think what it will be to be parted from the Painter!

Oh you who cannot bear to be without this despicable world! How can you bear to be without God, oh friend, how?

Since you cannot bear to be without this black water, how can you bear to be without God's fountain? . . .

If you should see the Beauty of the Loving God for one instant and throw your soul and existence into the fire,

Then having seen the glory and splendor of His proximity, you would see these sweet beverages as carrion. . . .

Strive quickly to find Self in selflessness—and God knows best the right course.

[*Masnawi* 4:3209–13, 15–16, 18]

GLOSSARY

Allah   literally, God; the Muslim name for the single Deity who is creator and Judge.

Caliph   literally, successor. The political successors to Muhammad according to the Sunni tradition.

Companions   *sahaba* in Arabic; Muhammad's closest followers during his life who assumed leadership roles after his death.

Hadith   literally, speech; sacred collections of short narratives about Muhammad which are thought to have originated with his early companions.

Imam   literally, he who stands before; spiritual leaders of the Shi'a tradition beginning with Ali and continuing through a line of his descendants.

Ka'bah   literally, cube; a cubelike building in the open air Mosque of Mecca, which is the central shrine of Islam.

Qur'an   also Qur'an, literally, to recite; Islam's most holy text consisting of Muhammad's collected revelations.

Mahdi   literally, the guided one; the final and awaited Imam in Shi'a tradition who will establish an era of peace.

Muslim   literally, one who surrenders; a follower of Islam.

Shi'a   literally, separate party; branch of Islam comprising 10 percent of all Muslims who honor the spiritual leadership of Ali and the other Imams.

Sufi   literally, wool clad; practitioners of Sufism, Islam's mystical tradition, which emphasizes the mystical union of the believer with God.

Sunni   from the Arabic *sunnah*, meaning custom; branch of Islam comprising 90 percent of all Muslims who accept the leadership role of the Caliphate.

Twelver   from the Arabic, *Ithna 'Ashariyya*, meaning followers of the twelve Imams; division of Shi'a Islam comprising 80 percent of its number who acknowledge the leadership of twelve specific Imam.

SUGGESTIONS FOR FURTHER READING

ABDUL-RAUF, MUHAMMAD. *Islam: Creed and Worship,* Washington: Islamic Center, 1975.

COULSON, N. A. *History of Islamic Law.* Edinburgh: University Press, 1964.

FARAH, CAESAR E. *Islam.* Hauppauge NY: Barons, 1987.

HODGSON, G. S. *The Venture of Islam,* 3 vol. Chicago: Chicago University Press, 1974.

LEWIS, BERNARD, ed. *Islam and the Arab World.* New York: Knopf, 1976.

NIGOSIAN, S. A. *Islam: The Way of Submission.* Northants: Thorsons, 1987.

PETERS, F. E., ed. *A Reader on Classical Islam.* Princeton: Princeton University Press, 1994.

RIPPIN, ANDREW AND JAN KNAPPERT, eds. *Textual Sources for the Study of Islam.* Totowa NJ: Barnes and Noble, 1986.

SAVORY, R. M., ed. *Introduction to Islamic Civilisation.* Cambridge: Cambridge University Press, 1976.

SCHIMMEL, A. *Mystical Dimensions of Islam.* Chapel Hill: University of North Carolina Press, 1975.

SHAH, IDRIES. *The Way of the Sufi.* London: Penguin, 1968.

Baha'i Faith

The Baha'i Faith[1] began in middle 19th-century Persia, a Shi'ite Islamic society. Founded by Baha'u'llah and his forerunner the Bab, developed and guided by his son, Abdu'l-Baha, and great-grandson, Shoghi Effendi, it is now widely recognized as an independent world religion. The Baha'i Faith emphasizes the unity of all religions and world peace. "To be a Baha'i," according to Abdu'l-Baha, "simply means to love all the world; to love humanity and try to serve it; to work for universal peace and universal brotherhood." Baha'i doctrine is sometimes expressed in the "three onenesses." (1) The oneness of God: There is a single and ultimately unknowable God who is given different names. The knowledge we do have of God derives from his various prophets who instruct us. (2) The oneness of humankind: There is a single human race, and we are all members of it. (3) The oneness of religion: All religions are unified insofar as they are each stages in God's revelatory plan.

HISTORY OF BAHA'I FAITH

Baha'i Founders

The Baha'i Faith is historically founded on the Babi religion, which in turn rests on the Shi'ite Muslim doctrine of the Hidden Imam. According to this doctrine, the Mahdi, the final Imam—or spiritual successor to Ali—is alive, but was placed by God in a condition of occultation in which he can see others but others cannot see him (or at least they cannot recognize him). He will return at the end of time, take vengeance on the wicked, and initiate an era of peace. Shi'ite Islam has numerous denominations and sects that have differing views of the status of the Imams in general and of the Mahdi. The 19th-century Shaykhi sect, founded by Shaykh (Sheik) Ahmad al-Ahsa'i (1753–1826), maintained that Imams have an almost divine status and that each generation needs a gate (Bab) as an intermediary between the Hidden Imam and believers. Although one of the Shaykhi leaders claimed to be guided by the Mahdi in his dreams, no one initially claimed to be the Bab himself.

The forerunner to the Baha'i Faith was affiliated with the Shaykhi sect—either formally or as a sympathizer. Sayyid Ali-Muhammad Shiraz (1819–1850) was born into a merchant family in south Persia; his father died soon after his birth, and he was raised by his uncle. He married at 22 and subsequently joined the Shaykhi. In 1844, while on a pilgrimage to Mecca, he claimed to be the Bab, which was a more extreme claim than his Shaykhi predecessors made. It is this event which Baha'is designate as the beginning of their religion. Scholars believe that the Bab privately announced to his followers that he was the Mahdi himself; the public declaration of Babhood, though, was politically more safe to make. Even so, his declaration quickly attracted followers, but it also raised political concerns, and for the next six years—the remainder of his life—he was exiled or imprisoned. After his announcement, the Bab formed a religious group called the Babis. The first 18 of his followers were sent out as proselytizers. Later the Bab publicly claimed to be the Imam Mahdi himself, and in 1848, in an important work called the *Bayan*, he declared that he was a manifestation of God, superseding Muhammad. The *Bayan* also presents a constitution for the coming Babi state and a series of laws. In perhaps the most controversial section, it maintains that believers can take all possessions of nonbelievers. The severity of some of the Bab's laws dramatized his messianic role and rhetorically underscored his legislative authority. However, these laws were counterbalanced by others that prohibit harming or offending others, especially nonbelievers. In any event, only a few of the Bab's laws were ever implemented.

He summoned the Shah of Persia to acknowledge his authority, and in 1848 the Babis distanced themselves from Islam. The same year about 300 Babis set off on a march that prompted armed confrontation. They defended themselves, but were quickly crushed by the Persian government. Massive persecution of Babis followed, and the Bab was executed by a firing squad in 1850. Witnesses reported that he and a follower were suspended by rope. The first volley only severed their ropes and they dropped to the ground. Seeing this as a divine sign, the commander of the regiment withdrew the troops, but a new group of soldiers was brought in, and they finished the task. The Bab's body was secretly retrieved by his followers and, after a number of years, transported to its final resting place at the Mausoleum of the Bab in Haifa, Israel. His immediate successor as Babi leader was Mirza Yahya (Subh-i-Azal), who resided in Baghdad. Before the Bab died, he foretold of a leader, greater than himself, who would finish his work.

The Baha'i Faith's second founder was Baha'u'llah (1817–1892), an honorific title that means "Glory of God." Baha'u'llah, originally named Mirza Husayn-Ali Nur, was born in Tehran, the capital of Persia. He had no formal education and was eldest son of a distinguished minister of state. When 22, his father died and he was left to manage the estate and care for his family. At age 26 (1844) he espoused Babism and became one of the Bab's earliest followers, although, as some Baha'i historians maintain, he never personally met the Bab. In 1852 a Babi named Sadiq attempted to assassinate the Iranian Shah in retaliation for the execution of the Bab. Sadiq and 80 others were killed, and many more were imprisoned or exiled. Baha'u'llah's property was confiscated and he was imprisoned for four months, after which he was exiled to Baghdad. Mirza Yahya (the Bab's provisional successor) went into hiding and made his way to Baghdad when he heard that Baha'u'llah was there. This initial period of exile lasted until 1863 and was relatively peaceful. Baha'u'llah retreated to the desert for two years (1854–1856), and when he returned he ably met challenges by the Muslim Mullas in defense of Babism. He wrote several books while in Baghdad, the most important of these being *The Book of Certitude (Kitab-i-Iqan)*, which explained how prophets from one dispensation anticipate the prophets of the next.

In 1863 Baha'u'llah was summoned to Constantinople (Istanbul). While preparing for the journey his house overflowed with well-wishers, and for 12 days he, and later his family, were compelled to camp in a garden, later named Ridvan (paradise). At this time he privately announced that he was the leader foretold by the Bab. As such, he declared himself to be the manifestation or appearance of God. This announcement is known to Baha'is as the Declaration at Ridvan, and is the basis of their most important festival celebrated each year from April 21 to May 2. Baha'u'llah, his family, and 26 followers went to Constantinople, where they were confined to squalid conditions for four months, and then they moved to Adrianople (Edirne), Turkey, where they remained until 1868. There he attracted more followers and openly announced his mission. He wrote letters to the Shah and other world leaders, including Napoleon III, Pope Pius IX, Czar Nicholas II, and Queen Victoria. In 1868, a long-standing tension between Baha'u'llah and Mirza Yahya culminated in division, principally owing to Baha'u'llah's claim of a new dispensation and universal religion. Contrary to Baha'u'llah's wishes, their quarreling led to violence among the two factions; Mirza Yahya was deported to Cyprus, where ultimately his followers abandoned him. Baha'u'llah was deported to Acre, Palestine (then part of Syria), which was a prison city for criminals of the Turkish Empire. For two years he and 80 followers were confined to army barracks; the conditions were so harsh that several of the followers died. When the barracks were needed to house troops, Baha'u'llah was moved to a small house in the city in which he stayed for six years. During these years his followers grew substantially in number. At this time he wrote *The Most Holy Book (Kitab-i-Aqdas)*, his most important work, which lays out the basic laws and principles for his followers and establishes the basis of Baha'i administration. In 1877 he was released from the prison city although the prison sentence was never removed. After a two-year stay in a house north of Acre, Baha'u'llah moved to a more regal estate, known as Bahji, secured through donations from his followers. He spent the remaining years of his life writing and teaching while administrative functions were taken over by his eldest son, Abdu'l-Baha (1844–1921). Upon Baha'u'llah's death in 1892 Abdu'l-Baha was appointed successor, as designated in Baha'u'llah's will. Baha'u'llah's burial site—a garden building near the main mansion at Bahji—is the most holy site for the Baha'i Faith.

Abdu'l-Baha ("servant of Baha") was born in Tehran, and was only nine when his father was first imprisoned (1852). He was a dutiful companion to his father, attending him throughout his years of exile and closely guarding him. After Baha'u'llah's death, the transition of leadership was not smooth, particularly as Abdu'l-Baha was opposed by several family members. After Baha'u'llah's death, Abdu'l-Baha built the shrine on Mount Carmel as a burial site for the Bab. Abdu'l-Baha's dissenting relatives reported to the Turkish government that he was constructing a fortress, and in 1901 he was confined to Acre for seven years. There he lived an austere life, teaching and visiting the sick. In 1907 a tribunal met to determine his fate. Coincidentally, a revolution broke out in the Ottoman Empire, and the tribunal members were called to Istanbul. The new leaders of the Empire (the Young Turks) released all political and religious prisoners in the empire. Thus, after a total of 40 years of imprisonment in Palestine, Abdu'l-Baha too was released (1908). In 1911–1913 he traveled to Great Britain, France, Germany, Hungary, the United States, Canada, and Egypt, where he met with religious and political leaders, scientists, and philosophers. He spoke at universities, charitable organizations, and institutions of various religions. Accordingly, Abdu'l-Baha is responsible for spreading the Baha'i Faith beyond the Middle East and into the Western world. He continued adapting the Baha'i Faith to modern social ideas. In his role as a spiritual leader, he maintained exclusive authority in interpreting scripture, as appointed to him by Baha'u'llah, although he did not consider his own writings to be equally authoritative. During the years of World War I, Abdu'l-Baha and the Baha'is in Palestine were under wartime restrictions and had only limited contact with outside pilgrims. Their efforts focused on securing food supplies for the Baha'is and the surrounding poor. After the war, Palestine was occupied by the British and Abdu'l-Baha was officially honored with Knighthood. He died in 1921, stating in his will that leadership should be passed to his 24-year-old grandson, Shoghi Effendi (1897–1957), whom he appointed "Guardian of the Cause."

Studying abroad at the time, Shoghi Effendi was surprised at the news of his position. During his tenure as leader, he established the administrative structure of the Baha'i Faith and became responsible for the subsequent formalized organization of Baha'is around the world. He established teaching plans to spread the Baha'i Faith worldwide, including North America. His definitive English translations and clarifications of Baha'u'llah's writings helped secure the Baha'i Faith in non-Islamic Western countries. Perhaps most importantly, he arranged for the long-awaited election of members to the Universal House of Justice (Bayt al-Adl al-Azam), which would succeed him after his death by overseeing the Baha'i community and elucidating doctrine. The plan for this task was Abdu'l-Baha's Will and Testament which, in turn, draws from the Aqdas. The first election of the members of the Universal House of Justice took place in 1963, six years after his death. Members reside in Haifa, Israel, meet almost daily, and are reelected every five years. Today, the Baha'i Faith has over five million followers in more than 230 countries worldwide, and is one of the world's fastest growing religions. It remains the largest religious minority in Iran, the cradle of the Baha'i Faith , with more than a quarter million believers. However, since the Iranian Islamic revolution of 1979, more than 200 Baha'is have been executed, and thousands more persecuted.

Baha'i Teaching

The Baha'i Faith now reflects little of its original Imami theology, although Shi'ite elements are more present in Iranian Baha'i traditions. Because of Baha'u'llah's appearance, the function of the Bab is no longer considered primary. A central tenet of Baha'i teaching holds that God's nature is unknowable. Everything around us, though, exhibits different attributes of the divine as each is created by God and endowed with different sets of attributes. Most generally, God is a single infinite power, which implies the nonexistence of evil: Evil is only the absence of good, just as darkness is the absence of light. Neither darkness nor evil have a reality, but are only names we give to the absence of the reality in question. The most striking aspect of Baha'i theology is its notion of the unity of religions. Revelation is thought to be progressive, and prophets deliver messages appropriate to their own times. All true prophets from the various religions should be acknowledged as genuine—including Moses, Zoroaster, Jesus, Muhammad, Krishna, and Buddha. The prophets are *manifestations* of God and have special insight into the spiritual realm. Baha'i revelation is seen as the fulfillment of all previous revelations.

In its eschatological teachings, the Baha'i Faith holds that there is life after death through the continuation of a disembodied soul. However, heaven, hell, and final judgment are symbolic. Baha'u'llah is the messianic figure spoken of by previous prophets, and the "final judgment" is the appearance of each new manifestation/prophet of God. Institutionally, the Baha'i Faith has no official priests, no monastic component, and all Baha'is are expected to participate in teaching. Local spiritual assemblies assist with life cycle rites, such as weddings and funerals, plan community events, counsel members, and coordinate Baha'i education programs. Nine Baha'is are elected annually by secret ballot (April 21) to help supervise the local assemblies. National spiritual assemblies oversee the local spiritual assemblies, and the Universal House of Justice oversees these. Baha'is follow a 19-month calendar, each month having 19 days with four intercalary days between the last two months. One month is designated for fasting.

In their social and moral beliefs, Baha'is teach racial and gender equality, monogamy, abstinence from alcohol and narcotics, and the voluntary sharing of property. Strong emphasis is placed on world peace and the unity of all humankind, as indicated in the statement by Baha'u'llah that "You are all fruits of one tree, the leaves of one branch, the flowers of one garden." The Baha'i founders and the Universal House of Justice variously advocated a universal language, a universal league of nations, and an international court of arbitration. Although Baha'is believe in the doctrine of a just war, military aggression is rejected.

BAHA'I SCRIPTURES

The most sacred group of Baha'i texts are the writings of the Bab and Baha'u'llah, which are considered to be revelations. Second to those are the writings of

Abdu'l-Baha, which, while not revealed, are considered to be inspired. The writings of Shoghi Effendi are not on a par with either of these groups, but are still considered authoritative. The letters of the Universal House of Justice are also authoritative, but are not scriptural either. The complete corpus of Baha'i scriptures is perhaps two hundred volumes, although some items are still in manuscript form. The Bab, Baha'u'llah, and Abdu'l-Baha were imprisoned and exiled for much of their lives, and, since they were prohibited from public speaking under these conditions, they devoted their time to writing.

The Bab composed about 50 volumes of writings. His most important work is the *Qayyum al-Asma'* (1844), a commentary on the Surah of Joseph in the Qur'an, which Baha'is consider to be the Bab's first revealed work. The foremost doctrinal works of the Bab are the Persian and Arabic *Bayan* ("exposition"). Although they share the same title, they are two independent works with some overlapping themes. The Persian *Bayan* (1848) is larger, although intentionally left incomplete, and is his principal doctrinal work. The Arabic *Bayan* (1850) was composed during the last few months of the Bab's life.

Baha'u'llah penned over one hundred volumes of writings, including letters to world leaders, prayers, and laws. Many of these are published as compilations. His most important writings are *The Book of Certitude (Kitab-i-Iqan)*, *Most Holy Book (Kitab-i-Aqdas)*, *The Hidden Words*, *The Seven Valleys*, *Tablet of the Holy Mariner*, and *Tablet of Glad-Tidings*. Abdu'l-Baha's writings include *Tablets of the Divine Plan*, *A Traveler's Narrative*, *Memorials of the Faithful*, and *Secret of Divine Civilization*. Important talks were also published, including *Promulgation of Universal Peace* and *Some Answered Questions*. Abdu'l-Baha composed about 50 volumes of text, some of which are in the form of letters to Baha'is as well as to those outside the faith. Shoghi Effendi composed about 35 volumes of text. His key works are *The Dispensation of Baha'u'llah*, *The Advent of Divine Justice*, *The Promised Day Is Come*, and *The World Order of Baha'u'llah*. His book *God Passes By* is his interpretation of Baha'i history. His writings also include letters and translations of the writings of the Bab, Baha'u'llah, and Abdu'l-Baha. *The Baha'i World*, an ongoing series of volumes founded by Shoghi Effendi (19 most recently), is a compilation of official Baha'i writings since 1925. It includes religious calendars, festival descriptions, poetry, music, administrative information, articles on theological topics, maps, bibliographies, transliterations, and definitions.

SELECTIONS FROM THE BAB[2]

THE IMPRISONED BAB

In 1844, Sayyid Ali-Muhammad Shirazi announced that he was indeed the "The Bab," and for the next six years, until the end of his life, he was imprisoned or exiled. In the following selections from an "Epistle to Muhammad Shah," the Bab recounts his plight from 1844–1848.

God beareth Me witness, I was not a man of learning, for I was trained as a merchant. In the year sixty [i.e., 1844] God graciously infused my soul with the conclusive evidences and weighty knowledge which characterize Him Who is the Testimony of God—may peace be upon Him—until finally in that year I proclaimed God's hidden Cause and unveiled its well-guarded Pillar, in such wise that no one could refute it. "That he who should perish might perish with a clear proof before him and he who should live might live by clear proof." [Qur'an 8:44]

In that same year I despatched a messenger and a book unto thee, that thou mightest act towards the Cause of Him Who is the Testimony of God as befitteth the station of thy sovereignty. But inasmuch as dark, dreadful and dire calamity had been irrevocably ordained by the Will of God, the book was not submitted to thy presence, through the intervention of such as regard themselves the well-wishers of the government. Up to the present, when nearly four years have passed, they have not duly presented it to Your Majesty. However, now that the fateful hour is drawing nigh, and because it is a matter of faith, not a worldly concern, therefore I have given thee a glimpse of what hath transpired.

I swear by God! Shouldst thou know the things which in the space of these four years have befallen Me at the hands of thy people and thine army, thou wouldst hold thy breath from fear of God, unless thou wouldst rise to obey the Cause of Him Who is the Testimony of God and make amends for thy shortcomings and failure.

While I was in *Shiraz* the indignities which befell Me at the hands of its wicked and depraved Governor waxed so grievous that if thou wert acquainted with but a tithe thereof, thou wouldst deal him retributive justice. For as a result of his unmitigated oppression, thy royal court hath become, until the Day of Resurrection, the object of the wrath of God. Moreover, his indulgence in alcohol had grown so excessive that he was never sober enough to make a sound judgement. Therefore, disquieted, I was obliged to set out from *Shiraz* with the aim of attaining the enlightened and exalted court of Your Majesty. The *Mu'tamidu'd-Dawlih* then became aware of the truth of the Cause and manifested exemplary servitude and devotion to His chosen ones. When some of the ignorant people in his city arose to stir up sedition, he defended the divine Truth by affording Me protection for a while in the privacy of the Governor's residence. At length, having attained the good-pleasure of God, he repaired to his habitation in the all-highest Paradise. May God reward him graciously. . . .

Following his ascension to the eternal Kingdom, the vicious *Gurgin*, resorting to all manner of treachery, false oaths and coercion, sent Me away from *Isfahan* with an escort of five guards on a journey which lasted seven days, without providing the barest necessities for My travel (Alas! Alas! for the things which have touched Me!), until eventually Your Majesty's order came, instructing Me to proceed to *Maku*. . . .

I swear by the Most Great Lord! Wert thou to be told in what place I dwell, the first person to have mercy on Me would be thyself. In the heart of a mountain is a fortress [*Maku*] . . . the inmates of which are confined to two guards and four dogs. Picture, then, My plight . . . I swear by the truth of God! Were he who hath been willing to treat Me in such a manner to know Who it is Whom he hath so treated, he, verily, would never in his life be happy. Nay—I, verily, acquaint thee with the truth of the matter—it is as if he hath imprisoned all the Prophets, and all the men of truth and all the chosen ones. . . .

When this decree was made known unto Me, I wrote to him who administereth the affairs of the kingdom, saying: "Put Me to death, I adjure thee by God, and send My head wherever thou pleasest. For surely an innocent person such as I, cannot reconcile himself to being consigned to a place reserved for criminals and let his life continue." My plea remained unanswered. Evidently His Excellency the *Haji*, is not fully aware of the truth of our Cause. It would be far more heinous a deed to sadden the hearts of the faithful, whether men or women, than to lay waste the sacred House of God. . . .

In brief, I hold within My grasp whatsoever any man might wish of the good of this world and of the next. Were I to remove the veil, all would recognize Me as their Best Beloved, and no one would deny Me. Let not this assertion astound Your Majesty; inasmuch as a true believer in the unity of God who keepeth his eyes directed towards Him alone, will regard aught else but Him as utter nothingness. I swear by God! I seek no earthly goods from thee, be it as much as a mustard seed. Indeed, to possess anything of this world or of the next would, in My estimation, be tantamount to open blasphemy. For it ill beseemeth the believer in the unity of God to turn his gaze to aught else, much less to hold it in his possession. I know of a certainty that since I have God, the Ever-Living, the Adored One, I am the possessor of all things, visible and invisible. . . .

In this mountain I have remained alone, and have come to such a pass that none of those gone before Me have suffered what I have suffered, nor any transgressor endured what I have endured! I render praise unto God and yet again praise Him. I find Myself free from sorrow, inasmuch as I abide within the good-pleasure of My Lord and Master. Methinks I am in the all-highest Paradise, rejoicing at My communion with God, the Most Great. Verily this is a bounty which God hath conferred upon Me; and He is the Lord of unbounded blessings.

[Selections from "Epistle to Muhammad Shah"]

THE QAYYUMU'L-ASMA': A NEW QUR'AN

The Qayyumu'l-Asma', a commentary on the Surah of Joseph in the Qur'an, was composed in 1844 and is the first book the Bab wrote after his Declaration. The first chapter was written in the presence of his first believer, Mulla Husayn, and, according to the Bab, the whole book was written in 40 days. Baha'is consider it his first revealed text and his most important work. He declares a new day, comparing the book itself to the Qur'an, and thereby announcing a new revelation from God. The Qayyumu'l-

Asma' continually draws on passages and themes from the Qur'an, replicating many of its laws. It is also in the literary style of the Qur'an—even to the point that the Bab intended it to be recited like the Qur'an. The passages below establish a fundamental theme in Baha'i faith: The Bab is a continuation in the line of the prophets acknowledged by Islam, most notably Moses, Jesus, and Muhammad.

1. ALL praise be to God Who hath, through the power of Truth, sent down this Book unto His servant, that it may serve as a shining light for all mankind. . . . Verily this is none other than the sovereign Truth; it is the Path which God hath laid out for all that are in heaven and on earth. Let him then who will, take for himself the right path unto his Lord. Verily this is the true Faith of God, and sufficient witness are God and such as are endowed with the knowledge of the Book. This is indeed the eternal Truth which God, the Ancient of Days, hath revealed unto His omnipotent Word—He Who hath been raised up from the midst of the Burning Bush. This is the Mystery which hath been hidden from all that are in heaven and on earth, and in this wondrous Revelation it hath, in very truth, been set forth in the Mother Book by the hand of God, the Exalted. . . .

61. Verily, Christ is Our Word which We communicated unto *Mary*; and let no one say what the Christians term as 'the third of three," inasmuch as it would amount to slandering the Remembrance Who, as decreed in the Mother Book, is invested with supreme authority. Indeed God is but one God, and far be it from His glory that there should be aught else besides Him. All those who shall attain unto Him on the Day of Resurrection are but His servants, and God is, of a truth, a sufficient Protector. Verily I am none other but the servant of God and His Word, and none but the first one to bow down in supplication before God, the Most Exalted; and indeed God witnesseth all things.

62. O People of the *Qur'an*! Ye are as nothing unless ye submit unto the Remembrance of God and unto this Book. If ye follow the Cause of God, We will forgive you your sins, and if ye turn aside from Our command, We will, in truth, condemn your souls in Our Book, unto the Most Great Fire. We, verily, do not deal unjustly with men, even to the extent of a speck on a date-stone.

63. O Peoples of the earth! Verily the resplendent Light of God hath appeared in your midst, invested with this unerring Book, that ye may be guided aright to the ways of peace and, by the leave of God, step out of the darkness into the light and onto this far-extended Path of Truth.

[Qur'an 5:15–18]. . . .

O peoples of the earth! Verily His Remembrance is come to you from God after an interval during which there were no *Messengers*, that He may purge and purify you from uncleanliness in anticipation of the Day of the One true God; therefore seek ye whole-heartedly divine blessings from Him, inasmuch as We have, in truth, chosen Him to be the Witness and the Source of wisdom unto all that dwell on earth . . .

Whenever the faithful hear the verses of this Book being recited, their eyes will overflow with tears and their hearts will be deeply touched by Him Who is the Most Great Remembrance for the love they cherish for God, the All-Praised. He is God, the All-Knowing, the Eternal. They are indeed the inmates of the all-highest Paradise wherein they will abide for ever. Verily they will see naught therein save that which hath proceeded from God, nothing that will lie beyond the compass of their understanding. There they will meet the believers in Paradise, who will address them with the words "Peace, Peace" lingering on their lips. . . .

68. Say, O peoples of the world! Do ye dispute with Me about God by virtue of the names which ye and your fathers have adopted for Him at the promptings of the Evil *One*? God hath indeed sent down this Book unto Me with truth that ye may be enabled to recognize the true names of God, inasmuch as ye have strayed in error far from the Truth. Verily We have taken a covenant from every created thing upon its coming into being concerning the Remembrance of God, and there shall be none to avert the binding command of God for the purification of mankind, as ordained in the Book which is written by the hand of the *Bab.*

[*Qayyumu'l-Asma'*, 1, 61–63, 68]

THE *BAYAN:* A BOOK FOR A NEW DISPENSATION

The Persian Bayan *is the central book of the Babi religion insofar as it establishes a new system of laws and religious principles. The Bab here declares himself to be the independent manifestation of God, whereas in his previous writings he refers to himself as the Mahdi or the Promised One. The following selection explains the relation of the* Bayan *to previous divine books, particularly the Qur'an.*

True knowledge, therefore, is the knowledge of God, and this is none other than the recognition of His Manifestation in each Dispensation. Nor is there any wealth save in poverty in all save God and sanctity from aught else but Him—a state that can be realized only when demonstrated towards Him Who is the Dayspring of His Revelation. This doth not mean, however, that one ought not to yield praise unto former Revelations. On no account is this acceptable, inasmuch as it behooveth man, upon reaching the age of nineteen, to render thanksgiving for the day of his conception as an embryo. For had the embryo not existed, how could he have reached his present state? Likewise had the religion taught by Adam not existed, this Faith would not have attained its present stage. Thus consider thou the development of God's Faith until the end that hath no end.

[*Bayan* V, 4]

Twelve hundred and seventy years have elapsed since the declaration of *Muhammad,* and each year unnumbered people have circumambulated the House of God [Mecca]. In the concluding year of this period He Who is Himself the Founder of the House went on pilgrimage. Great God! There was a vast concourse of pilgrims from every sect. Yet not one recognized Him, though He recognized every one of them—souls tightly held in the grasp of His former commandment. The only person who recognized Him and performed pilgrimage with Him is the one round whom revolve eight *Vahids* [i.e., sections of the *Bayan*], in whom God hath gloried before the Concourse on high by virtue of his absolute detachment and for his being wholly devoted to the Will of God. This doth not mean that he was made the object of a special favour, nay, this is a favour which God hath vouchsafed unto all men, yet they have suffered themselves to be veiled from it.

[*Bayan* IV, 18]

Everyone is eagerly awaiting His appearance, yet since their inner eyes are not directed towards Him sorrow must needs befall Him. In the case of the Apostle of God—may the blessings of God rest upon Him—before the revelation of the *Qur'an* everyone bore witness to His piety and noble virtues. Behold Him then after the revelation of the *Qur'an.* What outrageous insults were levelled against Him, as indeed the pen is ashamed to recount. Likewise behold the Point of the *Bayan.* His behaviour prior to the declaration of His mission is clearly evident unto those who knew Him. Now, following His manifestation, although He hath, up to the present, revealed no less than five hundred thousand verses on different subjects, behold what calumnies are uttered, so unseemly that the pen is stricken with shame at the mention of them. But if all men were to observe the ordinances of God no sadness would befall that heavenly Tree.

[*Bayan* VI, 11]

COMING OF HE WHOM GOD WILL MAKE MANIFEST

In the Bayan, *the Bab announced the coming of a future prophet—the Sun of Truth— or, more generally described as "He Whom God Shall Manifest." The Bab depicts him in eschatological terms and notes that his nature is reflected in the* Bayan. *Baha'is believe that the Bab is foretelling the coming of Baha'u'llah.*

IF at the time of the appearance of Him Whom God will make manifest all the dwellers of the earth were to bear witness unto a thing whereunto He beareth witness differently, His testimony would be like unto the sun, while theirs would be even as a false image produced in a mirror which is not facing the sun. For had it been otherwise their testimony would have proved a faithful reflection of His testimony.

I swear by the most sacred Essence of God that but one line of the Words uttered by Him is more sublime than the words uttered by all that dwell on earth. Nay, I beg forgiveness for making this comparison. How could the reflections of the sun in the mirror compare with the wondrous rays of the sun in the visible heaven? The station of one is that of nothingness, while the station of the other, by the righteousness of God—hallowed and magnified be His Name—is that of the Reality of things. . . .

If in the Day of His manifestation a king were to make mention of his own sovereignty, this would be like unto a mirror challenging the sun, saying: "The light is in me." It would be likewise, if a man of learning in His Day were to claim to be an exponent of knowledge, or if he who is possessed of riches were to display his affluence, or if a man wielding power were to assert his own authority, or if one invested with grandeur were to show forth his glory. Nay, such men would become the object of the derision of their peers, and how would they be judged by Him Who is the Sun of Truth!

[*Bayan* III, 12]

IT is not permissible to ask questions from Him Whom God will make manifest, except that which well beseemeth Him. For His station is that of the Essence of divine Revelation. . . . Whatever evidence of bounty is witnessed in the world, is but an image of His bounty; and every thing owes its existence to His Being. . . . The *Bayan* is, from beginning to end, the repository of all of His attributes, and the treasury of both His fire and His light. Should anyone desire to ask questions, he is allowed to do so only in writing, that he may derive ample understanding from His written reply and that it may serve as a sign from his Beloved. However, let no one ask aught that may prove unworthy of His lofty station. For instance, were a person to inquire the price of straw from a merchant of rubies, how ignorant would he be and how unacceptable. Similarly unacceptable would be the questions of the highest-ranking people of the world in His presence, except such words as He Himself would utter about Himself in the Day of His manifestation.

[*Bayan* III, 13]

THE DAY OF RESURRECTION

The Bab believed that the resurrection, judgment, heaven, and hell were to be understood metaphorically. In the following selection, he explains that the "day of resurrection" refers to the advent of a new dispensation that "resurrects" the previous one. For example, the Qur'an is resurrected in the Bayan, *and the* Bayan *ultimately will be resurrected in the advent of "He whom God will make manifest."*

The substance of this chapter is this, that what is intended by the Day of Resurrection is the Day of the appearance of the Tree of divine Reality, but it is not seen that any one of the followers of *Shi'ih Islam* hath understood the meaning of the Day of Resurrection; rather have they fancifully imagined a thing which with God hath no reality. In the estimation of God and according to the usage of such as are initiated into divine mysteries, what is meant by the Day of Resurrection is this, that from the time of the appearance of Him Who is the Tree of divine Reality, at whatever period and under whatever name, until the moment of His disappearance, is the Day of Resurrection.

For example, from the inception of the mission of Jesus—may peace be upon Him—till the day of His ascension was the Resurrection of Moses. For during that period the Revelation of God shone forth through the appearance of that divine Reality, Who rewarded by His Word everyone who believed in Moses, and punished by His Word everyone who did not believe; inasmuch as God's Testimony for that Day was that which He had solemnly affirmed in the Gospel. And from the inception of the Revelation of the Apostle of God—may the blessings of God be upon Him—till the day of His ascension was the Resurrection of Jesus—peace be upon Him—wherein the Tree of divine Reality appeared in the person of *Muhammad*, rewarding by His Word everyone who was a believer in Jesus, and punishing by His Word everyone who was not a believer in Him. And from the moment when the Tree of the *Bayan* appeared until it disappeareth is the Resurrection of the Apostle of God, as is divinely foretold in the *Qur'an*; the beginning of which was when two hours and eleven minutes had passed on the eve of the fifth of *Jamadiyu'l-Avval*, 1260 A.H. [May 22, 1844], which is the year 1270 of the Declaration of the Mission of *Muhammad*. This was the beginning of the Day of Resurrection of the *Qur'an*, and until the disappearance of the Tree of divine Reality is the Resurrection of the *Qur'an*. The stage of perfection of everything is reached when its resurrection occurreth. The perfection of the religion of *Islam* was consummated at the beginning of this Revelation; and from the rise of this Revelation until its setting, the fruits of the Tree of *Islam*, whatever they are, will become apparent. The Resurrection of the *Bayan* will occur at the time of the appearance of Him Whom God shall make manifest. For today the *Bayan* is in the stage of seed; at the beginning of the manifestation of Him Whom God shall make manifest its ultimate perfection will become apparent. He is made manifest in order to gather the fruits of the trees He hath planted; even as the Revelation of the *Qa'im* [He Who ariseth], a descendant of *Muhammad*—may the blessings of God rest upon Him—is exactly like unto the Revelation of the Apostle of God Himself [*Muhammad*]. He appeareth not, save for the purpose of gathering the fruits of *Islam* from the *Qur'anic* verses which He [*Muhammad*] hath sown in the hearts of men. The fruits of *Islam* cannot be gathered except through allegiance unto Him [the *Qa'im*] and by believing in Him. At the present time, however, only adverse effects have resulted; for although He hath appeared in the midmost heart of *Islam*, and all people profess it by reason of their relationship to Him [the *Qa'im*], yet unjustly have they consigned Him to the Mountain of *Maku*, and this notwithstanding that in the

Qur'an the advent of the Day of Resurrection hath been promised unto all by God. For on that Day all men will be brought before God and will attain His Presence; which meaneth appearance before Him Who is the Tree of divine Reality and attainment unto His presence; inasmuch as it is not possible to appear before the Most Holy Essence of God, nor is it conceivable to seek reunion with Him. That which is feasible in the matter of appearance before Him and of meeting Him is attainment unto the Primal Tree.

[*Bayan* II, 7]

CALL TO BELIEF

Acceptance of the Bab's message was not as widespread as he had hoped. The Bab compared his situation to the initial disbelief Muhammad's contemporaries had demonstrated towards Muhammad—just as Muhammad compared his situation to the rejected prophets from the past. The following selections are from "An Address to a Muslim Divine" (Abdu's-Sahib). And, again, like Muhammad, the Bab warns of divine punishment for disbelievers.

Thy vision is obscured by the belief that divine revelation ended with the coming of *Muhammad*, and unto this We have borne witness in Our first epistle. Indeed, He Who hath revealed verses unto *Muhammad*, the Apostle of God, hath likewise revealed verses unto *Ali-Muhammad*. For who else but God can reveal to a man such clear and manifest verses as overpower all the learned? Since thou hast acknowledged the revelation of *Muhammad*, the Apostle of God, then there is no other way open before thee but to testify that whatever is revealed by the Primal Point hath also proceeded from God, the Help in Peril, the Self-Subsisting. Is it not true that the *Qur'an* hath been sent down from God and that all men are powerless before its revelation? Likewise these words have also been revealed by God, if thou dost but perceive. What is there in the *Bayan* which keepeth thee back from recognizing these verses as being sent forth by God, the Inaccessible, the Most Exalted, the All-Glorious? . . .

Thou contendest, "How can we recognize Him when we have heard naught but words which fall short of irrefutable proofs?" Yet since thou hast acknowledged and recognized *Muhammad*, the Apostle of God, through the *Qur'an*, how canst thou withhold recognition from Him Who sent thee the Book, despite thy calling thyself "His servant?" Verily He doth exercise undisputed authority over His revelations unto all mankind. . . .

We enjoin thee to save thyself and all the inhabitants of that land from the fire, then to enter the peerless and exalted Paradise of His good-pleasure. Otherwise the day is approaching when thou shalt perish and enter the fire, when thou shalt have neither patron nor helper from God. We have taken compassion on thee, as a sign of Our grace, inasmuch as thou hast related thyself unto Us. Verily We are aware of all things. We are cognizant of thy righteous deeds, though they shall avail thee nothing; for the whole object of such righteousness is but recognition of God, thy Lord, and undoubted faith in the Words revealed by Him.

[Selections from "An Address to a Muslim Divine"]

SELECTIONS FROM BAHA'U'LLAH

KITAB-I-IQAN: DIFFERENT MANIFESTATIONS IN DIFFERENT DISPENSATIONS

Between 1861–62, while exiled in Baghdad, Baha'u'llah composed the Kitab-i-Iqan *(The Book of Certitude), perhaps the most influential Baha'i scripture. The work explains how different periods of time had their own prophets who subtly anticipated future prophets in future dispensations. Followers of these prophets invariably misinterpreted their messages. Baha'u'llah believes that special attention to key passages in their writings and symbolic terms will show that each prophet indeed announced the coming of the next. The work was composed one or two years prior to his Declaration at Ridvan, and, thus, he does not include himself in the chain of prophets.[3]*

Consider the past. How many, both high and low, have, at all times, yearningly awaited the advent of the Manifestations of God in the sanctified persons of His chosen Ones. How often have they expected His coming, how frequently have they prayed that the breeze of divine mercy might blow, and the promised Beauty step forth from behind the veil of concealment, and be made manifest to all the world. And whensoever the portals of grace did open, and the clouds of divine bounty did rain upon mankind, and the light of the Unseen did shine above the horizon of celestial might, they all denied Him, and turned away from His face—the face of God Himself. Refer ye, to verify this truth, to that which hath been recorded in every sacred Book.

Ponder for a moment, and reflect upon that which hath been the cause of such denial on the part of those who have searched with such earnestness and longing. Their attack hath been more fierce than tongue or pen can describe. Not one single Manifestation of Holiness hath appeared but He was afflicted by the denials, the repudiation, and the vehement opposition of the people around Him. Thus it hath been revealed: "O the misery of men! No Messenger cometh unto them but they laugh Him to scorn"

[Qur'an 36:30].

Again He saith: "Each nation hath plotted darkly against their Messenger to lay violent hold on Him, and disputed with vain words to invalidate the truth."

[Qur'an 40:5]. . . .

Among the Prophets was Noah. For nine hundred and fifty years He prayerfully exhorted His people and summoned them to the haven of security and peace. None, however, heeded His call. Each day they inflicted on His blessed person such pain and suffering that no one believed He could survive. How frequently they denied Him, how malevolently they hinted their suspicion against Him! . . . And after Noah the light of the countenance of *Hud* shone forth above the horizon of creation. For well-nigh seven hundred years, according to the sayings of men, He exhorted the people to turn their faces and draw nearer unto the *Ridvan* of the divine presence. What showers of afflictions rained upon Him, until at last His adjurations bore the fruit of increased rebelliousness, and His assiduous endeavours resulted in the wilful blindness of His people. . "And their unbelief shall only increase for the unbelievers their own perdition."

[Qur'an 35:39]

And after Him there appeared from the *Ridvan* of the Eternal, the Invisible, the holy person of *Salih,* Who again summoned the people to the river of everlasting life. For over a hundred years He admonished them to hold fast unto the commandments of God and eschew that which is forbidden. His admonitions, however, yielded no fruit, and His pleading proved of no avail. Several times He retired and lived in seclusion. All this, although that eternal Beauty was summoning the people to no other than the city of God.

Later, the beauty of the countenance of the Friend of God [i.e., Abraham] appeared from behind the veil, and another standard of divine guidance was hoisted. He invited the people of the earth to the light of righteousness. The more passionately He exhorted them, the fiercer waxed the envy and waywardness of the people, except those who wholly detached themselves from all save God, and ascended on the wings of certainty to the station which God hath exalted beyond the comprehension of men. It is well known what a host of enemies besieged Him, until at last the fires of envy and rebellion were kindled against Him. And after the episode of the fire came to pass, He, the lamp of God amongst men, was, as recorded in all books and chronicles, expelled from His city.

And when His day was ended, there came the turn of Moses. Armed with the rod of celestial dominion, adorned with the white hand of divine knowledge, and proceeding from the *Paran* of the love of God, and wielding the serpent of power and everlasting majesty, He shone forth from the Sinai of light upon the world. He summoned all the peoples and kindreds of the earth to the kingdom of eternity, and invited them to partake of the fruit of the tree of faithfulness. . . .

And when the days of Moses were ended, and the light of Jesus, shining forth from the dayspring of the Spirit, encompassed the world, all the people of Israel arose in protest against Him. They clamoured that He Whose advent the Bible had foretold must needs promulgate and fulfill the laws of Moses, whereas this youthful Nazarene, who laid claim to the station of the divine Messiah, had annulled the law of divorce and of the sabbath day—the most weighty of all the laws of Moses. Moreover, what of the signs of the Manifestation yet to come? These people of Israel are even unto the present day still expecting that Manifestation which the Bible hath foretold! How many Manifestations of Holiness, how many Revealers of the light everlasting, have appeared since the time of Moses, and yet Israel, wrapt in the densest veils of satanic fancy and false imaginings, is still expectant that the idol of her own handiwork will appear with such signs as she herself hath conceived!

. . . There is yet another verse in the Gospel wherein He saith: "Heaven and earth shall pass away: but My words shall not pass away" [Luke 21:33]. Thus it is that the adherents of Jesus maintained that the law of the Gospel shall never be annulled, and that whensoever the promised Beauty is made manifest and all the signs are revealed, He must needs re-affirm and establish the law proclaimed in the Gospel, so that there may remain in the world no faith but His faith. This is their fundamental belief. And their conviction is such that were a person to be made manifest with all the promised signs and to promulgate that which is contrary to the letter of the law of the Gospel, they must assuredly renounce him, refuse to submit to his law, declare him an infidel, and laugh him to scorn. This is proved by that which came to pass when the sun of the *Muhammadan* Revelation was revealed. Had they sought with a humble mind from the Manifestations of God in every Dispensation the true meaning of these words revealed in the sacred books—words the misapprehension of which hath caused men to be deprived of the recognition of the *Sadratu'l-Muntaha*, the ultimate Purpose— they surely would have been guided to the light of the Sun of Truth, and would have discovered the mysteries of divine knowledge and wisdom.

From all that We have stated it hath become clear and manifest that before the revelation of each of the Mirrors reflecting the divine Essence, the signs heralding their advent must needs be revealed in the visible heaven as well as in the invisible, wherein is the seat of the sun of knowledge, of the moon of wisdom, and of the stars of understanding and utterance. The sign of the invisible heaven must needs be revealed in the person of that perfect man who, before each Manifestation appeareth, educateth, and prepareth the souls of men for the advent of the divine Luminary, the Light of the unity of God amongst men.

[Selections from *Kitab-i-Iqan*]

KITAB-I-AQDAS: BAHA'I LAWS

In around 1873, 10 years after his declaration at Ridvan and midway into his ministry, Baha'u'llah penned the Kitab-i-Aqdas (Most Holy Book), *which is principally a compendium of Baha'i law. Although the* Bayan *also contains laws, Baha'is believe that the* Bayan *has been superseded by the* Aqdas. *Accordingly, the* Aqdas *follows some of the* Bayan's *laws and ignores others. Section 42 below describes the function of the Universal House of Justice, which was later instituted by Shoghi Effendi as the ruling body of the Baha'i Faith.*[4]

1. The first duty prescribed by God for His servants is the recognition of Him Who is the Dayspring of His Revelation and the Fountain of His laws, Who representeth the Godhead in both the Kingdom of His

Cause and the world of creation. Whoso achieveth this duty hath attained unto all good; and whoso is deprived thereof hath gone astray, though he be the author of every righteous deed. It behoveth every one who reacheth this most sublime station, this summit of transcendent glory, to observe every ordinance of Him Who is the Desire of the world. These twin duties are inseparable. Neither is acceptable without the other. Thus hath it been decreed by Him Who is the Source of Divine inspiration.

12. It hath been ordained that obligatory prayer is to be performed by each of you individually. Save in the Prayer for the Dead, the practice of congregational prayer hath been annulled. He, of a truth, is the Ordainer, the All-Wise.

13. God hath exempted women who are in their courses from obligatory prayer and fasting. Let them, instead, after performance of their ablutions, give praise unto God, repeating ninety-five times between the noon of one day and the next "Glorified be God, the Lord of Splendour and Beauty". Thus hath it been decreed in the Book, if ye be of them that comprehend.

14. When travelling, if ye should stop and rest in some safe spot, perform ye—men and women alike—a single prostration in place of each unsaid Obligatory Prayer, and while prostrating say "Glorified be God, the Lord of Might and Majesty, of Grace and Bounty". Whoso is unable to do this, let him say only "Glorified be God"; this shall assuredly suffice him. He is, of a truth, the all-sufficing, the ever-abiding, the forgiving, compassionate God. Upon completing your prostrations, seat yourselves cross-legged—men and women alike—and eighteen times repeat "Glorified be God, the Lord of the kingdoms of earth and heaven". Thus doth the Lord make plain the ways of truth and guidance, ways that lead to one way, which is this Straight Path. Render thanks unto God for this most gracious favour; offer praise unto Him for this bounty that hath encompassed the heavens and the earth; extol Him for this mercy that hath pervaded all creation.

16. O Pen of the Most High! Say: O people of the world! We have enjoined upon you fasting during a brief period, and at its close have designated for you *Naw-Ruz* as a feast. Thus hath the Day-Star of Utterance shone forth above the horizon of the Book as decreed by Him Who is the Lord of the beginning and the end. Let the days in excess of the months be placed before the month of fasting. We have ordained that these, amid all nights and days, shall be the manifestations of the letter *Ha*, and thus they have not been bounded by the limits of the year and its months. It behoveth the people of *Baha*, throughout these days, to provide good cheer for themselves, their kindred and, beyond them, the poor and needy, and with joy and exultation to hail and glorify their Lord, to sing His praise and magnify His Name; and when they end—these days of giving that precede the

season of restraint—let them enter upon the Fast. Thus hath it been ordained by Him Who is the Lord of all mankind. The traveler, the ailing, those who are with child or giving suck, are not bound by the Fast; they have been exempted by God as a token of His grace. He, verily, is the Almighty, the Most Generous.

30. The Lord hath ordained that in every city a House of Justice be established wherein shall gather counsellors to the number of *Baha*, and should it exceed this number it doth not matter. They should consider themselves as entering the Court of the presence of God, the Exalted, the Most High, and as beholding Him Who is the Unseen. It behoveth them to be the trusted ones of the Merciful among men and to regard themselves as the guardians appointed of God for all that dwell on earth. It is incumbent upon them to take counsel together and to have regard for the interests of the servants of God, for His sake, even as they regard their own interests, and to choose that which is meet and seemly. Thus hath the Lord your God commanded you. Beware lest ye put away that which is clearly revealed in His Tablet. Fear God, O ye that perceive.

31. O people of the world! Build ye houses of worship throughout the lands in the name of Him Who is the Lord of all religions. Make them as perfect as is possible in the world of being, and adorn them with that which befitteth them, not with images and effigies. Then, with radiance and joy, celebrate therein the praise of your Lord, the Most Compassionate. Verily, by His remembrance the eye is cheered and the heart is filled with light.

32. The Lord hath ordained that those of you who are able shall make pilgrimage to the sacred House, and from this He hath exempted women as a mercy on His part. He, of a truth, is the All-Bountiful, the Most Generous.

33. O people of *Baha*! It is incumbent upon each one of you to engage in some occupation—such as a craft, a trade or the like. We have exalted your engagement in such work to the rank of worship of the one true God. Reflect, O people, on the grace and blessings of your Lord, and yield Him thanks at eventide and dawn. Waste not your hours in idleness and sloth, but occupy yourselves with what will profit you and others. Thus hath it been decreed in this Tablet from whose horizon hath shone the day-star of wisdom and utterance. The most despised of men in the sight of God are they who sit and beg. Hold ye fast unto the cord of means and place your trust in God, the Provider of all means.

37. Whoso layeth claim to a Revelation direct from God, ere the expiration of a full thousand years, such a man is assuredly a lying impostor. We pray God that He may graciously assist him to retract and repudiate such claim. Should he repent, God will, no doubt, forgive him. If, however, he persisteth in his error, God will, assuredly, send down one who will deal mercilessly with him. Terrible, indeed, is

God in punishing! Whosoever interpreteth this verse otherwise than its obvious meaning is deprived of the Spirit of God and of His mercy which encompasseth all created things. Fear God, and follow not your idle fancies. Nay, rather, follow the bidding of your Lord, the Almighty, the All-Wise. Erelong shall clamorous voices be raised in most lands. Shun them, O My people, and follow not the iniquitous and evil-hearted. This is that of which We gave you forewarning when We were dwelling in *Iraq,* then later while in the Land of Mystery, and now from this Resplendent Spot.

42. Endowments dedicated to charity revert to God, the Revealer of Signs. None hath the right to dispose of them without leave from Him Who is the Dawning-place of Revelation. After Him, this authority shall pass to the *Aghsan,* and after them to the House of Justice— should it be established in the world by then—that they may use these endowments for the benefit of the Places which have been exalted in this Cause, and for whatsoever hath been enjoined upon them by Him Who is the God of might and power. Otherwise, the endowments shall revert to the people of *Baha* who speak not except by His leave and judge not save in accordance with what God hath decreed in this Tablet—lo, they are the champions of victory betwixt heaven and earth—that they may use them in the manner that hath been laid down in the Book by God, the Mighty, the Bountiful.

49. God hath imposed a fine on every adulterer and adulteress, to be paid to the House of Justice: nine *mithqals* of gold, to be doubled if they should repeat the offence. Such is the penalty which He Who is the Lord of Names hath assigned them in this world; and in the world to come He hath ordained for them a humiliating torment. Should anyone be afflicted by a sin, it behoveth him to repent thereof and return unto his Lord. He, verily, granteth forgiveness unto whomsoever He willeth, and none may question that which it pleaseth Him to ordain. He is, in truth, the Ever-Forgiving, the Almighty, the All-Praised.

63. God hath prescribed matrimony unto you. Beware that ye take not unto yourselves more wives than two.[5] Whoso contenteth himself with a single partner from among the maidservants of God, both he and she shall live in tranquillity. And he who would take into his service a maid may do so with propriety. Such is the ordinance which, in truth and justice, hath been recorded by the Pen of Revelation. Enter into wedlock, O people, that ye may bring forth one who will make mention of Me amid My servants. This is My bidding unto you; hold fast to it as an assistance to yourselves.

65. It hath been laid down in the *Bayan* that marriage is dependent upon the consent of both parties. Desiring to establish love, unity and harmony amidst Our servants, We have conditioned it, once the couple's wish is known, upon the permission of their parents, lest enmity and rancour should arise amongst them. And in this We have yet other purposes. Thus hath Our commandment been ordained.

149. Recite ye the verses of God every morn and eventide. Whoso faileth to recite them hath not been faithful to the Covenant of God and His Testament, and whoso turneth away from these holy verses in this Day is of those who throughout eternity have turned away from God. Fear ye God, O My servants, one and all. Pride not yourselves on much reading of the verses or on a multitude of pious acts by night and day; for were a man to read a single verse with joy and radiance it would be better for him than to read with lassitude all the Holy Books of God, the Help in Peril, the Self-Subsisting. Read ye the sacred verses in such measure that ye be not overcome by languor and despondency. Lay not upon your souls that which will weary them and weigh them down, but rather what will lighten and uplift them, so that they may soar on the wings of the Divine verses towards the Dawning-place of His manifest signs; this will draw you nearer to God, did ye but comprehend.

155. Gambling and the use of opium have been forbidden unto you. Eschew them both, O people, and be not of those who transgress. Beware of using any substance that induceth sluggishness and torpor in the human temple and inflicteth harm upon the body. We, verily, desire for you naught save what shall profit you, and to this bear witness all created things, had ye but ears to hear.

[*Kitab-i-Aqdas* 1, 12–14, 16, 30–33, 37, 42, 49, 63, 65, 149, 155]

PROMOTING PEACE

Many of Baha'u'llah's writings focus on the place of the Baha'i Faith in God's scheme of revelation, and also on laws which govern the Baha'i community. Some writings, though, focus on the larger issue of world peace—a distinguishing feature of the Baha'i Faith. Such themes are seen in the following from the Lawh-i-Dunya (Tablet of the World).[6]

Whilst in the Prison of *Akka,* We revealed in the *Crimson Book* that which is conducive to the advancement of mankind and to the reconstruction of the world. The utterances set forth therein by the Pen of the Lord of creation include the following which constitute the fundamental principles for the administration of the affairs of men:

First: It is incumbent upon the ministers of the House of Justice to promote the Lesser Peace so that the people of the earth may be relieved from the burden of exorbitant expenditures. This matter is imperative and absolutely essential, inasmuch as hostilities and conflict lie at the root of affliction and calamity. Second: Languages must be reduced to one common language to be taught in all the schools of the world. Third: It behoveth man to adhere tenaciously unto that which will promote fellowship, kindliness and unity. Fourth: Everyone, whether man or woman, should hand over to a trusted person a portion of what he or she earneth through trade, agriculture or other occupation, for the training and education of children, to be spent for this purpose with the knowledge of the Trustees of the House of Justice. Fifth: Special regard must be paid to agriculture. Although it hath been mentioned in the fifth place, unquestionably it precedeth the others. Agriculture is highly developed in foreign lands, however in Persia it hath so far been grievously neglected. It is hoped that His Majesty the *Shah*—may God assist him by His grace—will turn his attention to this vital and important matter.

Were men to strictly observe that which the Pen of the Most High hath revealed in the Crimson Book, they could then well afford to dispense with the regulations which prevail in the world. Certain exhortations have repeatedly streamed forth from the Pen of the Most High that perchance the manifestations of power and the dawning-places of might may, sometime, be enabled to enforce them. Indeed, were sincere seekers to be found, every emanation of God's pervasive and irresistible Will would, for the sake of His love, be revealed. But where are to be found earnest seekers and inquiring minds? Whither are gone the equitable and the fair-minded? At present no day passeth without the fire of a fresh tyranny blazing fiercely, or the sword of a new aggression being unsheathed. Gracious God! The great and the noble in Persia glory in acts of such savagery that one is lost in amazement at the tales thereof.

[Selections from Lawh-i-Dunya]

PARADISE

Just as the Bab reinterpreted the traditional notion of the "Day of Judgment," so too does Baha'u'llah give a broader interpretation to the notion of "paradise" and "hell." They are partly experienced here on earth, although they are more vast in the afterlife. The following selection is from the Suriy-i-Vafa *(Tablet to Vafa).[7]*

As to Paradise: It is a reality and there can be no doubt about it, and now in this world it is realized through love of Me and My good-pleasure. Whosoever attaineth unto it God will aid him in this world below, and after death He will enable him to gain admittance into Paradise whose vastness is as that of heaven and earth. Therein the Maids of glory and holiness will wait upon him in the daytime and in the night season, while the day-star of the unfading beauty of his Lord will at all times shed its radiance upon him and he will shine so brightly that no one shall bear to gaze at him. Such is the dispensation of Providence, yet the people are shut out by a grievous veil. Likewise apprehend thou the nature of hell-fire and be of them that truly believe. For every act performed there shall be a recompense according to the estimate of God, and unto this the very ordinances and prohibitions prescribed by the Almighty amply bear witness. For surely if deeds were not rewarded and yielded no fruit, then the Cause of God—exalted is He—would prove futile. Immeasurably high is He exalted above such blasphemies! However, unto them that are rid of all attachments a deed is, verily, its own reward. Were We to enlarge upon this theme numerous Tablets would need to be written.

[Selections from the *Suriy-i-Vafa*]

SELECTIONS FROM ABDU'L-BAHA

BAHA'U'LLAH'S TEACHINGS

Several of Abdu'l-Baha's writings are formal religious texts and resemble the style of the Bayan *or* Kitab-i-Iqan. *Other texts, though, are more informal in nature, such as those based on public lectures. The effect of these is the communication of Baha'i doctrine to a wider circle of people. Such is the case with the following summary of Baha'u'llah's teachings from Abdu'l-Baha's "Discourse at the London Theosophical Headquarters," September 30, 1911.*[8]

[Baha'u'llah] declared the most human virtues; He manifested the Spiritual powers, and put them into practice in the world around Him.

Firstly: He lays stress on the search for Truth. This is most important, because the people are too easily led by tradition. It is because of this that they are often antagonistic to each other, and dispute with one another. But the manifesting of Truth discovers the darkness and becomes the cause of Oneness of faith and belief: because Truth cannot be two! That is not possible.

Secondly: Baha'u'llah taught the Oneness of humanity; that is to say, all the children of men are under the mercy of the Great God. They are the sons of one God; they are trained by God. He has placed the crown of humanity on the head of every one of the servants of God. Therefore all nations and peoples must consider themselves brethren. They are all descendants from Adam. They are the branches, leaves, flowers and fruits of One Tree. They are pearls from one shell. But the children of men are in need of education and civilization, and they require to be polished, till they become bright and shining. Man and woman both should be educated equally and equally regarded. It is racial, patriotic, religious and class prejudice, that has been the cause of the destruction of Humanity.

Thirdly: Baha'u'llah taught, that Religion is the chief foundation of Love and Unity and the cause of Oneness. If a religion become the cause of hatred and disharmony, it would be better that it should not exist. To be without such a religion is better than to be with it.

Fourthly: Religion and Science are inter-twined with each other and cannot be separated. These are the two wings with which humanity must fly. One wing is not enough. Every religion which does not concern itself with Science is mere tradition, and that is not the essential. Therefore science, education and civilization are most important necessities for the full religious life.

Fifthly: The Reality of the divine Religions is one, because the Reality is one and cannot be two. All the prophets are united in their message, and unshaken. They are like the sun; in different seasons they ascend from different rising points on the horizon. Therefore every ancient prophet gave the glad tidings of the future, and every future has accepted the past.

Sixthly: Equality and Brotherhood must be established among all members of mankind. This is according to Justice. The general rights of mankind must be guarded and preserved. All men must be treated equally. This is inherent in the very nature of humanity.

Seventhly: The arrangements of the circumstances of the people must be such that poverty shall disappear, and that every one as far as possible, according to his position and rank, shall be comfortable. Whilst the nobles and others in high rank are in easy circumstances, the poor also should be able to get their daily food and not be brought to the extremities of hunger.

Eighthly: *Baha'u'llah* declared the coming of the Most Great Peace. All the nations and peoples will come under the shadow of the Tent of the Great Peace and Harmony—that is to say, by general election a Great Board of Arbitration shall be established, to settle all differences and quarrels between the Powers; so that disputes shall not end in war.

Ninthly: *Baha'u'llah* taught that hearts must receive the Bounty of the Holy Spirit, so that Spiritual civilization may be established. For material civilization is not adequate for the needs of mankind and cannot be the cause of its happiness. Material civilization is like the body and spiritual civilization is like the soul. Body without soul cannot live.

This is a short summary of the Teachings of *Baha'u'llah*. To establish this *Baha'u'llah* underwent great difficulties and hardships. He was in constant confinement and He suffered great persecution. But in the fortress (*Akka*) He reared a spiritual palace and from the darkness of His prison He sent out a great light to the world. It is the ardent desire of the *Baha'is* to put these teachings into common practice: and they will strive with soul and heart to give up their lives for this purpose, until the heavenly light brightens the whole world of humanity.

[Selections from "Discourse at the London Theosophical Head Quarters"]

PANTHEISM

In another informal work, Some Answered Questions *(written between 1904–1906), Abdu'l-Baha considers the issue of pantheism—the theological position that God is identical to the universe as a whole. He distinguishes between two types of pantheism: that of the Sufis and that of the prophets. The pantheism of the Sufis maintains that individual beings (people, animals) are subcomponents of God's essence. This he rejects, since it implies that God becomes a lower form of existence. The pantheism of the prophets sees the world as an emanation of God, distinct from, yet illuminated by God's being. This maintains the immanence of God's attributes, while still conserving God's transcendence. Baha'u'llah endorses this view as* true Pantheism.[9]

Question—How do the Theosophists and the *Sufis* understand the question of pantheism? What does it mean, and how nearly does it approximate to the truth?

Answer—Know that the subject of pantheism is ancient. It is a belief not restricted to the Theosophists and the *Sufis*; on the contrary, some of the sages of Greece believed in it, like Aristotle, who said, "The simple truth is all things, but it is not any one of them." In this case, "simple" is the opposite of "composed"; it is the isolated Reality, which is purified and sanctified from composition and division, and which resolves Itself into innumerable forms. Therefore, Real Existence is all things, but It is not one of the things. Briefly, the believers in pantheism think that Real Existence can be compared to the sea, and that beings are like the waves of the sea. These waves, which signify the beings, are innumerable forms of that Real Existence; therefore, the Holy Reality is the Sea of Preexistence, and the innumerable forms of the creatures are the waves which appear.

. . . The *Sufis* admit God and the creature, and say that God resolves Himself into the infinite forms of the creatures, and manifests like the sea, which appears in the infinite forms of the waves. These phenomenal and imperfect waves are the same thing as the Preexistent Sea, which is the sum of all the divine perfections. The Prophets, on the contrary, believe that there is the world of God, the world of the Kingdom, and the world of Creation: three things. The first emanation from God is the bounty of the Kingdom, which emanates and is reflected in the reality of the creatures, like the light which emanates from the sun and is resplendent in creatures; and this bounty, which is the light, is reflected in infinite forms in the reality of all things, and specifies and individualizes itself according to the capacity, the worthiness and the intrinsic value of things. But the affirmation of the *Sufis* requires that the Independent Wealth should descend to the degree of poverty, that the Preexistent should confine itself to phenomenal forms, and that Pure Power should be restricted to the state of weakness, according to the limitations of contingent beings. And this is an evident error. Observe that the reality of man, who is the most noble of creatures, does not descend to the reality of the animal, that the essence of the animal, which is endowed with the powers of sensation, does not abase itself to the degree of the vegetable, and that the reality of the vegetable, which is the power of growth, does not descend to the reality of the mineral.

Briefly, the superior reality does not descend nor abase itself to inferior states; then how could it be that the Universal Reality of God, which is freed from all descriptions and qualifications, notwithstanding Its absolute sanctity and purity, should resolve Itself into the forms of the realities of the creatures, which are the source of imperfections? This is a pure imagination which one cannot conceive. On the contrary, this Holy Essence is the sum of the divine perfections; and all creatures are favored by the bounty of resplendency through emanation, and receive the lights, the perfection and the beauty of Its Kingdom, in the same way that all earthly creatures obtain the bounty of the light of the rays of the sun, but the sun does not descend and does not abase itself to the favored realities of earthly beings.

[Selections from *Some Answered Questions*]

UNIVERSAL LOVE

A key theme in the Baha'i religion is a love of humanity. One of the most dramatic statements of this doctrine is from Abdu'l-Baha's public talk in Paris, October 24, 1911, on the subject of "The Universal Love."[10]

An Indian said to *Abdu'l-Baha*: "My aim in life is to transmit as far as in me lies the message of Krishna to the world."

Abdu'l-Baha said: The Message of Krishna is the message of love. All God's prophets have brought the message of love. None has ever thought that war and hate are good. Every one agrees in saying that love and kindness are best. Love manifests its reality in deeds, not only in words—these alone are without effect. In order that love may manifest its power there must be an object, an instrument, a motive. There are many ways of expressing the love principle; there is love for the family, for the country, for the race, there is political enthusiasm, there is also the love of community of interest in service. These are all ways and means of showing the power of love. Without any such means, love would be unseen, unheard, unfelt—altogether unexpressed, unmanifested! Water shows its power in various ways, in quenching thirst, causing seed to grow, etc. Coal expresses one of its principles in gas-light, while one of the powers of electricity is shown in the electric light. If there were neither gas nor electricity, the nights of the world would be darkness! So, it is necessary to have an instrument, a motive for love's manifestation, an object, a mode of expression.

We must find a way of spreading love among the sons of humanity. Love is unlimited, boundless, infinite! Material things are limited, circumscribed, finite. You cannot adequately express infinite love by limited means. The perfect love needs an unselfish instrument, absolutely freed from fetters of every kind. The love of family is limited; the tie of blood relationship is not the strongest bond. Frequently members of the same family disagree, and even hate each other. Patriotic love is finite; the love of one's country causing hatred of all others, is not perfect love! Compatriots also are not free from quarrels amongst themselves. The love of race is limited; there is some union here, but that is insufficient. Love must be free from boundaries! To love our own race may mean hatred of all others, and even people of the same race often dislike each other. Political love also is much bound up with hatred of one party for another; this love is very limited and uncertain. The love of community of interest in service is likewise fluctuating; frequently competitions arise, which lead to jealousy, and at length hatred replaces love. A few years ago, Turkey and Italy had a friendly political understanding; now they are at war! All these ties of love are imperfect. It is clear that limited material ties are insufficient to adequately express the universal love.

The great unselfish love for humanity is bounded by none of these imperfect, semi-selfish bonds; this is the one perfect love, possible to all mankind, and can only be achieved by the power of the Divine Spirit. No worldly power can accomplish the universal love. Let all be united in this Divine power of love! Let all strive to grow in the light of the Sun of Truth, and reflecting this luminous love on all men, may their hearts become so united that they may dwell evermore in the radiance of the limitless love. . . . The animal creation is captive to matter, God has given freedom to man. The animal cannot escape the law of nature, whereas man may control it, for he, containing nature, can rise above it. The power of the Holy Spirit, enlightening man's intelligence, has enabled him to discover means of bending many natural laws to his will. He flies through the air, floats on the sea, and even moves under the waters. All this proves how man's intelligence has been enabled to free him from the limitations of nature, and to solve many of her mysteries. Man, to a certain extent, has broken the chains of matter. The Holy Spirit will give to man greater powers than these, if only he will strive after the things of the spirit and endeavour to attune his heart to the Divine infinite love.

When you love a member of your family or a compatriot, let it be with a ray of the Infinite Love! Let it be in God, and for God! Wherever you find the attributes of God love that person, whether he be of your family or of another. Shed the light of a boundless love on every human being whom you meet, whether of your country, your race, your political party, or of any other nation, colour or shade of political opinion. Heaven will support you while you work in this in-gathering of the scattered peoples of the world beneath the shadow of the almighty tent of unity. You will be servants of God, who are dwelling near to Him, His divine helpers in the service, ministering to all Humanity. All Humanity! Every human being! never forget this! Do not say, he is an Italian, or a Frenchman, or an American, or an Englishman, remember only that he is a son of God, a servant of the Most High, a man! All are men! Forget nationalities; all are equal in the sight of God!

[Selections from "The Universal Love"]

ABDU'L-BAHA'S WILL

Abdu'l-Baha died in 1921, and in his will he appointed Shoghi Effendi to succeed him as the Guardian of the Cause of the Baha'i Faith. The following selections, from the conclusion of his will, describe this appointment.[11]

O ye the faithful loved ones of *Abdu'l-Baha*! It is incumbent upon you to take the greatest care of Shoghi Effendi, the twig that hath branched from and the fruit given forth by the two hallowed and Divine Lote-Trees, that no dust of despondency and sorrow may stain his radiant nature, that day by day he may wax greater in happiness, in joy and spirituality, and may grow to become even as a fruitful tree.

For he is, after *Abdu'l-Baha*, the Guardian of the Cause of God, the *Afnan*, the Hands (pillars) of the Cause and the beloved of the Lord must obey him and turn unto him. He that obeyeth him not, hath not obeyed God; he that turneth away from him, hath turned away from God and he that denieth him, hath denied the True One. Beware lest anyone falsely interpret these words, and like unto them that have broken the Covenant after the Day of Ascension (of *Baha'u'llah*) advance a pretext, raise the standard of revolt, wax stubborn and open wide the door of false interpretation. To none is given the right to put forth his own opinion or express his particular conviction. All must seek guidance and turn unto the Center of the Cause and the House of Justice. And he that turneth unto whatsoever else is indeed in grievous error.

[Selections from *The Will And Testament Of Abdu'l-Baha*]

SELECTIONS FROM SHOGHI EFFENDI

POSSIBILITIES FOR THE FUTURE

A principal achievement of Shoghi Effendi's leadership was the establishment of the formal Baha'i administrative structure. As a visionary, many of his writings and talks map out achievement goals and multiyear plans to accomplish these. Some of his goals, such as the establishment of the Universal House of Justice, did not come into being until after his death. The following selection from The Advent of Divine Justice, a December 25, 1938, address to American and Canadian Baha'is, lists goals for the future.[12]

I can only for the moment cite at random certain of these opportunities which stand out preeminently, in any attempt to survey the possibilities of the future: The election of the International House of Justice and its establishment in the Holy Land, the spiritual and administrative center of the *Baha'i* world, together with the formation of its auxiliary branches and subsidiary institutions; the gradual erection of the various dependencies of the first *Mashriqu'l-Adhkar*[13] of the West, and the intricate issues involving the establishment and the extension of the structural basis of *Baha'i* community life; the codification and promulgation of the ordinances of the *Most Holy Book* [*Kitab-i-Aqdas*], necessitating the formation, in certain countries of the East, of properly constituted and officially recognized courts of *Baha'i* law; the building of the third *Mashriqu'l-Adhkar* of the *Baha'i* world in the outskirts of the city of *Tihran*, to be followed by the rise of a similar House of Worship in the Holy Land itself; the deliverance of *Baha'i* communities from the fetters of religious orthodoxy in such Islamic countries as Persia, *Iraq*, and Egypt, and the consequent recognition, by the civil authorities in those states, of the independent status and religious character of *Baha'i* National and Local Assemblies; the precautionary and defensive measures to be devised, coordinated, and carried out to counteract the full force of the inescapable attacks which the organized efforts of ecclesiastical organizations of various denominations will progressively launch and relentlessly pursue; and, last but not least, the multitudinous issues that must be faced, the obstacles that must be overcome, and the responsibilities that must be assumed, to enable a sore-tried Faith to pass through the successive stages of unmitigated obscurity, of active repression, and of complete emancipation, leading in turn to its being acknowledged as an independent Faith, enjoying the status of full equality with its sister religions, to be followed by its establishment and recognition as a State religion, which in turn must give way to its assumption of the rights and prerogatives associated with the *Baha'i* state, functioning in the plenitude of its powers, a stage which must ultimately culminate in the emergence of the worldwide *Baha'i* Commonwealth, animated wholly by the spirit, and operating solely in direct conformity with the laws and principles of *Baha'u'llah.*

[Selection from *The Advent of Divine Justice*]

UNITY OF RELIGIONS, RACES, AND GOD

The writings of the Bab and Baha'u'llah reflect the fact that their initial audience was Muslim. The unity of religions, races, and God are indeed pervasive themes of their writings; however, these themes are often presented in contexts that defend the Bab's and Baha'u'llah's roles as legitimate prophets in the line of Moses, Jesus, and Muhammad. In Shoghi Effendi's writings, the Muslim context is less important and the themes of unity are brought to the fore on their own merits. This is evident in the following selections from the Preface to The Promised Day Is Come *(1941).*[14]

The fundamental principle enunciated by *Baha'u'llah* . . . is that religious truth is not absolute but relative, that Divine Revelation is a continuous and progressive process, that all the great religions of the world are divine in origin, that their basic principles are in complete harmony, that their aims and purposes are one and the same, that their teachings are but facets of one truth, that their functions are complementary, that they differ only in the nonessential aspects of their doctrines, and that their missions represent successive stages in the spiritual evolution of human society. . . .

. . . His mission is to proclaim that the ages of the infancy and of the childhood of the human race are past, that the convulsions associated with the present stage of its adolescence are slowly and painfully preparing it to attain the stage of manhood, and are heralding the approach of that Age of Ages when swords will be beaten into plowshares, when the Kingdom promised by Jesus Christ will have been established, and the peace of the planet definitely and permanently ensured. Nor does *Baha'u'llah* claim finality for His own Revelation, but rather stipulates that a fuller measure of the truth He has been commissioned by the Almighty to vouchsafe to humanity, at so critical a juncture in its fortunes, must needs be disclosed at future stages in the constant and limitless evolution of mankind.

The *Baha'i* Faith upholds the unity of God, recognizes the unity of His Prophets, and inculcates the principle of the oneness and wholeness of the entire human race. It proclaims the necessity and the inevitability of the unification of mankind, asserts that it is gradually approaching, and claims that nothing short of the transmuting spirit of God, working through His chosen Mouthpiece in this day, can ultimately succeed in bringing it about. It, moreover, enjoins upon its followers the primary duty of an unfettered search after truth, condemns all manner of prejudice and superstition, declares the purpose of religion to be the promotion of amity and concord, proclaims its essential harmony with science, and recognizes it as the foremost agency for the pacification and the orderly progress of human society. . . .

Mirza Husayn-'Ali, surnamed *Baha'u'llah* (the Glory of God), a native of *Mazindaran*, whose advent the *Bab* [Herald and Forerunner of *Baha'u'llah*] had foretold, . . . was imprisoned in *Tihran*, was banished, in 1852, from His native land to *Baghdad*, and thence to Constantinople and Adrianople, and finally to the prison city of *Akka*, where He remained incarcerated for no less than twenty-four years, and in whose neighborhood He passed away in 1892. In the course of His banishment, and particularly in Adrianople and *Akka*, He formulated the laws and ordinances of His Dispensation, expounded, in over a hundred volumes, the principles of His Faith, proclaimed His Message to the kings and rulers of both the East and the West, both Christian and Muslim, addressed the Pope, the Caliph of *Islam*, the Chief Magistrates of the Republics of the American continent, the entire Christian sacerdotal order, the leaders of *Shi'ih* and *Sunni Islam*, and the high priests of the Zoroastrian religion. In these writings He proclaimed His Revelation, summoned those whom He addressed to heed His call and espouse His Faith, warned them of the consequences of their refusal, and denounced, in some cases, their arrogance and tyranny. . . .

The Faith which this order serves, safeguards and promotes is . . . essentially supernatural, supranational, entirely non-political, non-partisan, and diametrically opposed to any policy or school of thought that seeks to exalt any particular race, class or nation. It is free from any form of ecclesiasticism, has neither priesthood nor rituals, and is supported exclusively by voluntary contributions made by its avowed adherents. Though loyal to their respective governments, though imbued with the love of their own country, and anxious to promote at all times, its best interests, the followers of the *Baha'i* Faith, nevertheless, viewing mankind as one entity, and profoundly attached to its vital interests, will not hesitate to subordinate every particular interest, be it personal, regional or national, to the overriding interests of the generality of mankind, knowing full well that in a world of interdependent peoples and nations the advantage of the part is best to be reached by the advantage of the whole, and that no lasting result can be achieved by any of the component parts if the general interests of the entity itself are neglected. . . .

[*The Promised Day is Come*, "Preface"]

SELECTION FROM THE UNIVERSAL HOUSE OF JUSTICE

PROMISE OF WORLD PEACE

Shoghi Effendi died in 1957. One of his principal concerns was to establish the Universal House of Justice to succeed him when he died. The Universal House of Justice was officially elected in 1963, and since then has overseen Baha'i administration, interpreted Baha'i scripture, and produced its own authoritative Baha'i texts. The following selections are from one such text, The Promise of World Peace, *addressed to the world on October 1985.*

The Great Peace towards which people of good will throughout the centuries have inclined their hearts, of which seers and poets for countless generations have expressed their vision, and for which from age to age the sacred scriptures of mankind have constantly held the promise, is now at long last within the reach of the nations. For the first time in history it is possible for everyone to view the entire planet, with all its myriad diversified peoples, in one perspective. World peace is not only possible but inevitable. It is the next stage in the evolution of this planet—in the words of one great thinker, "the planetization of mankind." . . .

A candid acknowledgement that prejudice, war and exploitation have been the expression of immature stages in a vast historical process and that the human race is today experiencing the unavoidable tumult which marks its collective coming of age is not a reason for despair but a prerequisite to undertaking the stupendous enterprise of building a peaceful world. That such an enterprise is possible, that the necessary constructive forces do exist, that unifying social structures can be erected, is the theme we urge you to examine. . . .

No serious attempt to set human affairs aright, to achieve world peace, can ignore religion. Man's perception and practice of it are largely the stuff of history. An eminent historian described religion as a "faculty of human nature". That the perversion of this faculty has contributed to much of the confusion in society and the conflicts in and between individuals can hardly be denied. But neither can any fair-minded observer discount the preponderating influence exerted by religion on the vital expressions of civilization. Furthermore, its indispensability to social order has repeatedly been demonstrated by its direct effect on laws and morality. . . .

Banning nuclear weapons, prohibiting the use of poison gases, or outlawing germ warfare will not remove the root causes of war. However important such practical measures obviously are as elements of the peace process, they are in themselves too superficial to exert enduring influence. Peoples are ingenious enough to invent yet other forms of warfare, and to use food, raw materials, finance, industrial power, ideology, and terrorism to subvert one another in an endless quest for supremacy and dominion. Nor can the present massive dislocation in the affairs of humanity be resolved through the settlement of specific conflicts or disagreements among nations. A genuine universal framework must be adopted. . . .

The emancipation of women, the achievement of full equality between the sexes, is one of the most important, though less acknowledged prerequisites of peace. The denial of such equality perpetrates an injustice against one half of the world's population and promotes in men harmful attitudes and habits that are carried from the family to the workplace, to political life, and ultimately to international relations. There are no grounds, moral, practical, or biological, upon which such denial can be justified. Only as women are welcomed into full partnership in all fields of human endeavour will the moral and psychological climate be created in which international peace can emerge.

[Selections from *The Promise of World Peace*]

GLOSSARY

Bab   Arabic for "gate"; the term refers to a person who is an intermediary between the Hidden Imam and believers. This is the title adopted by Sayyid Ali-Muhammad Shiraz (d. 1850), who declared himself to be the Bab.

Babi religion (Babism)   The religion founded by the Bab (Sayyid Ali-Muhammad Shirazi), which was the precursor to the Baha'i Faith.

Baha   Literally "Glory" or "Splendor"; a title that designates Baha'u'llah. The phrase "People of Baha" refers to followers of Baha'u'llah (superseding People of the Bayan). This designation of *Baha'i* as a follower of Baha'u'llah became current during the later years of Baha'u'llah's residence in Adrianople.

Baha'u'llah   Literally "Glory of God." Founder of the Baha'i Faith , born Mirza Huasayn-Ali Nur (d. 1892). Baha'is believe him to be the *Manifestation of God*, commissioned by God to unify the modern world through a theory and practice of unity.

Bayan   Literally "exposition"; the title of two distinct books by the Bab (one in Persian, the other in Arabic); the term "Bayan" is also used by the Bab as a reference to the whole of his revelation in a generic sense.

Dispensation   A divinely appointed age in which God reveals himself through a prophet.

House of Justice (Bayt al-Adl al-Azam)   Internationally elected Baha'i administrative institution which oversees the Baha'i community. First described by Baha'u'llah and officially elected in 1963.

Manifestation   Appearance of God; a prophet of God's revelation in a given dispensation.

Point, Primal   Symbol of the Bab. In Persian mysticism, all knowledge originates from a single dot, or point.

Qa'im   Literally, "He who shall arise" from a descendant of Muhammad; also known as the the Mahdi, "The Guided One."

SUGGESTIONS FOR FURTHER READING

BUCK, CHRISTOPHER. *Symbol and Secret: Qur'an Commentary in Baha'u'llah's Kitab-i Iqan*, in *Studies in the Babi and Baha'i Religions*, vol. 7. Los Angeles: Kalimat Press, 1995.

ESSLEMONT, JOHN EBENEZER. *Baha'u'llah and the New Era*. Wilmette, IL: Baha'i Pub. Committee, 1950.

GOUVION, COLETTE AND PHILIPPE JOUVIONS. *The Gardeners of God: An Encounter with Five Million Baha'is*. Oxford: Oneworld, 1993.

HATCHER, WILLIAM S. AND MARTIN, J. DOUGLAS. *The Baha'i Faith*. San Francisco: HarperCollins, 1958.

MACEOIN, DENIS. *Rituals in Babism and Baha'ism*. London: British Academic Press, 1994.

MOMEN, WENDI. *A Basic Baha'i Dictionary*. Oxford: George Ronald, 1989.

SMITH, PETER. *A Short History of the Baha'i Faith*. Oxford; Rockport, MA: Oneworld Publications, 1996.

Endnotes

ZOROASTRIANISM

1. The name "Zoroaster," which he is often called, is a Greek translation of "Zarathushtra."
2. Bruce Lincoln writes, "At present, the majority opinion among scholars probably inclines toward the end of the second millennium or the beginning of the first, although there are still those who hold for a date in the seventh century." *Death, War, and Sacrifice* (1991), p. 150.
3. Zaehner argues that the haoma ritual itself wasn't condemned by Zarathushtra, but its association with blood sacrifices (*Dawn and Twilight of Zoroastrianism*, 1961).
4. The meaning of the Avestan term "yama," "twin," in the Gathic verse in question is widely debated. Some suppose it means "sons of Ahura Mazda," but this is nowhere stated clearly and is contradicted by other texts.
5. Many Parsis, however, live in abject poverty in some parts of rural India.
6. The alphabet was specifically created for recording the Avesta phonemes accurately (probably for purposes of liturgical precision). It was based on the ambiguous Pahlavi alphabet, which had its origins in the Aramaic script. Pahlavi was written with as few as 13 graphemes, and the Avestan alphabet has 49.
7. Translation by Joseph H. Peterson; copyright 1997 Joseph H. Peterson.
8. William W. Malandra, *An Introduction to Ancient Iranian Religion: Readings from the Avesta and Achaemenid Inscriptions* (Minneapolis: University of Minnesota Press, 1983).
9. Adapted from James Hope Moulton, *Early Zoroastrianism* (London: Williams and Northgate, 1913).
10. Adapted from James Darmesteter, *The Zend-Avesta*, Part 1 (Oxford: Clarendon Press, 1880).
11. Ibid.
12. In Zoroastrian literature, the terms "*Aspahe-ashtra*" and "*Sraosho-charana*" are used to quantify sin, and by contrast, designate what measure of good works are needed for atonement. The terms may date back to prehistoric times and it is uncertain if physical punishment was meant literally in Zoroastrian literature. In any case, it has not been interpreted or practised in that way by modern Zoroastrians.
13. In Zoroastrian practise, the receptacle is a pit in the center of the *dakhma* where bones are swept after they are picked clean, rain-washed, and sun-bleached.
14. [The day is divided into five watches or *Gahs*. If the man dies a natural death, the Druj comes directly; if the death be violent and unlooked for, the Druj is taken unawares, and it requires time for her to be warned of it and to come. —J. Darmesteter]

15. Adapted from the 1876 English translation by Ratanshah E. Kohiyar in *The Dinkard*, edited by Peshotun Dustoor Behramjee Sunjana (Bombay, Printed at the Duftur Ashkara Press, 1874–1928).
16. Adapted from E. W. West, *Pahlavi Texts*, Part 2 (Oxford: Clarendon Press, 1882).
17. [The intermediate place for those not good enough for heaven and not bad enough for hell, where such souls remain in a passive immovable state till the resurrection. It is divided into two parts, one for those nearly righteous, and one for those nearly wicked. —E. W. West]
18. Adapted from E. W. West, *Pahlavi Texts*, Part 1 (Oxford: Clarendon Press, 1880).
19. The Ahunvar is as follows: "As a heavenly lord is to be chosen, so is an earthly master, for the sake of righteousness, to be a giver of the good thoughts of the actions of life towards Mazda; and the dominion is for the lord (Ahura) whom he (Mazda) has given as a protector for the poor." —E. W. West]
20. Adapted from E. W. West, *Pahlavi Texts*, Part 5 (Oxford: Clarendon Press, 1897).
21. [Quoting from the (now lost) *Spend Nask*.]
22. Adapted from E. W. West, *Pahlavi Texts*, Part 5 (Oxford: Clarendon Press, 1880).
23. Adapted from E. W. West, *Pahlavi Texts*, Part 1 (Oxford: Clarendon Press, 1880).
24. [Ice and slopes are the work of evil spirits.]
25. Adapted from E. W. West, *Pahlavi Texts*, Part 3 (Oxford: Clarendon Press, 1885).
26. *The Wisdom of the Sasanian Sages (Denkard VI)*, tr. Shaul Shaked (Boulder, Colorado: 1979), pp. 11, 173.
27. Mary Boyce, *Textual Sources for the Study of Zoroastrianism* (Chicago: University of Chicago Press, 1984), pp. 97–98.

JUDAISM

1. See Richard Elliott Friedman, *Who Wrote the Bible?* (San Francisco: HarperCollins, 1987). Friedman argues that E emphasizes northern heroes, cities, and institutions such as Moses, Joshua, Samuel, Shiloh, the Mosaic covenant, and the Tabernacle. J, by contrast, emphasizes counterparts associated with Judah and Jerusalem, such as the Patriarchs, Aaron, Hebron, the Abrahamic covenant, the ark of the covenant, and Aaron's line of priesthood.
2. It is also suggested that an exiled editor put the finishing touches on the Deuteronomistic History to explain the Babylonian exile and dissolution of the royal line of David.
3. All selections from the Tanakh are from *Tanakh: The Holy Scriptures* (Philadelphia: Jewish Publication Society, 1985).
4. From *The Old Testament Pseudepigrapha*, ed. James Charlesworth (New York: Doubleday, 1983), Vol. 1, pp. 34–38.
5. From *New American Bible* (Confraternity of Christian Doctrine, 1970).
6. From *The Dead Sea Scrolls in English*, 3rd ed., tr., G. Vermes (New York: Penguin Books, 1987), pp. 64–67.
7. From *The Old Testament Pseudepigrapha*, ed. James Charlesworth (New York: Doubleday, 1983), Vol. 1, pp. 388–389.
8. From *The Talmud*, tr. Ben Zion Bokser (New York: Paulist Press, 1989), pp. 219–221.
9. From *The Talmud*, tr. Ben Zion Bokser (New York: Paulist Press, 1989), pp. 184–185.

10. [The case seems trivial but an important principle in law was involved here. According to biblical law (Lv 15:13), vessels may be contaminated with ritual uncleanliness. This stove had apparently been contaminated, and the owner, to evade the law that calls for its destruction, broke it into tiles, which were separated from each other by sand and plastered over with cement. Objectively the stove was no longer a "whole" vessel, and thus no longer under the biblical law. On the other hand, it could still be used; functionally it was still a vessel, and therefore subject to the biblical law. R. Eliezer generally ignored subjectivity in his interpretation of the law, and therefore ruled it clean, while his colleagues countered (i.e., responded) the subjective factors and therefore ruled it in effect a whole vessel, subject to the law of levitica impurity. It has been suggested that Akhnai was the owner of the stove, but the fact that *akhna* means a snake led the Talmud to offer a homiletical interpretation.—Ben Zion Bokser]
12. From *The Talmud*, tr. Ben Zion Bokser (New York: Paulist Press, 1989), pp. 131–132.
13. From *Zohar, The Book of Slendor*, ed. Gershom Scholem, (New York: Schocken Books, 1949).
14. From *Nahman of Bratslav: the Tales* (New York: Paulist Press, 1978), pp. 274–277.

CHRISTIANITY

1. See Richard A. Horsley, *Bandits, Messiahs, and Prophets* (San Francisco: Harper-Collins, 1985).
2. Robert W. Funk, *The Five Gospels* (New York: Macmillan, 1993) p. 5.
3. Kenneth Ewing Bailey, *Poet and Peasant* (Grand Rapids: Eerdmans, 1976).
4. From *The Holy Bible, New International Version* (International Bible Society, 1984).
5. Selections from Mark, Matthew, Luke, and John are from *The Complete Gospels: Annotated Scholars Version*, ed. Robert J. Miller (Polebridge Press, Harper San Francisco, 1994).
6. Selections from Acts, Galatians, and 1 Corinthians are from *The Holy Bible, New International Version* (International Bible Society, 1984).
7. Translation by James Fieser.
8. From *The Complete Gospels: Annotated Scholars Version*, pp. 387–392.
9. Ibid.
10. Ibid.
11. Ibid.
12. From *The Book of Common Prayer* (London: 1855).
13. From *Psuedo-Dionysus: The Complete Works*, tr. Colm Luibheid, (New York: Paulist Press, 1987), pp. 138–141.
14. From *The Philokalia: The Complete Text*, tr. G.E.H. Palmer, et als, Vol. 1, pp. 179–196.
15. From *Interior Castle*, tr. E. Allison Peers, (Garden City, NY: Doubleday, 1961), pp. 104–106.

ISLAM

1. *Surah 9*, which deals with divine judgment, omits the opening statement, "In the name of God, the Merciful, the Compassionate."

2. Narratives of Arabian origin include those of Thamud, Luqman, dhu 'l-Qarnayn, and the seven sleepers.
3. Three other less revered Sunni *Hadith* collections are the *Muwatta* of Malik Ibn Anas (d. 795), which was the first collection recorded, the *Musnad* of Ibn Hanbal (d. 855), and that by Darimi (d. 869).
4. Selections from the Qur'an are from *The Koran*, tr. N. J. Dawood (London: Penguin Books, 1990).
5. [Revocable divorce, or the renunciation of one's wife on oath.—N. J. Dawood]
6. [By pronouncing the formula 'I divorce you' for the third time.—N. J. Dawood]
7. [At this time Muhammad had nine wives, apart from slave-girls.—N. J. Dawood]
8. Selections from *Sahih al-Bukhari* are from *The Translation of the Meanings of Sahih al-Bukhari*, 9 vols. tr. Muhammad Muhsin Khan (Chicago: Kazi Publications, 1979).
9. From *Islamic Jurisprudence: Shafi'i's Risala*, tr. Majid Khadduri (Baltimore: Johns Hopkins Press, 1961).
10. From *A Shi'ite Creed*, Ibn Babawayh al-Qummi, tr. Asaf A.A. Fyzee (London: Oxford University Press, 1942).
11. [Fyzee notes that "Some apparently believed that the Imams were miraculously translated to Heaven."]
12. From *Rabi'a: The Life and Work of Rabi'a*, Margaret Smith (London : Cambridge University Press, 1928).
13. From *The Faith and Practice of al-Ghazali*, tr. W. Montgomery Watt (London: George Allen and Unwin, 1953), pp. 26–27, 54–62.
14. From *The Sufi Path of Love: the Spiritual Teachings of Rumi*, tr. William C. Chittick (Albany: State University of New York Press, 1983), pp. 235–236.

BAHA'I FAITH

1. Baha'is refer to their religion as the "Baha'i Faith," as opposed to "Baha'ism" or "Baha'i." The term "Baha'i" alone is either an adjective or is a noun meaning a follower of the faith.
2. *Selections from the Writings of the Bab* (Baha'i World Centre, 1982 ed.).
3. *Kitab-i-Iqan* (Baha'i World Centre, 1989).
4. *Kitab-i-Aqdas* (Baha'i World Centre, 1992).
5. Abdu'l-Baha interpreted this to mean that Baha'is are limited to taking only one wife: "Know thou that polygamy is not permitted under the law of God. For contentment with one wife hath been clearly stipulated. Taking a second wife is made dependent upon equity and justice being upheld between the two wives, under all conditions. However, observance of justice and equity towards two wives is utterly impossible. The fact that bigamy has been made dependent upon an impossible condition is clear proof of its absolute prohibition. Therefore it is not permissible for a man to have more than one wife." *Kitab-i-Aqdas*, p. 206 (note 89)
6. *Tablets of Baha'u'llah Revealed After the Kitab-i-Aqdas* (U.S., 1988 pocket-size ed.).
7. Ibid.
8. *Abdu'l-Baha in London* (U.K., 1982 reprint).
9. *Some Answered Questions* (U.S., 1990 reprint of pocket-size ed.)
10. *Paris Talks*, 11th ed. (U.K., 1972 reprint).
11. *Will and Testament of Abdu'l-Baha* (U.S., 1990 reprint)

12. *The Advent of Divine Justice* (U.S., first pocket-size edition 1990) .
13. *"Mashriqu'l-Adhkar"* refers to national Baha'i houses of worship. The first one in the west is the House of Worship in Wilmette, Illinois. "Dependencies" of the houses of worship are specific social institutions that are to be built nearby. There are five dependencies: a hospital, pharmacy, hospice, orphanage, and a university.
14. *The Promised Day Is Come* (U.S., Revised Edition 1980).

Acknowledgments

ZOROASTRIANISM

Excerpts from *The Wisdom of the Sasanian Sages* (Denkard VI), tr. Shaul Shaked (Boulder, Colorado: 1979). Reprinted by permission of Shaul Shaked.

Translation of excerpts from Zoroastrian texts, by Joseph Peterson. Reprinted by permission.

JUDAISM

Excerpts from *TANAKH: The New JPS Translation of the Holy Scriptures According to the Masoretic Text.* Used by permission.

Excerpts from *The Old Testament Pseudepigrapha* by James H. Charlesworth. Copyright © 1983, 1985 by James H. Charlesworth. Used by permission of Doubleday, a division of Bantam Doubleday Dell publishing Group, Inc.

Excerpt from *The Dead Sea Scrolls in English,* third edition, Tr., G. Vermes (New York: Penguin Books, 1987). Reproduced by permission of Frederick Warne & Co.

Excerpts reprinted from *The Talmud,* translated by Ben Zion Bokser. Copyright © 1989 by Baruch M. Bokser. Used by permission of Paulist Press.

Excerpts from *Zohar, The Book of Slendor,* by Gershom Scholem. Copyright © 1949, renewed 1977 by Schocken Books, Inc. Reprinted by permission of Schocken Books, distributed by Pantheon Books, a division of Random House, Inc.

Excerpts reprinted from *Nahman of Bratslav: the Tales.* Copyright © 1978 by Arnold J. Band. Used by permission of Paulist Press.

CHRISTIANITY

Excerpts from the *New American Bible* Copyright © 1970 Confraternity of Christian Doctrine, Washington, D.C. and are used by permission of the copy-

ISLAM

BAHA'I FAITH

Extracts from Baha'i scriptures reprinted by permission from the National Spiritual Assembly of the Bahais of the United States.